PEARSON

ALWAYS LEARNING

W9-ATQ-681

Public Speaking for Success

Third Edition

Gerald L. Wilson
University of South Alabama

Megan S. Sparks
University of South Alabama

April DuPree Taylor
University of South Alabama

Cover Art: created by Melissa Meinhold

Pearson Learning Solutions, 501 Boylston Street, Suite 900, Boston, MA 02116
A Pearson Education Company
www.pearsoned.com

Printed in the United States of America

9   16

000200010271873031

TS/VP

ISBN 10: 1-269-86094-1
ISBN 13: 978-1-269-86094-9

Preface

Public Speaking for Success is written for students enrolled in the basic public speaking course. This book is intended to be thorough without being tedious. It meets the abilities and needs of undergraduate students while maintaining intellectual integrity. This book maintains the strengths of the previous editions, while addressing new important topics.

We all want to be successful in the many situations we will find ourselves. This is especially true when we are facing an audience. In order to do this, we must strive to develop excellence in the many skills and understanding needed to achieve this goal. These skills and understandings are here to be achieved through careful study and practice of the principles presented in this book.

The skills presented in *Public Speaking for Success* are useful beyond the public speech. They translate into effectiveness and success in many other areas of your life. For example, if you learn to make an excellent persuasive argument in your classroom speaking assignment, you will be able to make an excellent argument in a one-on-one situation at work. The ability to pull together the many principles for creating a successful speech and also to apply them well is a significant achievement.

We believe *Public Speaking for Success* can have a dramatic impact on your success in the many challenges you will face in your lifetime if you study it seriously and practice the skills taught. We also believe that, more than any other course in the college curriculum, this course teaches you a set of skills to navigate life. This public speaking course offers significant practical knowledge and skills that will point you to the path of personal development and the success you desire.

Ordinary people like us accomplish extraordinary things through the art of public speaking. We sincerely expect great things from each of you as you strive to have a positive impact at your work, in your community groups, and in your family through the skills taught in this book.

NEW TO THE THIRD EDITION

We have added several new topics that we judge to be significant in advancing our theme of successful public speaking. We have also added references to support the material as well as updating references for existing material. Here are the additions and changes, chapter by chapter:

Chapter 1:
1. Added to the section titled, Your Personal Life.
2. Added definitions for encoding and decoding.

Chapter 2:
3. Added a section on avoiding pandering.

Chapter 3:
4. Added a paragraph describing the passivity syndrome.
5. Added a section on listening to the nonverbal behavior of the speaker.

Chapter 5:

    6. Added a new section discussing the role of taste and judgment in selecting a topic.

Chapter 6:

    7. Added a section on blogs.

Chapter 8:

    8. Strengthened our understanding of the power in telling a story.

Chapter 9:

    9. Added a section on comparisons.
    10. Added a section on contrasts.

Chapter 11:

    11. Added a section on adaptation of language to diverse audiences.

Chapter 16:

    12. Added a section on counter persuasion.

Chapter 17:

    13. Added the full text of the speech, "Here's to Kat."

PEER FEEDBACK FORMS

We believe in the significant effect that peer critique has on the learning process. To accomplish this purpose, we have provided critique forms at the end of this book. These forms are perforated for easy removal and use in critiques that provide the speaker feedback.

ACKNOWLEDGMENTS

Manuscripts are turned into successful books by those who provide developmental and editorial help. The people at Pearson are exceptional in their skill and professionalism. We really enjoy working with them.

    We thank Pearson's extraordinarily dedicated editors, especially Joshua A. Uehlin, Anthony Howard, and Traci Sobocinski, for sharing their expertise and knowledge in the production of this book. We give special thanks to Melissa Meinhold for sharing her exceptional talent in the design of the cover of this book. Beth Whitehurst and Brett Holmes provided the encouragement we needed to undertake and complete this project. Thank you so much.

    Finally, we wish to thank Lin Wilson, Jason Sparks and Coustaur Taylor for their patience, understanding, and encouragement during the revision of this book.

Gerald L. Wilson
Megan S. Sparks
April DuPree Taylor
Mobile, Alabama

This book is lovingly dedicated to our spouses and children

Jason Cecil Sparks
Anna Grace Sparks
Brady Sebastian Sparks

Coustaur Devon Taylor
Chandler DuPree Taylor
Chesney DuPree Taylor

Linda Stewart Wilson
Hannah Beth Wilson
Ryan Stewart Wilson

Brief Contents

Contents

Chapter 1
Speaking in Public

Courtesy of Richard Lewishon/Alamy.

WHY IS IT IMPORTANT TO STUDY PUBLIC SPEAKING?

It is likely you are enrolled in the public speaking course to fulfill a requirement to complete your degree. Many colleges require all students, not just students who major in communication or liberal arts, to complete a public speaking course. Why do nearly all colleges require the study and practice of public speaking? The answer is simple. The faculties of these colleges believe this course provides essential skills that lead to success in your profession, regardless of what that profession is. This is why your authors have titled this book *Public Speaking for Success*. We believe each chapter provides information you need to understand the skills you will use in delivering speeches. We also believe this book will enhance the skills you will need to present mini speeches you will make in meetings and persuasive presentations. We will have more to say about how public speaking will impact your life shortly.

The number of colleges and universities requiring basic public speaking began to increase in the 1980s, and this requirement has continued to the present day. Even though the faculty of your college have concluded that a class devoted to teaching effective public speaking is essential for the students' core curriculum, students often question the importance of this type of course. It is true that some of the students who enroll in the public speaking course are not motivated to take the class. So, if you are a bit reticent about taking the course, know that you are not alone. However, generally speaking, by the end of the semester, most students recognize the importance of the course and appreciate the skills they learn and enhance by taking the course.

Typical comments faculty get at the end of the public speaking course include these we received:

"I cannot believe how much I learned in this class! I am an Information Technology major. One of the reasons I chose this major was because I figured I could never learn the skills to speak in public. But I have learned so many skills that I know have helped me become a better speaker."

"Before taking this class I would get so nervous when I was called on to answer a question in class. After taking this class I feel more confident when I am called on to talk and have been given very little time to prepare."

"This course has been one of the most useful courses in my college career!"

Hopefully, as you go through the course, you too will appreciate the benefits of studying public speaking and how skill in it can lead to your success. We believe becoming an effective public speaker will be beneficial to you in three primary segments of your life: your life as a student, your professional life and your personal life.

Your Life as a Student

Preparing speeches involves numerous skills that you can use in other courses and also groups to which you belong. Almost all college courses require students to engage in creative thinking to complete assignments, conduct research for class projects, make oral presentations and engage in basic

Courtesy of Bob Adelman/Corbis Images.

"Becoming an effective speaker will benefit your life as a student, your professional life, and your personal life."

communication. Consider the following example to further explain what we mean when we assert the idea that this class will help improve your life as a student:

Dr. Jennings, a sociology professor, assigned a project to her students requiring them to explore diversity. In the assignment, students were instructed to find a group or organization that was different from them or that they would not ordinarily join (creative thinking). After identifying the group, students were required to locate at least three sources about the group (conducting research). After doing a little research, Dr. Jennings urged her students to visit a group meeting and talk with members of the group (basic communication and research). Finally, the students had to present their discoveries concerning diversity to the sociology class (oral presentation).

It's likely you have had professors in other classes who have given similar assignments—assignments which required you to use creative thinking, conduct research, employ basic communication and give an oral presentation. If so, it is our hope that in this class you will learn other strategies to help you get more proficient with these types of assignments. If you have not had to use these skills in your college classes yet, believe us, you will. And the concepts you learn in this class will help ensure you are prepared when you do.

Your Professional Life

If you take a look at the Classified Ads in any Sunday newspaper, you might notice that public speaking skills top the list of sought-after skills by many organizations. Organizations from the large-scale ones to the smaller ones recognize that good communication skills are essential to being a productive organization. Employers are well aware that good communication skills empower their employees to convey information, persuade and motivate others.

In a survey conducted by the National Association of Colleges and Employers (NACE) Job Outlook, employers reported the characteristic they prized the most in the "perfect" job candidate category was good communication skills. Additionally, Paul Baruda, an employment expert for the site Monster.com, has said:

> Articulating thoughts clearly and concisely will make a difference in both a job interview and subsequent job performance. . .the point is, you can be the best physicist in the workplace, but if you can't tell people what you do or communicate it to your co-workers, what good is all of that knowledge? I can't think of an occupation, short of living in a cave, where being able to say what you think cogently at some point in your life isn't going to be important.

Your Personal Life

The scholastic benefits and the personal benefits of studying public speaking are usually pretty obvious. But maybe not so obvious is the benefit to your personal life of becoming an effective public speaker. Learning basic public speaking skills are essential in helping us communicate personal concerns in our community.

Bing Dictionary defines **community** as a group of people with a common background or with a shared interest. There are many communities in which you might participate. Think of groups that share your interests to which you belong or might join with in the future. The broad categories where people get involved are recreational activities, church activities, environmental concerns, political issues, and political campaigns. These represent some of the many areas that you as a college graduate are likely to find yourself involved.

Your public speaking skills position you to exercise your "public voice" in expressing yourself in both political and civic activities as well as environmental concerns. You will want to stand up for your own interests and have an impact that will make a difference. Your success as a public speaker is tied to learning the crucial skills taught in this course. All of us want to make a positive difference in our society; we want to make our mark in our corner of the world.

All of us are passionate about something. This passion can be a driving force to cause you to speak out to defend your beliefs and values when it comes to directions and actions groups take. Finding your voice as a speaker will help you better present and, if necessary, defend your beliefs and values. For example, as you become a more confident speaker, you may be compelled to attend a student government meeting at your college or university to express your concerns about the lack of lighting surrounding the student dormitories or some other issue which is important to you.

Public speaking skills allow you to have a sense of power over the direction of your life as it pertains, not only carrying out civic responsibilities, but also personal interests. You will want to have an impact in the organizations to which you belong—environmental, recreational, church and others. You may not think there is much opportunity for public speaking in these group situations. But, when the occasion comes—and it likely will—you will want to make a powerful speech. In addition to these formal public speaking occasions, there will be many opportunities to make statements and present arguments in the meetings of these groups. This speaking requires the same skills that are required for a formal public speech.

Because you are more closely involved in the activities of the groups you join, your impact is very important to you. It is kind of like a member's participation in the monthly meeting of his or her fraternity or sorority. The person cares, so he or she wants to have impact in these meetings on the direction the fraternity or sorority is taking. The more important the issue, the more this person feels the need to exercise the power that comes from effective public speaking. Of course, the opportunities to speak will also flow from various leadership positions you take in these groups.

We believe that this community involvement pertains directly to you. Throughout your life there will be many issues that deeply concern you. Your impact on these issues will be greatly enhanced by the skills you will gain throughout this course.

WHAT IS PUBLIC SPEAKING?

When we say public speaking, we may be thinking something different than you are. As we explore the definition of public speaking, it is important to remember that public speaking is an interactive process. It is not static. A speech is an action performed with the help of listeners.

Public speaking is defined as the process of speaking to a group of people in a structured, deliberate manner that is intended to inform, persuade, or entertain listeners. This definition is significant because it establishes that public speeches should have a purpose. Also, this definition recognizes the importance of the listeners. This definition further drives home the point that while almost everybody can speak, it takes effort to become an effective public speaker. Public speaking involves more than a person standing behind a podium if the speaker is to have an impact on the listeners.

The process of delivering a public speech involves eight essential elements. These elements include the following: the sender, the receiver, the message, the channels, noise, feedback, the context, and the shared meaning among the speaker and the listener. We will now turn to a discussion of these.

THE PROCESS OF COMMUNICATION

In 1954, Wilbur Schramm developed a model that is useful in helping you visualize how effective communication works. The model is illustrated in Figure 1.1.

Schramm's Process Model of Communication illustrates some important concepts in public speaking. First, the model presents the public speaking process as circular communication between the sender and receiver. The diagram suggests that both the sender and the receiver take turns playing the role of encoding and decoding messages in communication. Simply put, the **sender** is the person who talks or sends the message (the encoder). The **receiver** is the person who listens or receives the message (the decoder).

In the model, the **message** is the information the sender and receiver send to each other. These messages must be encoded by the sender and decoded by the receiver. **Encoding** means to put the ideas or information into specific language the speaker selects to convey his or her ideas. **Decoding** means for the listener to interpret the verbal and nonverbal content of a message to give it meaning. These messages can be verbal (talking) and/or nonverbal (a head nod). The **channels** are the mediums through which the messages are sent and they can be verbal (a radio program) or nonverbal (a newspaper).

Schramm's model also emphasizes the element of feedback in communication. **Feedback**

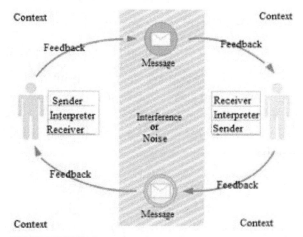

FIGURE 1.1
Schramm's Model of Communication

is the information the receiver sends back to the sender to let the speaker know how well the sender's messages are being understood. Like messages and channels, feedback can also be verbal (an answer "yes" to a question) or nonverbal (a smile or a yawn).

Although noise, or interference, is not desired in the communication setting, it is always there in some form or another. So, noise is worth identifying in the communication model. **Noise** is defined as anything that interferes with the message exchange between the sender and receiver. Noise can be internal (thought processes) or external (the hum of an air conditioner). Because of the **context**—where communication takes place—some external noise can not be eliminated. However, senders and receivers should work hard to reduce internal noise they have during the communication event.

Finally, shared meaning must be accomplished in any communication event. **Shared meaning** is accomplished when both the sender and receiver have an understanding of the messages delivered in the communication. Many communication scholars suggest that shared meaning is the primary goal of communication. So, if shared meaning is not accomplished, there really has not been effective communication.

NERVOUSNESS IN PUBLIC SPEAKING

If you are nervous about standing up in front of a whole room of people and delivering a speech, you are not alone. In a revealing thought, actor and comedian Jerry Seinfeld is quoted as saying, "According to most studies, people's number one fear is public speaking. Number two is death. Death, number two? Does this seem right? This means, to the average person, if you have to go to a funeral, you're better off in the casket than doing the eulogy"—the speech that lifts the virtues of the diseased.

In several studies, researchers found the following interesting statistics:

- Fear of public speaking is often ranked higher than death.
- 70-75% of adults fear public speaking (McCroskey, 2009)
- 76% of experienced speakers have fear before giving a speeches (Knowles, 1990)

So again, if you are nervous about taking this class and delivering speeches, you are not alone. Also, you should be relieved to know that there are strategies you can adopt to help you manage the anxiety. The most common techniques speakers use to help manage their apprehensions are relaxation techniques, attitude modifications, cognitive restructuring and visualization.

Briefly, **relaxation techniques** help you reduce your apprehension by helping you associate relaxed feelings, instead of anxious feelings, with public speaking. This association is accomplished by having you imagine speech scenes while in a state of deep relaxation (Ayres &Hopf, 1985; Ellis, 2001). **Attitude modifications** are accomplished by allowing you to complete several lessons on how to develop a speech, and then allowing you to complete

This speaker understands that noise can disrupt communication.

drill and practice sessions until you are comfortable with the speech (Ellis, 2001; Phillips, 1991). **Cognitive restructuring** is a strategy which helps you replace irrational thoughts with rational ones. You can accomplish this by identifying negative self-statements and replacing them with positive statements (Ellis, 2001).**Visualization** is used to help reduce communication apprehension by helping you create, or recreate, sensations associated with the your speaking experience (Ayres, Hopf, & Ayres, 1997).

So, while you are totally normal to feel some nervousness about taking this public speaking class, there are methods you can use to help you cope with the nervousness. Your public speaking instructor will be eager to help you succeed!

SUMMARY

In this chapter we discussed why it is important to study public speaking. Specifically, we outlined how studying public speaking can enhance your life as a student, your life as a working professional and your personal life. We also defined public speaking and presented a diagram of Schramm's process model of communication. In the process model, we emphasized the speaker, the receiver, messages, the channels, feedback, noise, the context, and shared meaning as the essential elements in the process of communication.

Finally, we addressed the nervousness you may experience as a speaker in your public speaking class. We assured you that your nervousness is normal. Also, we gave you suggestions you can use to help cope with the nervousness. The strategies we suggested for you include relaxation techniques, attitude modifications, cognitive restructuring and visualization. In the subsequent chapters of this text, your authors will continue to provide you with valuable information to help you become a successful public speaker.

REFERENCES

Ayres, J., & Hopf, T. S. (1985). Visualization: A mean of reducing speech anxiety. *Communication Education, 34*, 318–232.

Ayres, J., & Hopf, T. S. (1987). Visualization, systematic desensitization, and rational emotive therapy: A comparative evaluation. *Communication Education*, 36(3), 236–240.

Ellis, A. (2001). *New directions for rational emotive therapy*. New York, NY: Prometheus.

NACE Job Outlook (2012). Retrieved April 22, 2012, from http://www.naceweb.org/Research/Job_Outlook.aspx.

McCroskey, J. C. (2009) Communication apprehension: What we have learned in the last four decades. *Human Communication*,12, 179–187.

Knowles, M. S. (1990). *The adult learner: A neglected species.* Houston, TX: Gulf Publishing Company.

McKay, J. (2005). Employers complain about communication skills. In *The Pittsburg Post Gazette*. Retrieved on April 22, 2012 from http://old.post.com/pg/05037/453170-28.stm

Phillips, G. M. (1991). *Communication incompetencies: A theory of training oral performance behavior*. Carbondale, IL: Southern Illinois University Press.

Rogers, E. M. (1994). *A history of communication study: A biographical approach*. New York: Free Press.

Schramm, W. (1997). *The beginnings of communication study in America: A personal memoir*. Thousand Oaks, CA: Sage.

Seinfeld, J. (nd). Retrieved on April 22, 2012 from http://thinkexist.com/quotation/according_to_most_studies-people-s_number_one/9010.html

Chapter 2
Ethics in Public Speaking

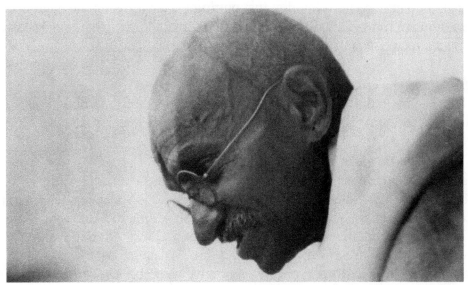

Courtesy of Bettmann/Corbis Images.

WHY IS ETHICAL BEHAVIOR IMPORTANT?

Ethics is a very "hot topic" today because we hear about persons whose unethical behavior has been in the news and some are actually in court defending their behavior. Of course, you would not connect the word honesty with any of this behavior.

All of us believe we are honest. In fact, we make a great effort to be honest and see ourselves as successful in this effort. That is why we are disgusted by this unethical behavior when we hear about it. If honesty is all there is to being ethical we would not be writing this chapter—there is much more. Let's turn first to why ethical behavior is important before we explain what we mean by there is more to ethical behavior than honesty.

You are aware that the title of this book is *Public Speaking for Success*. Our title answers the question, "Why is ethical behavior important?" A speaker's success depends on his or her being ethical—and this means being more than honest. We will begin by presenting the ethical demands of a speaker that will lead to success. This chapter is divided into three sections: Ethical Public Speaking, Plagiarism, and Ethical Listening.

ETHICAL PUBLIC SPEAKING

The word, ethics, has its roots in the Greek word **ethos**, which is translated as the character of the speaker. Aristotle, the author of *The Rhetoric*, observed that audiences trust speakers

11

who demonstrate positive character. We have come to believe that this positive character refers to trustworthiness, straightforwardness, honest presentation of ideas and respect for the audience. We conclude that **ethical communication** is that which fosters "truthfulness, fairness, responsibility, personal integrity, and respect for self and others" (Credo of Communication Ethics, 1999, p. 27). You may be thinking that just putting these words on the page is not very helpful. Of course, you are right. This next section will help you know what they mean and how to implement these characteristics of ethical communication.

GUIDELINES FOR ETHICAL SPEAKING

This section will allow you to discover why ethics is more than honesty. You will also learn why speakers who violate these guidelines are generally not successful speakers.

Have a Clear and Responsible Goal

History provides us with numerous examples of speakers who did not have a clear and responsible goal. Undoubtedly, the best known example is found in speeches delivered by Aldof Hitler during World War II. His speeches incited the German people to hatred and genocide. They stirred the people to accept invasion of other countries and war. No one would claim that Hitler's goals were responsible or ethical.

Today through news broadcasts and online reports we hear about speakers who engage in irresponsible behavior to achieve their personal goals. We have preachers who persuade their audiences to make contributions—part of which support their lavish lifestyles. We have politicians who manipulate the public trust for personal gain. We have business leaders who persuade people to invest in their questionable enterprises and defraud them of millions of dollars. Of course, none of these are responsible or worthy goals.

Perhaps you are saying, "These are extreme cases. I do not see how a student speaking in the classroom can violate this guideline." Here is one example experienced by one of your authors. The assignment was to prepare an informative speech on a topic chosen by the speaker. One student prepared a sermon with the purpose of converting class members to his religion. Please understand that this is a captive audience in that they do not have the choice to be there to listen to this fellow student who is attempting to convert them to his religion. Many are persons of faith, but do they want to be "converted" to another faith? Many are persons of no particular faith. Do they want to be "converted" to this person faith? But, they have no choice other than to listen or leave the room. (Remember also that the assignment was to write and deliver an informative speech.)

You probably see the ethical problem here, but we will point it out. Is it ethical to present a persuasive speech when the assignment is an informative speech and try to "convert" the audience to the speaker's faith? Remember the audience has no choice about being in attendance. We think not. The point we are making is to be sure your goal for your speech is ethical. You can ask the question, "Is it right for me to pursue this goal?" "Would reasonable people see my goal for this speech as appropriate?"

Prepare Thoroughly

Let's begin by answering the question, "What does it mean to be fully prepared?" You will discover more about what this means as you progress in this course. For now, let's say it means to carefully analyze your audience, thoroughly research your topic, carefully organize your ideas, support your ideas with credible information and evidence, and present what you say clearly so your audience will understand.

There are many reasons for the advice to prepare thoroughly. First, you may miss some really important information or evidence if you do not prepare thoroughly. The lack of preparation could easily result in you presenting inaccurate information or evidence. You see there very well may be missing pieces. In a persuasive speech, you may even be misleading your audience because of missing critical information or evidence and probably not know you are doing so. You are expected to know your topic thoroughly. Preparing thoroughly guards against these problems.

Second, you may be wasting the audience members' time if you do not prepare thoroughly. This is the case, because of the missing pieces, you may not be giving them the kind of quality they deserve and expect. Superficial treatment of a topic is not what a responsible speaker provides. And it is not what the audience expects. This violates the ethical principle that a speaker respects his or her audience.

Be Honest, Trustworthy and Responsible

Audiences expect that the words of the speaker can be trusted, unless given some reason to doubt this. Knowingly presenting false or misleading information to an audience is a violation of ethics—as we all know. But, we do not have to turn far to see that speakers do not follow this principle.

Consider this well-known example. In 1998 President Clinton declared in a public forum "I did not have sexual relations with that woman—Miss Lewinsky." We all would agree that evidence later proved this to be a lie. This serious breach of ethics was the source of serious trouble for Clinton as some were able to forgive, but others were not. Of course, there are other examples, but the point has been made clear by this one.

Trustworthiness combines honesty with dependability. We have spoken about honesty, but what about dependability. We depend on the speaker to have done the research on the topic as we would have done it, if we had the time and energy to do it ourselves. The key phrase here is "as we would have done it." We are honest and we expect the speaker to be honest. We depend on the speaker to be honest and thorough in his or her research and preparation.

There are several other types of dishonesty that bear mention. These are just as dishonest although they may seem to some as not being so. These include:

- Misquoting somebody
- Misrepresenting sources of information or evidence
- Paraphrasing too closely the original form

13

This speaker has credibility because of her reputation for being trustworthy and responsible.   Courtesy of Ellis Photography.

- Manipulating statistics
- Not telling the whole story
- Citing cases as typical that are actually unusual
- Quoting out of context
- Distorting the evidence so that it is a "half-truth"

Perhaps you are thinking there are many levels of honesty and some are harmless and may even protect another person—for example, sometimes telling the truth might be hurtful to the other and may not seem to be important. The truth may not even seem to be particularly relevant to the situation. In this case, it may be tactless and imprudent to tell the truth. Here is another example.

Suppose the President of the United States is conducting secret negotiations with another country and speaking the truth could easily jeopardize the negotiations. Should his press secretary tell the truth when asked about this situation? Or perhaps a friend shows you a new outfit that she clearly enjoys and you think it doesn't suit her at all. Do you tell her the truth? We often consider this kind of dishonesty to be a "white lie," equivocation or evasion (Wilson, 2014). We are not completely honest and open because it can be damaging in some way.

What are we saying about telling "white lies?" There are times when telling the whole truth is damaging in some way to people you wish to protect. If the situation is serious, you will undoubtedly tell. If it is not, you may decide to be prudent in what you say.

Avoid Pandering

Merely telling an audience what you think they want to hear or indicating agreement with the audience on all issues when you really don't is called **pandering**. This approach is attractive to the speaker because it seems like a good audience adaptation technique that will get the audience on their side. All of us like a positive response, but this is not the ethical way to get one.

Those who have contributed to our long rhetorical tradition worried about this issue. The ancient philosopher and rhetorician, Plato, in his dialogue Gorgias, urges speakers to avoid merely reinforcing their audiences' opinions rather than showing the audience what is best for their interests. Politicians are often seen as panderers when they tell interest-groups that they share their point of view and will support them if they will cast their ballot to elect them.

The ethical problem here centers on the inauthentic relationship the speaker develops with the audience. The speaker neglects to voice his or her opinion so as to appear in complete agreement with the audience. Pandering runs the risk, of course, of building barriers between the speaker and the audience once the speaker is found out to be less than truthful. It would be ethical, of course, for the speaker to honestly acknowledge differences of opinion and then make an effective persuasive argument to move the audience to his or her position.

Do Not Engage in Name Calling

Many of us grew up being told that "sticks and stones can break my bones, but words can never hurt me." Of course, this was told to protect us from those who would say hurtful things. The message was to ignore these things; do not "take them to heart." But, we know that words can be hurtful and that it is very difficult to ignore them. We all know that words are powerful and when aimed at hurting they can do that and scar us psychologically—maybe, permanently.

We know who we are by how others react to us. The words they speak, the names they use to describe us, are their reaction to us and help to define who we are. For example, if we are labeled as disabled, and may actually be disabled, the constant communicating this to us can cause us to focus on it as a major part of our identity. The opposite can also be true. When others focus on different attributes and do not constantly communicate disabled, we develop a different, perhaps healthier definition of who we are even if we are disabled.

Name-calling is the use of abusive words to demean or defame another person. Sometimes the name-calling is directed toward some group. Groups are often maligned for their gender, ideology, ethnic background, religion, sexual orientation or disabilities. The speaker's name-calling has as its aim suggesting the groups are in some way inferior and because of this do not need to be treated with the same respect as others. The speaker is basically attempting to dehumanize and devalue the group.

The effect of name-calling goes beyond the speaker's situation. Name-calling can have a cumulative effect. Over time, if it is used often, it contributes to reinforcing attitudes of others so that a cultural stereotype develops. Hate crimes and civil rights violations are but two of the well-documented effects of stereotyping (Tsesis, 2002). The ethical issue here is one of respecting the dignity of diverse people and groups.

Recognize that Legal Speech may not be Ethical Speech

The United States of America is well-known for providing a platform for citizens to speak freely. This right was so important to those who wrote the U.S. Constitution that the First Amendment clearly guarantees our right to "speak our mind." This amendment states, "Congress shall make no law . . . abridging the freedom of speech." Courts have attempted to define further what this means. There is a clear dilemma here. How do you achieve a balance between free speech and protecting those who can be harmed by the speech? Does a group have the right to argue racial superiority, for example? Courts have found that arguing racial superiority falls within the right to free speech. Of course, this is offensive and we believe not ethical speech.

The First Amendment also allows a speaker to defame a public official as long as what is said is not a reckless disregard for the truth. If a speaker crosses this line, he or she may be sued for libel. We do not consider this kind of speech to be ethical.

People who engage in speech that is not protected by the First Amendment can be tried and, if convicted, jailed. So, what kinds of speech are not protected? Speech that provokes violence or some unlawful act is not protected. Defamatory falsehoods are also not protected. These are speeches that aim to destroy an individual's reputation and, if delivered, can lead to a charge of libel. In addition, the first Amendment does not permit threats against the life of the President. Even a threat made in jest may lead to the person's arrest. All of these are illegal and also do not pass the fundamental test of ethics: Does the speech harm others and is the truth being told?

Now, let us turn to an area of ethics that is often confusing to some.

PLAGIARISM

Plagiarism is the act of using another's ideas or language as if it is your own. You are probably thinking, "Not me!" Perhaps you are correct and will not find this a problem. We do find though that some students who cross into plagiarism territory do not know they are there. Obviously, this kind of behavior does not lead to the success we want for you as a speaker. Beyond this, if caught, a plagiarist will likely suffer serious penalties that range from a failing grade on the assignment to failing the course. In business and industry, it can result in the loss of a job.

Plagiarism can also lead to public humiliation. One example will make this point clear. Senior Pastor Glenn Wagner, pastor of one of the largest churches in Charlotte, North Carolina, revealed his plagiarism and resigned. He said, "On a number of occasions, when I felt literally empty and devoid of any creative ability, I used material from sermons of some of my brother preachers, in part or in whole, for my sermons, and did not give them credit. This was wrong" (*The Charlotte World*, September 13, 2004).

Types of Plagiarism

Identifying situations that fit into the area of plagiarism can more easily be understood if we examine the various kinds of plagiarism.

Use of an Entire Work   The most obvious kind of plagiarism is the **use of an entire work** of another person without giving credit to the author. In this case, giving credit may be misunderstood. Perhaps you think that some statement like, "I derived this information I am presenting from that which I found in the *New York Times*," is sufficient acknowledgment for using the material. It is not. Perhaps you think if you take the material and tweak it in several spots you are not guilty of wholesale stealing. The truth of the matter is that this does not make it an original piece of work that you can claim as your own.

Why are speakers lured into committing this kind of plagiarism? Often the answer is, "I put off working on my speech until there just wasn't enough time to complete it. I had to have a speech so this seemed like the only option." So, the student gets on line and downloads a speech to solve the problem. Another version of solving this problem is to get someone else's speech, "borrow" it with their permission—perhaps it is a speech presented by a friend in a previous term. Finally, a student might solve this problem by making a close paraphrase of a magazine article.

Of course, there is an ethical problem here in all of these cases. But, there is also an additional problem that students who engage in this kind of behavior almost never consider. Someone else's work only rarely sounds like it fits with the student who delivers it. The instructor will likely know this and many will do some checking on the Internet to see if the work is actually someone else's. We also know of cases where an instructor recognizes a speech that he or she heard delivered by another student.

The best way to avoid this problem is to pick your topic early and begin shortly thereafter researching and constructing your speech. This allows you plenty of time to research and write the speech and plenty of time to practice it. The obvious outcome is a better speech and a better grade.

Piecing Together from Several Sources   The speech of this kind involves selecting material from several sources, taking them word for word and joining them together in a way that makes sense. It is often referred to as "**cut and paste**." This cut and paste job cannot really be claimed as your original material. In fact, it is nearly all somebody else's. The ideas need to be your own and expressed in your own words.

The key to avoiding this trap is to start early in collecting your information and collect enough of it that you are well-informed about the topic. You will begin to see patterns of topics that are central to the topic. This will make it easy for you to formulate your own main points. Group the information—you should have plenty—as it pertains to the points. Now put what these people are saying in your own words. Give credit if it is a clear paraphrase. At this point in preparing there is more work to do; topics that will be addressed in other chapters. The good news, as you can see, is that you have avoided plagiarism.

Quoting or Paraphrasing Others without Giving Credit   **Quoting** is the use of another's exact words or a text. **Paraphrasing** is the restatement, rewording or a summary in your own words of what somebody said or something printed in a text.

We all know a quotation can be a powerful addition to any speech and, especially, to a persuasive speech. There are three specific requirements to keep in mind when you use a quotation. First, check carefully that you have the exact words of the text or person you are quoting. Next, be sure you use this wording exactly as it was reported. The best way to ensure this is to write the text out on a note card that you will be able to read to your audience. Finally, give credit to the source.

It is not complicated to avoid plagiarism when quoting a text. This process is very much like crediting the source in written work you do, but this time the citation is verbal and connected to the quotation you use. For example, you might say, "As reported on the NBC Nightly News on September 7th, 2012, Reporter Brian Williams said, '[quote whatever he said].' " Here is another example. "On August 28, 1963, on the steps of the Lincoln Memorial in Washington D.C., Dr. Martin Luther King, Jr. delivered his "I Have a Dream" speech. Dr. King spoke these words, 'Five score years ago, a great American, in whose symbolic shadow we stand signed the Emancipation Proclamation. This momentous decree came as a great beacon of light of hope to millions of Negro slaves who had been seared in the flames of withering injustice.' "

Recall that paraphrasing is taking another's material and restating it or summarizing it in your own words. Paraphrasing is ethical and not plagiarism, of course, if you do it properly. Properly, in this case, means to give credit when you use the person's phrasing with some wording changes. Also, give credit if you are retaining the person's overall organization of the ideas and basic sentence structures. Beyond this, you may use information that is common knowledge among those who are informed about the topic—you can tell this if you find several sources saying the same thing. In this case, bring this information together in your own words and do not worry about giving credit.

Avoid all this kind of plagiarism by personally analyzing and summarizing your material and convey the content in your own words.

Using Internet Documents without Giving Credit   Many of us make extensive use of the Internet to collect information for use in a speech. It seems like this is an area where more plagiarism appears than any other. Why? Perhaps it is the ease of collecting this information and transporting it directly into a speech. Perhaps this is because the Internet has become a major source of retrieving information. Regardless of the reason, you need to understand that you must give credit just as you would if the information came from some other source.

You will be creating problems for yourself if you download a copy of the information but do not also copy the source. You will not be able to cover-up by merely saying, "According to the internet. . . ." or "I found this on a Web site. . . ." Providing the citation of the source is an important ethical responsibility. The listener will not be able to evaluate the quality of your information without knowing the source.

A very serious problem in the use of materials found on the Internet is the use of intact speeches that are for sale. This practice is definitely risky and, of course, highly unethical. Here is the reason this is risky behavior. Almost all of these speeches are such that the language does not sound like what a student would use. When this is suspected, the instructor can easily go on the Internet and find the speech. Many schools also have computer programs that are designed to detect such a problem. In most schools, discovery of this kind of plagiarism will yield an "F" for the speech or possibly an "F" for the course or perhaps dismissal from the school. It is a very risky business to present a speech that has been acquired on the Internet.

ETHICAL LISTENING
Our examination of ethics in public speaking would not be complete without turning our attention to ethical listening. **Ethical listening** is behaving responsibly when receiving and processing what the speaker is saying. We have three guidelines that when followed will help you to be an ethical listener.

Give the Speaker Your Full Attention
It may be difficult to give the speaker your full attention if you are suffering from sleep deprivation. Let's face it; most of us are not in this situation. There are several other reasons we can cite. Perhaps the problem is that the topic does not interest you very much, so you resort to

other things. We find most often this "other thing" is holding a cell phone under the desk top and texting somebody. The next most prevalent form of coping with this problem is to study for some other course. Perhaps you do have an examination in the course, but studying earlier should be the solution.

Consider how it would feel if you were the speaker. Perhaps you see this behavior as inconsiderate or worse—rude. You have put in a whole lot of time preparing this speech. You constructed the best introduction you could think of so that you could capture your audience's attention. You have given "your best shot" at including examples and illustrations that your audience can relate to. Now you notice that several of your classmates are not giving their full attention. You gave them your full attention when they were speaking! You can see how this unethical and rude behavior can be demoralizing. Inattentive behavior like this is especially disturbing to people who are in the public speaking learning process—they are not likely to have the skills to cope with it.

Do Not Prejudge the Speaker

There are many reasons a listener may form a judgment of the speaker. Most of these reasons are related to some kind of prejudice—things like race, appearance or lifestyle. Another reason may rest on the audience member's understanding of the reputation of the speaker. These things, then, spill over into the listener's evaluation of the speech. They can even cause the listener to be closed-minded.

We believe you should strive to respect the speaker. We believe you should listen carefully and use what you hear as the basis of your opinion. Of course, you have a right to your opinion. We encourage you, though, to hold your evaluation until you have heard all the speaker has to say. We also encourage you to understand your prejudices, if you have any, and understand these biases may be having an effect on how you judge the speaker's message.

Try to Fully Understand the Speaker's Position

Finally, understand that nearly every speech you hear has something in it for you—something you can use. You cannot find that "something" if you tune the speaker out and retreat into your private world. Give the speaker your full attention so that you can find what is in that speech that is especially for you.

We are not naïve. We know that there are some speeches that are so bad that you will not find anything useful in them. We ask you to recall that the speaker put out some effort, but failed somehow. This presents an opportunity for you. Learn from this speaker by figuring out what the mistakes are. Imagine ways you could improve this speech. The speaker is giving you a lesson in what not to do—so use it.

Put Ethics into Practice to be Successful

We believe that all of us think ethics is important. But, do we practice it?

If we are going to be ethical and successful we must act ethically—we must practice being ethical. You might be tempted to say to yourself, "How about paraphrasing this section from another rather than citing the author." Or, you might—and this is more likely—just paraphrase the material without ever thinking about citing the author. Our point is this: You must be vigilant in every step in writing a speech to avoid slipping into areas of unethical behavior like these.

SUMMARY

Concern about ethical behavior is strong because we are confronted in the news with incidents of people being cited for their dishonesty. All of us believe we are honest and see ourselves as making a great effort to do what is right. It is important to fully understand the ethics of public speaking and listening if we are to be successful in these efforts.

Ethics has its roots in the Greek word ethos, the character of the speaker. We have come to understand this means the trustworthy, straightforward and honest presentation of ideas as well as respect for the audience.

Ethical speakers are marked by these characteristics:

- They have a clear and responsible goal.

- They prepare thoroughly.

- They are honest, trustworthy and responsible.

- They do not engage in name calling.

- They recognize that legal speech may not be ethical speech.

Plagiarism is an ethical problem for some speakers. Plagiarism is the act of using another's ideas or language as if it is your own. All of us think we obey the rules for avoiding plagiarism, but there are clearly some subtle ways that we may break the rules and not know it.

These are the kinds of plagiarism that are understood to be wrong by most people.

- Use of an Entire Work

- Piecing Together from Several Sources (Cut and Paste)

- Quoting or Paraphrasing Others without Giving Credit

- Using Material from the Internet without Giving Credit

Some aspects of quoting and paraphrasing may cause trouble. First, be sure you quote accurately and give credit to the source. Second, making minor alterations of the text is not paraphrasing and constitutes plagiarism. Third, you must give credit when you paraphrase using

21

the person's overall organization of ideas and basic sentence structure, even if the words are mostly your own.

A very serious act of plagiarism is use of intact speeches, whether you paid for the speech or not. This behavior is easily detected through retrieving the same speech used from the Internet.

Finally, the issue of ethical listening was addressed. Ethical listening is behaving responsibly when receiving and processing what the speaker has said. Three guidelines will help you to be an ethical listener.

- Give the speaker your full attention.
- Do not prejudge the speaker.
- Try to fully understand the speaker's position.

We all believe that ethics is important. But, do we practice it? If we are going to be an ethical speaker, we must practice being ethical.

REFERENCES

Burgoon, J. K., Guerrero, L. K., & Floye, K. (2010). *Nonverbal communication.* Boston: Allyn & Bacon, p. 317.

Credo of Communication Ethics, National Communication Association, 1999.

Leathers, D., & Eaves, M. H. (2008). *Successful nonverbal communication,* 4th ed. Boston: Allyn & Bacon, p. 5.

The Charlotte World, September 13, 2004.

Tsesis, A. (2002). *Destructive messages: How speech paves the way for harmful social movements.* New York: New York University Press.

Wilson, G. L. (2014). *Relational Communication.* Boston: Pearson.

Chapter 3
Listening

Courtesy of Brendan Smialowski/AP Images.

WHY IS LISTENING IMPORTANT?

Listing is the communication activity we spend the most time doing. You probably spend about 90 percent of your class time listening. Of course, that does not surprise you. But did you know that students who listen more effectively learn better and, as a result, earn better grades than students who do not (Barker, Edwards, Gaines, & Holley, 1980; Hunsaker, 1991)?

Effective listening is also seen by employers as vital. Research points out that employees spend 55 to 60 percent of their time listening. Poor listening can lead to costly mistakes, a fact that employers are well aware of and consequently offer listening training for their employees (Hiam, 1997; Linowes, 1998;

Wolvin & Coakley, 1991). A survey of executives found that 80 percent believed listening to be one of the most important skills in the corporate world (Salopeck, 1999).

Listening is more important than ever in our communication-oriented world that depends so heavily on it. Business managers rank listening as the number one communication skill that is most critical to their jobs (Wolvin & Coakley, 1991). The same study found that effective listeners held higher positions and were promoted more often than people who were ineffective listeners.

We begin our study of listening by presenting a model of the listening process that illustrates that hearing is only one step. We describe this process so you can understand what is involved when you listen effectively. Next, we address listening problems that emerge from bad listening habits and then provide suggestions for improving your listening. Then, we provide advice for sharpening your critical listening skills. We also believe that you can and should help your audience listen better. To that end, we provide some advice. Finally, we know that as an audience member in a public speaking class you will be evaluating speeches of your classmates. We provide information that will be help you carry out this role successfully.

HEARING IS NOT LISTENING

You may hear the words and see the nonverbal communication behaviors when you say you are listening, but how well are you attending to the message? How well do you understand? How well do remember? To understand the point we are making here, focus on the sounds around you. Perhaps you can hear the air conditioner or heater functioning. Perhaps you can hear people talking. If you are indoors, perhaps you can hear sounds from outside, such as cars or birds. Locate one of those sounds. Why didn't you sense this before? If it was there, you could have sensed it. However, you did not complete the listening process until we urged you to do so. Listening involves much more than sensing or hearing. It also involves attending, understanding, remembering, and responding.

"You are not hearing me" usually means, "You are not listening to me and understanding me." You see, listening is much more complex than merely hearing. Listening is an active process of receiving verbal and nonverbal messages. It has four components, each of which is essential to effective listening. These are sensing, attending, understanding, and remembering. We have placed these in a model to help you visualize the process (Figure 3.1).

We are often not aware of the components of the listening process because they blend into the

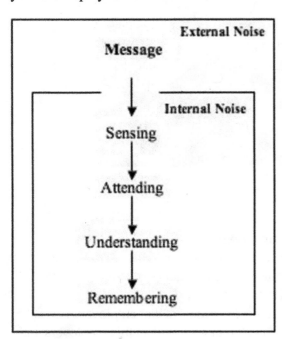

FIGURE 3.1
Components of the Listening Process

24

nearly instantaneous act of listening. Our hope is that considering each component individually will help you increase your awareness of them.

THE LISTENING PROCESS

Sensing

Sensing is receiving information through the five senses. This information is often referred to as a stimulus. A **stimulus** is something that incites your senses to their functional activity. We think primarily of audio and visual stimuli, but of course there are others. For example, touch and smell may be two we might be aware of in a romantic encounter. How is it, then, that you were not aware of some stimuli until they are pointed out? The reason is that there are so many things to sense that *we have to* intentionally filter some things out in order to focus on what we see as important.

Attending

You may not have been aware of the clock because you did not attend to it—you did not select its sound from the many of which you were conscious. **Attending** is the selective act of focusing on stimuli.

Hundreds of stimuli are available for your attention. You select only those that seem relevant to the particular situation and ignore the others. This is why you were able to sense but did not listen. You may have determined the stimulus from the clock was not relevant, and ignored it.

Selective attention suggests that we focus on something. This kind of attention is good in that it helps you concentrate on the message. It allows you to block out what you choose to ignore. This selectivity also contributes to poor listening if you ignore important aspects of the message. Consider the consequences, for example, of "accidentally" filtering out an important message you hear from your teacher.

Understanding

Understanding refers to the interpretation and evaluation of what you choose to attend to. Understanding involves more than merely paying attention to what is heard; it implies that you assign a meaning that, hopefully, is close to what the speaker intended. Remember that meaning is related to more than mere sensing. You get important data from you experience that helps you interpret what you hear. Perhaps you will show up for class without an important assignment if you do not understand.

Remembering

Remembering, the process of recalling by an effort of memory, is a difficult task for many people. Would you dare not take notes if you wanted to remember what was said in a lecture? Most of us would take careful notes. Your reluctance to skip note taking is for a good reason.

Retention of information falls off rapidly. You actually lose a lot of what is said almost as soon as it has been said. Your notes provide a record of what was said.

Just as you perceive and attend selectively, you remember selectively. You remember some ideas more easily than others because you have found them useful. Sometimes you remember because you are intrigued by the thought or see a potential payoff. You encounter problems when you choose not to remember something that later turns out to be important.

Responding

Responding to a message means to give observable feedback. This step is necessary to complete the listening process since communication in our view is transactional. **Transactional** is a back and forth "negotiation" of meaning. The speaker and listener are responding to each other as they seek to create a common understanding of the meaning. Each audience member becomes an active participant, not a passive listener.

You may become prey to the **passivity syndrome** when you believe that the speaker is entirely responsible for the meaning and do not participate actively because of your belief. You *and* the speaker are responsible for completing and understanding the message. You, as a listener, can fulfill this responsibility by working to pay close attention and following the suggestion provided in this chapter.

Lewis and Reinsch (1988) studied the behavior of good listeners. They found that these people are attentive in that they maintained appropriate eye contact and displayed appropriate facial expressions that suggested they were listening. They also demonstrated their attention verbally by exchanging ideas and answering questions.

Although Lewis and Reinsch did not study responses of poor listeners, all of us have experienced them and would find them easy to describe. These people seem bored and their eye contact wanders away from us when we are speaking. Often their posture is less alert as they slump. Sometimes they are even rude enough to be having a text conversation on their cell phone while "listening" to us.

Effective listening is not a passive activity. Listeners need to be active participants in the communication. We will address active listening shortly, but first we will turn to listening problems.

LISTENING PROBLEMS

Something seemingly simple as bad habits often account for our inability to listen effectively. Of course, not all of these habits may apply to your listening, but just one can cause you trouble. Here are several listening problems that are often experienced:

We Have Trouble Concentrating

You might say, "My mind wanders," when you speak of your listening. This wandering phenomenon is actually quite understandable. This is why it is. Our brain processes at about 400 to 800 words per minute. We talk at a rate of 120 to 150 words per minute (Wolff & Marsnick, 1992). What this means is we can let our brain wander and still get the point. But, of course, the opposite can happen too. We lose track of the point. As we are thinking about other things, our brain may not tune back in when we should actually be listening.

Another difficulty that affects our concentration is becoming distracted. There are many sources of distraction, beyond the wandering mind. Noise is the other primary distracter. **Noise** is any interference that distorts the message exchange. It can be physiological or psychological. **Physical noise** is such things as aches, pains, or other discomforts like a room that is so hot that people are feeling uncomfortable and sleepy. So a person might feel pain and this draws his or her attention. Physical noise also includes physiological problems like hearing and vision loss. **Psychological noise** can come from worry or concern. Perhaps the person has an important job interview or has experienced a significant disappointment. These concerns occupy some of the psychological space that would normally be devoted to listening to the speaker and, thus, make effective listening difficult.

We Decide We Know What the Speaker Will Say

We believe we know what the speaker will say so we tune out. Of course no one can predict the "future," but we think we can. Once this decision is made that we know what the speaker will say, listening stops and we have violated a principle of great listening—*hear the speaker out before you decide you know what will be said.*

Another situation brings us to decide the speaker is going to say something we do not want to hear. We decide we do not like what the speaker is saying and think where he or she is going or decide we disagree with the speaker and so we stop listening. If you continued to listen carefully, you might discover the speaker has ideas that never occurred to you. Perhaps the speaker has things to say that would cause you to rethink your position on the topic. A fresh approach may be very useful to you, but you will never know it if you tune out.

You will find that nearly all speeches have something useful to you—information, a different view point, or a different way to do something. You are the loser if you prejudge the speaker and decide not to listen. The choice is yours.

We Become Distracted by the Speaker's Appearance or His or Her Delivery

Not every speaker delivers a speech well. Not every speaker can afford to dress well. Not every speaker meets your expectations about appearance and delivery. A friend of ours would say, "So what? Does that mean the speaker does not have something important to say that would be useful to you?" This person has a simply stated and very good point. Give the speaker a fair chance. You cannot learn anything from the speaker if you tune out. You will often be pleasantly surprised at what you have learned.

We Become Too Attentive and Miss the Significant Ideas And Broad Picture

Sometimes we are so intent on "getting it all" that we try to retain every detail of what the speaker is saying. If you are doing this you may very well experience listening overload.

Resist distractions like these dark glasses that prevent eye contact.

Dr. Ralph Nichols, recipient of the Lifetime Achievement Award from the International Listening Association, called this bad habit listening for the facts.

So, why is working on getting the details a problem? This listener's focus on facts and the details makes it difficult to focus on the main ideas and their support and therefore the listener does not have a basis for understanding the "big picture." Without the big picture the listener does not have a framework to organize the facts and so he or she becomes "lost." We recommend you concentrate on the main ideas and evidence, a practice that will enhance your efficiency as a listener.

IMPROVING YOUR LISTENING

Be Willing To Expend Energy

A major assumption about listening for many people is that it does not take much effort. These people think they can sit back and absorb what is being said. We argue that you can follow this strategy, but you will not be listening very well. A statement often made by one of your authors is, "Just because you can does not mean you should." This applies here. Take the task of listening seriously. Excellent listening takes self-discipline.

Just relaxing is a mistake. Avoid this by assuming an alert posture. This means sitting up straight, leaning forward slightly, and maintaining eye contact. Of course, you can maintain this attentive posture and still not listen, but, rather than slouching, leaning back, looking away from the speaker or closing your eyes, remaining alert will give you a better shot at listening effectively. Read on; there is more you can do to help yourself listen effectively.

"Listen" to the Nonverbal Behavior

Of course the words are important, but much is also being said by the nonverbal behavior. You can often get a better understanding of the speaker's meaning if you look for the nonverbal cues. Notice the body language, physical appearance, facial expressions, and eye contact. Hear the emotional side of the message by noticing the speaker's tone of voice. Here are some aspects of nonverbal behavior to consider when evaluating a speaker's nonverbal behavior:

- How do the verbal message and nonverbal messages of the speaker match? There is an interesting situation if there is a mismatch. Often the nonverbal is believed over the verbal if there is a difference. Is there message value here?

- Are there changes in the speaker's vocal tone? Does the volume increase? A change in tone and increase in volume often signals a significant point.

- What emotions, if any, are expressed by the face? Judee Burgoon and her colleagues (2010, p. 317) report "the most significant nonverbal channels for emotional expression are the voice and the face."

We know that "slightly more than two-thirds of communicated meaning can be attributed to nonverbal messages" (Leathers & Eaves, 2008). Do you suppose that your attention to the nonverbal part of the message is important?

Resist Distractions

There are many things going on in an auditorium or classroom while the speaker is addressing his or her audience. People may be coughing or whispering. A "listener" in front of you may be using his or her cell phone to text a message. You may experience physical distractions, like a headache, a seat that is too hard or a room that is too hot or too cool. All of these are distractions you will want to overcome. How do you do this?

The answers to this question may not surprise you, but it can be difficult to achieve. The answer is active listening; but what does that mean? **Active listening** requires you to "will yourself" to pay attention. This means to pull your mind to what the speaker is saying and force yourself to keep it there. One way to do this is to review in your mind what the speaker has been saying. Here is an example of what that might be like: "So the speaker's point was. . . . And, this is being followed by this example." Or perhaps this is what you might say to yourself, "OK, the central idea of the speech is. . . . And she said that a good reason to know this is. . . . And now, the first point was. . . ." You can easily see that you can only do this if you are listening carefully.

Suspend Judgments

Of course, you may not agree with everything the speaker has to say. But consider that a speech "unfolds" as do arguments and ideas with their support. This suggests that you will not fully understand what the speaker is going to say until you hear the complete idea or argument, including its support.

A natural response to something being said with which we do not agree is to stop listening and formulate the reasons we do not like what we are hearing or perhaps construct counter arguments. What this means is that we are not listening effectively because our attention is drawn away from the speaker on to whatever we are working with in our mind. So our listening is being impaired.

What needs to be done is to avoid reaching conclusions until you have heard everything the speaker has to say. You will need to set aside your own prejudices in order to be successful at achieving this. An excellent way to achieve this is to try to identify with the speakers experiences, feelings and ideas.

Take Excellent Notes

A final technique for helping yourself focus your attention on the speaker is note taking. All of us have taken notes—we are or have been students after all. This may lead you to think there is not much to learn about note taking. Of course, that is possible, but please read on. What we say will be brief so we encourage you to read it carefully and use what seems right for you.

Some people take too many things down and error in writing too much. If it seems like you are running a race as you take notes—trying to keep up with the speaker with little success—you are probably writing down too much. You are not alone in this problem. One of your authors is guilty of attempting to get it all down. What happened is that the relatively neat writing turned to scribble with incomplete words. The result was difficult to read notes and then a place where the writing stopped. Your author just gave up listening. The speaker won the race. The opposite of this is writing down too few words. The result is notes that leave big gaps in what was said. These are difficult, and sometimes impossible, to read.

The solution is to follow two practices of effective listeners who choose to take notes. First, try to work with a key-word outline. This uses principles of outlining that you will find in Chapter 10. Second, begin with what you believe you can expect and write this

Courtesy of Ocean/Corbis Images.

Appreciative listening is something we do for enjoyment or pleasure.

down, leaving a space to place your notes when you hear them. Here are some key topics you can usually expect in a well-written speech:

I.   Thesis:
II. Preview:
III. First Main Point:
    A, B, etc. (Sub Points, if there are some):
      Support:
      1.
      2.
      3.
IV. Repeat this for each point/sub point.
V.   Special Remarks and Summary in the Conclusion

Of course, you will want to get some practice using this suggestion for note taking. Practice will hone your note-taking skills. We predict your effort will be rewarded with excellent results.

KINDS OF LISTENING

Wolvin & Coakley (1995) identify four kinds of listening. We will briefly discuss each so that you will understand how listening serves some very different purposes, depending on the context.

- **Appreciative listening** is listening we do for enjoyment or pleasure. An entertaining speech, listening to a stand-up comic or listening to music are examples of this type of listening.

- **Empathic listening** provides emotional support for the speaker. When a friend comes to you to talk about a problem he or she is experiencing, empathic listening is in order.

- **Comprehensive listening** involves listening for understanding of the message. This is the primary listening we do in the classroom or at a Monday morning meeting at our place of employment.

- **Critical listening** (sometimes called discriminative listening) is what we engage in when evaluating a message for the purpose of accepting or rejecting it. Persuasive speeches of all kinds fall into this category. A sales presentation, a political campaign speech, and various speeches in our legislatures are situations that require critical evaluation from the listener.

This is our next topic. Next, we will provide some pointers for careful listening.

HOW TO LISTEN CRITICALLY

Listening becomes easier if you know what you are looking for in the speech. We know what we are asking you to do is sometimes a judgment call. We also know that you will have more and more "tools" to help you in the evaluation process as you progress through this book and the course. The truth is, though, you have to start somewhere. Here we will lay a brief frame-work that will help you get started.

We pointed out in the section on note taking, above, the basic structure of most speeches. This is a central idea, main points, supporting materials, and a conclusion. Here are some rules about how these parts fit together and how to evaluate them:

The **thesis statement** provides the central idea of the speech. This should be found in the introduction to the speech's development.

Ask these questions about the thesis statement:

1. Is the thesis statement clear?
2. Is it stated as a simple declarative sentence?

The **main points** develop the thesis statement. They are the important things being said about the thesis. There should be no more than three or four of these.

Ask these questions about the main points:

1. Does each point represent some aspect of the thesis—does it fit?
2. Are the main points limited to three or four?
3. Are they clear statements?

The sub points develop main points. Their analysis follows the same as the main point analysis. (A short speech may not have any sub points.)

Supporting material expands on the main and sub points. It is meant to explain the point, provide an illustration or example of the point, and/or provide evidence as proof of an argument made by the point.

Ask these questions about the supporting material:

1. Does the example or illustration help you understand more about the point?
2. Is the evidence accurate?
3. Is the evidence cited taken from unbiased (objective) sources?
4. Does the evidence seem to relate to the speaker's claims?
5. Is there sufficient material presented to support the speaker's point?

The **conclusion** is used to summarize the points made during the speech. It often has a concluding statement that ties the speech together.

Ask these questions about the conclusion:

1. Are the main points reviewed?
2. Is there a statement that ties the speech together? How effective is it?

HELPING YOUR AUDIENCE LISTEN EFFECTIVELY

Some speakers do not think of helping their audience listen as a responsibility for them to fulfill. We do. If you look out at your audience in the middle of your speech and find many of they doing things other than listening, do you blame yourself or do you blame your audience? Did you, as a speaker, have anything to do with this situation? You bet you did. Of course the audience does bear some of the responsibility, but so do you. The following section lets you know some of the things you can try to do to avoid this embarrassing situation. Here are our guidelines:

Speak Up, Slow Down, and Repeat Yourself

Most speakers are not too loud, not too slow, and do not summarize too often. So, speak up, slow down, and repeat yourself is good advice.

Give Your Audience a Reason to Listen

We do not know of anybody who has turned down information that they really believe is useful. We do not know of anybody who has turned down information that they really believe is valuable.

One of the most important things you can do for yourself when you prepare a speech is to find out the answer to the question, "Why should my audience care about my topic?" This is a significant key to holding their attention. They will give you their attention if they think you have something important and valuable to say.

Emphasize Your Main Points

So, what does emphasizing your points do for you and how do you do it? Emphasizing your points helps your audience remember them more readily. Is that not a main goal you will have as a speaker? Of course it is.

Here is what you can do to provide emphasis and help your audience remember your main ideas:

- Give an initial summary, a preview of the main points in your introduction.

- Provide markers, "I will cover three points. (Say them.) First, let us consider. . . ." The word "first" is a marker. It lets the audience know a main point is coming. It helps the main point stand out.

- Provide vocal emphasis for your main points. Slow your rate a bit and raise your volume a bit when you say the main point.

- Summarize your main points when you present your conclusion.

Sharing Meanings Will Help with Understanding

People will understand better if you are able to put your ideas into a familiar framework. For example, a political candidate would be more persuasive if he or she provides examples to the audience from factory life if the audience members live every day in that environment. You would do well to know who is in your audience and select examples from their personal situations that relate to your topic.

Help Your Audience Remember through Use of Visuals

PowerPoint slides and other well-crafted visuals are a powerful aid to helping your audience pay attention. You will learn more about visuals in Chapter 12. It is a well-known fact that they help hold attention. It is much more difficult to let your attention wander if you are attending to PowerPoint visuals that are moving right along with the content of the speech.

EVALUATING THE SPEAKER

One of the most significant factors in improving your public speaking is receiving feedback. Of course, your instructor will provide feedback, but also your classroom colleagues may provide feedback too. These represent an important source of feedback.

We know that speakers profit from and learn from listening to others speakers. We believe you know when you have heard a very good or even excellent speech. We believe you can gain some "pointers" that will be useful in improving your own public speeches if you pay close attention.

Both of these, receiving feedback from others and gleaning ideas for improving your own speech through being an observer/critic, are vital to achieving the success you want and deserve. Your hard work as a listener is the key to this success.

Here are some guidelines to help you in this process:

1. Use a check list to guide you through the important considerations for your listening and note taking.

Figure 3.2 provides an example of such a check list:

CRITERIA FOR EVALUATING A SPEECH

The Introduction: *Comments:*
- Gained attention and interest
- Presented Need
- Introduced topic clearly
- Previewed the speech

CRITERIA FOR EVALUATING A SPEECH *(cont'd)*

The Development:
- Main points were clear
- Main points were organized appropriately
- Main points were supported
- A variety of support was used
- Language was clear and vivid
- Clear transition was made between points
- Topic was adapted to the audience
- Visual aids were effective

The Conclusion:
- Summarized main points or ideas
- Tied speech together

The Delivery:
- Maintained eye contact with the listeners
- Presented visual materials effectively
- Used gestures appropriately
- Voice had adequate volume, rate, variety

General Effectiveness:
- Topic seemed appropriate to this audience
- Topic was clearly focused to fit time limit
- Speech was within the time requirements

FIGURE 3.2
Checklist for Listening and Note Taking

2. *Listen carefully.*

3. *Take notes.*

4. *Note the strengths and weaknesses of the speaker.*

5. *Lead your critique with a strength and then an area that needs improvement if you are providing a critique.*

6. *Couple a need for improvement with your suggestion for improvement.*

SUMMARY

We began our discussion of listening by pointing out how vital it is to your success in many areas of your life. Business managers rank listening as the number one communication skill that is most critical to their jobs and those of their employees.

We began our study of listening by presenting a model of the listening process that illustrates that hearing is only one of the five steps in the listening process. These steps are: sensing, attending, understanding, remembering.

We continued with a discussion of listening problems. These are: trouble with concentrating, deciding we know what the speaker will say, being distracted by the speaker's appearance or delivery and being too attentive and missing the broad picture and significant ideas.

Next, we addressed ways to improve your listening. You must be willing to expend energy, resist distractions, suspend judgment and take excellent notes. A specific plan was presented to help you hone your note taking skills.

There are many kinds of listening, depending on the situation. These are appreciative listening, empathic listening, comprehensive listening and critical listening. We focused on critical listening because it is very important to your evaluation of speeches. Here we indicated the major parts of a speech with suggested questions to be asked to aid in evaluating them.

We also pointed out that the speaker can help his or her audience listen better. These require you, as the speaker, to speak up, slow down, and repeat yourself. Beyond this you can give your audience a reason to listen, emphasize your main points, share meaning by using audience experiences to illustrate points and create visuals that help the audience follow your presentation.

Finally, we presented criteria for you to use when you are evaluating a speech and providing a critique. These guidelines include specific criteria.

REFERENCES

Barker, L, Edwards, C., Gaines, K., & Holley, F. (1980). An investigation of proportional time spent in various communication activities. *Journal of Applied Communication Research*, 8, 101–109.

Hunsaker, R. (1991). Critical listening—a neglected skill. Presentation to the 77th annual meeting of the Speech Communication Association.

Hiam, A. (1997). Is anybody listening? *Workforce*, 76, 92.

Lewis, M. H., Reinsch, Jr., N. L. (1988). Listening in organizational environments. *Journal of Business Communication*, 23, 49–67.

Linowes, J. G. (1988). Listening between the lines. *Journal of Management in Engineering*, 14, 21–23.

Salopeck, J. J. (1999). Is anyone listening? *Training and Development*, 53, 58–60.

Wolff, F. I., & Marsnick, N. C. (1992). *Perceptive listening*, 2nd ed. Fort Worth, TX: Harcourt Brace Jovanovich.

Wolvin, A. D., & Coakley, C. G. (1991). A survey of the status of listening training in some Fortune 500 Corporations.*Communication Education*, 40, 152–162.

Wolvin, A. D., & Coakley, C. G. (1995). *Listening*, 2nd ed. Dubuque, IA: Brown and Benchmark.

Chapter 4
Analyzing the Audience

Courtesy of HO/Reuters/Corbis Images.

WHY BOTHER WITH AN AUDIENCE ANALYSIS?

The answer to this question is that you can increase the opportunity for success because your audience will identify more closely with you and what you say. **Audience-Centeredness** means that you do plan your speech so that it relates to the audience's experience. In other words, what you say connects with the experience of the members of your audience. You want audience members to believe you are talking directly to them. So, again, "Why worry about this, why bother?" You will be more successful and get a better grade on your presentation if you do; you will be less successful and, perhaps, unhappy with your grade if you don't.

Why is being audience-centered a great idea? There are several easily understood ideas that explain this. First, an audience will give more attention to something they see as relevant to themselves. Second, it helps you achieve the goals you set for your speech. Third, it boosts your ethos, credibility, because the experiences about which you speak seem similar to those your audience has experienced. Fourth, your audience is more likely to see you as knowledgeable and competent. Finally, your audience won't see you as insensitive because you are not delivering a speech that doesn't have anything to do with their interests and wasting their time.

The solution to achieving this kind of success is careful audience analysis. We will guide through this process in the remainder of this chapter. We begin by focusing on your classmates as your audience. Next, we address the psychology of this audience. We follow this by a discussion of common methods of audience analysis. Then, we will help you understand the factors you should consider in discovering just who the listeners are. Finally, we will discuss adapting your speech to the audience.

YOUR CLASSMATES AS AUDIENCE

You have an excellent opportunity to sharpen your public speaking skills while speaking with an audience where the members find themselves in the same situation as you do. The end result of this is that you will have empathic audience members who understand the difficulty of your task. In addition, they are folks with whom you share things in common and, because of this, you are likely to have some basic knowledge regarding what they know about your topic and how they will receive it. You might be tempted to conclude this means you will not need to do much in the way of audience analysis. Do not go down this road. It will certainly lead you in the wrong direction and decrease the chance that you will achieve excellence and success in your speaking assignments.

The best speeches are those that are adapted to the audience who receive them. In a sense, this kind of adaptation shows respect for your audience. Understanding your audience will allow you to pick a topic that is worthy of your and your audience's time. We hope that one of your goals in presenting the topic you select is that it will have impact in some way on your audience. How do you expect to achieve this if they do not relate to what you are saying? The answer to this is in understanding what causes your audience to pay attention.

THE PROCESS OF ATTENDING

All of us have a frame of reference we use as a filtering system. We perceive things and make decisions about whether to pay attention or not based on our frame of reference. The basic questions your audience members will ask are these: "Is this important?" "Is this useful to me?" "Does this affect my values, beliefs or well-being?" "Will knowing this have a positive impact on my life?" Answers to these questions affect their decisions about attending.

The process of answering these questions requires examining them in relation to each person's frame of reference. A **frame of reference** is our personal set of interlocking facts, ideas, beliefs, values, and attitudes that we use to filter what we hear and then make sense of it if we allow it to register in our brain. Perception is always selective. What this means is, because of this process, what you say as a speaker will not necessarily be the same message an audience member gets. So, the "why is this important or useful" is a very critical question. Your audience member will let more of what you say register in his or her brain when he or she sees what you are saying as important. In addition, the closer what you say is to the person's frame of reference, the more likely the meaning they give to what you have said will be to what you are thinking.

So what does this have to do with audience analysis? The answer to this question is simple: The speaker will hear what you say and judge it on the basis of their frame of reference. The audience analysis you do is meant to uncover what you can about the frames of references of your audience members. So when you use this as a basis for constructing your speech you will increase your chances of being successful. Now let's continue our journey through this chapter by providing pointers on how to gather information through audience analysis.

METHODS OF AUDIENCE ANALYSIS

Two basic methods for collecting information about your audience are direct and indirect. **Direct methods** are interviews, surveys and focus groups where you have personal contact with those from whom you are collecting information. The direct method you may not understand is the focus group. **A focus group** is a gathering of selected individual participants who are encouraged to talk in an unstructured way about questions posed by a facilitator. The discussion is generally recorded for analysis. You might use this technique if you know three or four members of your class who would be willing to talk to you as part of a group about their experiences with you topic. In this case, you would probably not bother to record what they say for future analysis.

Indirect methods are those you use when you do not have the opportunity to talk directly with those who might provide information about your audience. **Indirect methods** are observations, asking people other than group members and reviewing written documents to gather information. All of these allow you to make inferences about your audience.

One source of information for a classroom audience or, perhaps, a group in another setting where you are part of a group, is your direct observation. Using your class, for example, you might ask a group of questions like these to gather information. How many students are in this class? What ages are represented? What topics have been used in speeches that are similar to my proposed topic? How did they react to these? Do their views seem to be liberal or conservative or in between? If you are invited to speak to a group outside of your classroom situation, you can ask some of these questions of a person who represents the group. What is the purpose of the group? What are their common goals? What are their reasons for gathering on this occasion?

DEMOGRAPHIC AUDIENCE ANALYSIS

A demographic analysis can be of enormous help in providing information for your success on your speaking assignment. A **demographic analysis** is a technique used to draw inferences about your audience based on categories of information you have available. This analysis allows you to make decisions about various aspects of your speech as related to your audience. Some typical categories are age, gender, sex and ethnicity. Not all demographic variables will be of interest to you with respect to a particular topic and audience. So, your first task is to identify those that do relate to your particular speech.

Age

We do think of people as falling into age categories of all sorts. All of us have heard of Baby Boomers, Generation X, Generation Y and Generation 2K. Of course, these are merely labels, but there is enough commonality among the people born within the times of these brackets that they have been given names. One attribute of the people from these generational groups is they do like and represent things in common and have common interests. Each of these generations has relatively common values and experiences that make them different from another one. For example, older people tend to be uncomfortable with things like hip-hop, body piercing, and tattoos. Many younger people can recognize the names of historical people and events like the Vietnam War and President John F. Kennedy, but they do not really understand their place in history. Clearly, our particular generation means certain things.

Does this make a difference in the content of your speech? Of course it does. Age can affect the basic concerns of your audience because at different points in life people have different concerns. For example, career planning would likely be of interest to somebody who is completing a degree and launching a career. Of course, some college students are older, but most are not. Help in this area would be appreciated because of this. An older audience might be more interested in a speech that provides strategies for managing career changes. You need to be especially mindful when you select your topic for a speech.

You need to ask yourself about age at specific points in the speech construction process if this is an issue. First, and probably the most important, is to consider this in selecting your topic. Of course, the question here is, "Is this topic appropriate for this audience?" Second, in selecting supporting material you should ask, "Will my audience be able to relate to these examples and illustrations because in selecting them I took age into account?" Your examples and illustrations should relate to your audience's experiences and fit a person of the particular age group for which you are aiming.

What should you do if you have an audience that represents more than one generation? You might provide information that is useful to each. For example, you might provide information useful to apartment dwellers and home owners if you were talking about how to keep a residence safe.

Courtesy of Ed Kashi/Corbis Images.

Cultural differences represented by your audience can be a significant factor to take into account if your speech is to be successful.

Cultural Background

It is a well-known fact that the context in which you were raised has a profound impact on who you are because it shapes your values, beliefs, and attitudes (Stewart, 2012; Donavan & Rundle, 1997; Bashi & McDaniel, 1997). We hope you are not thinking that the basic label, Americans, describes the cultural background of your audience. Of course, in the broader sense this probably does define the cultural background in which you will speak. But, let's examine this more closely.

Suppose you were to pick the topic of gun control for your speech. Suppose, also, that several of your audience members grew up in the inner city of Chicago where gang violence and now-and-then shootings took place. Would you suppose they would have a view on gun control? Perhaps these audience members are thinking that their family needed to have a gun to protect their property and lives. Now, suppose that some audience members grew up in a rural area where hunting provided food and was a very important recreational activity. Would you suppose they have a view about gun control? Suppose, also, that some of your audience members grew up in a small urban community, perhaps Fairhope, Alabama, and never felt any need to own a gun. In fact, several of these people think there is no need to own a gun and that the more guns around, the more dangerous our world becomes. It only takes one additional step to suppose these people might also represent a particular cultural group. The people of the United States represent a great deal of cultural diversity. You may also find a number of international students in your audience. This surely will make a difference. Perhaps you can now see that speaking about gun control is not necessarily a simple matter. Finally, we bet you have a view on guns and gun control. How do you think it matches those of your audience? We conclude that you would be well-served by considering the cultural background of your listeners in relation to your view, the topic, and things you intend to say about it.

Gender

Ignoring the gender differences represented by your audience can get you into a lot of trouble. People can easily be offended if you make inappropriate remarks. And, of course, if you offend them you may kill your chance of success with your speech.

Suppose you are in the position to address a group of professionals and you use the male pronoun, "he," to refer to them. This is likely to be a big mistake regardless of what you think about this issue. How could this be a problem? It turns out that half of the audience is women who have worked especially hard to get where they are in their organization. It likely appears to them that you are insensitive to this fact and their situation by referring to them as "he." They may even think you are out of touch with today's reality.

Another place where you might run into problems is assuming that certain roles or interests align with a particular gender. Your male author is a very good cook, helps with the laundry, tends to the needs of children and participates in school activities. Women work in a variety of jobs, including construction, flying helicopters for the U. S. Army, and serving as athletic coaches for men's football. Clearly, men and women have broad aspirations for what they do in their spare time and directions for their vocation.

This issue is even more complicated by the fact there are some important similarities that tend to hold for most women and most men. In the field of interpersonal communication, we know that women are more likely to focus more attention on relational issues than on task issues (Wilson, 2014). This tendency can affect the construction of a speech. For example, a woman may focus on the relational issues when preparing a speech on teenage pregnancy. A man may focus on the task side of this issue—that is, the details of the problem, but not necessarily the harm to the relationships involved. Notice we said focus more on and not that they ignore the task or relationships. Knowing this information can dramatically affect the way you approach interpersonal communication. Perhaps you see the importance of gender on communication in your speech. We hope so.

Memberships in Groups

Citizens of the United States are very group oriented. We are joiners. You will find students in your audience who are members of religious groups, political groups, a variety of interest groups, groups that center on their academic major, sororities and fraternities and many more kinds of other groups. Group membership is one of the more difficult demographics to "read." Use of a survey analysis would help dramatically in this process. But, you do understand college students will likely have several similar affiliations. On the other hand, you may very well find it easy to discover significant affiliations for speeches you will deliver outside your university or college. Often these groups have a purpose that is well-known. You will be more successful if you are aware of this as you select the topic and construct the speech.

What do you do about this affiliation issue? Here is a plan that can work for you. Ask yourself what groups might have a position on your topic. Go to a second step after you identify these groups. Make a list of these groups and write next to the group name your best guess as to what their position might be. Examine this list and see if it informs you about an approach to your topic. We hope it does. If not, take a middle ground and try to be sensitive in your preparation of your speech.

Religion

Religious considerations can be important for topics that have religious implications. We probably think of our faith expression when we are addressing a sensitive topic. We often think that our view is the "correct view." Of course, a person of a different faith expression will likely think their view is the "correct view." Who is right? We often do not know. What we do know is that you will find it difficult to know where the problems lie if you do not know the beliefs of other faith expressions.

Our traditional grouping of Catholic, Protestant, and Jewish faiths are now joined by Buddhists, Hindus, Muslims, Sikhs, and others. Diana Ech, a scholar of religion, has declared the United States as "the most religiously diverse nation in the world (2001, p. 4). Perhaps you are still skeptical about the diversity of religion in the United States. Here are a few numbers that might interest you. There are more than twenty Buddhist temples in the greater Seattle area; five Hindu temples in San Diego; a Sikh gurundwara in Omaha; eight Muslim mosques in Dallas; a Jain temple in Allentown, Pennsylvania; and Baha's centers in Topeka, Kansas, and Anchorage, Alaska. There are more than 1,200 houses of worship for Muslims, 1,600 for Buddhists, and 600 for Hindus. (Sources of this information are found under "Religious Diversity Data" in the Reference section.)

As always, the "so what" question needs to be answered. The answer is simple. Attempt to know what the traditional religious groups think about your topic. You probably know someone from each of these faiths. Merely, explain that you will be giving a speech on (whatever the topic is) and you want to know if their faith expression members would have a view on it. If you can identify persons from these other groups in class, they may have delivered a speech that will give you a clue, ask them this same question.

Diversity of Sexual Orientation

We understand that those who have other than a heterosexual orientation are in the minority, but we also realize they are a factor that should be considered if you select certain topics. Often heterosexual people make the mistake of assuming that their audience is composed entirely of heterosexual individuals. Regardless of your view, religious or otherwise, it is a fact of life that our society includes a number of lesbian and homosexuals. We believe responsible and effective speakers will respect all diversities of their audience members.

We advise you to be careful in how you address your audience. It is a matter of being an ethical speaker for us. Why do we say ethical? We say this because ethical speakers treat all their audience members with respect.

What does this mean in a practical sense as you are planning and delivering your speech? First, avoid inflammatory language. Name calling and abusive language, regardless of the group being singled out, is offensive; avoid it. Second, and more subtle, is the assumption that all people who are living with a partner are married. So, instead of referring to these people as married couples, refer to them as couples.

SITUATIONAL ANALYSIS

Audience Size

The size of your audience means you will need to consider some adjustments in your delivery and visual materials as appropriate. It is likely that this situational dynamic will affect your delivery, not what you will have to say. These adjustments may be obvious, but they may bear mentioning so you will remember to take them into account if you find yourself addressing a large audience. First, you will definitely want to produce PowerPoint slides or large poster board displays so your audience can easily see your visuals. Second, you will need amplification of your voice; arrange for this if possible. If this is not possible, you will have to compensate. Sometimes, you can move closer to your audience and raise the volume of your voice a little if necessary.

The Physical Setting

The main thing you should consider about the physical setting is whether the situation will have any effect on the audience's attention span or their ability to hear you. The conditions related to these situational factors are not something you will want to try to address at the last minute. Perhaps you will need amplification for your voice and can ensure it will be available. You should discover what you can in advance so you have the best opportunity to deal with whatever it is. Perhaps the lighting needs repair such as replacement of burned out bulbs. You will want to talk to somebody about the setting and, perhaps, visit it several days in advance of your presentation. This will be the time for you to make any requests you need to make.

You may also want to arrive early for your presentation. This will give you the opportunity to ask for an adjustment of the room temperature or other physical setting issues if necessary. You may also be able to request an adjustment of the seating arrangement or even ask for a podium if there is not one already in place.

Suppose you have to speak in an undesirable physical situation. What do you do? We would suggest you do your best to make as lively, energetic and relatable speech as you can deliver. In other words, do what you can to hold the audience's attention.

The Audience's Disposition toward Your Topic

Of course, the chief aim of your audience analysis is to know a great deal about your audience so that you can make judgments that will allow you to be successful. This section helps you understand how to make specific inferences regarding reactions your audience could have with respect to your topic. There are three primary areas of interest regarding your audience and topic—their knowledge of the topic, their attitudes toward the topic and their interest in the topic.

Their Knowledge Your consideration of what your audience knows about your topic will be a significant part of your analysis. If your speech covers too many things they already know, you will bore them and they may decide you are wasting their time. If you go too far beyond what they know, some audience members may "tune out" because they are experiencing information overload and are uncomfortable. What you want to do is move this kind of audience forward from what they know so that they are satisfied. In other words, provide them some interesting "news." You will have to decide from your research and judgment how much they know and how far you can go. We believe it is better to error on the side of a bit too much "news." Just be careful to explain clearly and provide excellent supporting materials.

There is another issue here. What should you do if some of your audience members are knowledgeable and some are not? The trick you have to pull off here is to bring those who have little knowledge up to speed. Try to start simple and build to where you have "news" for everybody. You might prepare your audience for this by saying something like this. "I understand that some of you know more about (name the topic) than others. I will start by getting everyone up to speed with some basics. Then, I will move to some new ideas."

Their Interest There are a few circumstances where you will have a "captive audience." A **captive audience** is one where the people are required to attend. Your classmates compose a captive audience, as do your colleagues if your boss requires them to attend a presentation. Generally, however, people do not make the effort to go and hear a presentation that does not interest them. So, this speaking situation should have an inherent interest factor.

You will have to answer this question if you are going to successfully hold your audience's interest. "How does this topic affect my audience?" Another way to ask this question is, "How can my audience use this information?" You will want them to know the answers to these questions early in your speech. So, put them in your introduction. Work, also, to include examples and illustrations with which they may have experienced to hold their attention. That is, tie what you are saying to their life experience. Point out, and not just in your introduction, how this information is or will be of use to them. Refer to our Chapter 9 on supporting materials to find additional hints on how to make what you are saying interesting.

Their Attitude We are using the word **attitude** to mean where your audience stands on a continuum from in favor to opposed to your topic and ideas. Of course, you will find that all your audience does not fall conveniently into one category. You will find, we hope, that a carefully selected topic will find many of your audience members with a particular stance on it.

The most difficult audience to deal with is the one where people are opposed. You can begin to handle this problem by asking this question, "Why might they be opposed?" The answer or answers will let you know the issues you must address if you are to be successful. We will have much more to say about this problem when we talk about persuasive speaking in Chapters 15 and 16.

We have addressed your audience's view of your topic. Now we will move to the audience's view of you as a speaker.

The Audience's Disposition toward You as the Speaker

When you think about the audience's disposition toward you, the speaker, there is good news. You are in a classroom situation with people who will also have to speak to the class. This will likely provide a sympathetic audience because each of the members knows first-hand what is required to write and deliver a successful speech.

A positive audience disposition allows this speaker to be effective.

Of course, there is a circumstance where you could turn a sympathetic audience into one that is not. This circumstance is one where you lose your credibility as a speaker. If you do not prepare well, appear to be wasting their time and deliver your speech poorly, the audience might develop a negative attitude toward you. All of these issues are in your hands to control. Careful application of what we are telling you should be all you need to avoid this situation.

The Audience's Disposition toward the Occasion

Speeches you are invited to give outside of the classroom setting will undoubtedly have a stated purpose. Your contact person will certainly be happy to give you the specifics of the occasion. Your speech will also have a general time limit. Ask about this too. Our best advice is that you stick to the stated purpose of the speech and its time limit. Serious violation of these expectations will very likely lead to upsetting the audience and no invitation for a return visit.

There are also expectations surrounding the occasion of a classroom speech. The speech must conform to the assignment. The speaker must respect the audience and follow appropriate standards of taste. The speaker must also respect the time limit given in the assignment.

ADAPTING TO YOUR AUDIENCE

We began this chapter by discussing the need for an audience-centered speech. The two concerns you will have in meeting this goal are constructing a speech that adapts to your audience and delivering your speech so it adapts to your audience's expectations.

Constructing an Audience-Centered Speech

You will know that you are ready to take this step when you have an excellent "feel" for who the people in the audience are and what they think about the several aspects we discussed, above. We advise you to keep your audience constantly in your mind as you develop your speech. Ask how your audience responds at every stage in the construction of your speech. "How will they respond to my introduction?" "How will they respond to this first main point?" "How will they respond to my examples and explanations?" "How will they respond to my evidence?" "How will they respond to my conclusion?" "Have I said enough for them to understand this difficult point?" "Have I made my message meaningful to my audience?"

Here is one final bit advice that we hope you will use. Talk through a close outline of your speech with a classmate. Ask for advice on improving what you said. Next, do the same for this person who helped you. This really works if you both take the job seriously.

Delivering an Audience-Centered Speech

We have two suggestions that will help you achieve the delivery expected of an audience-centered speech. First, make great eye contact with your audience. This means devoting at least 90% or more of your time looking at your audience. You will need to know your speech well to do this, but that is what it takes to deliver an outstanding speech.

Next, look for feedback. Of course, most of you are not going to stray very far away from your prepared speech based on audience feedback. Generally, it is only the experienced speaker who can do this. But, if you see quizzical looks, you may want to try to explain your point again. On the other hand, if you see audience members lean forward in their seats, maintain eye contact and nod in approval, know that you are right on target.

SUMMARY

We began this chapter by discussing the importance of audience analysis. Basically, this allows you to craft a speech that your audience appreciates because you have taken an audience-centered approach. This means that it takes them into account at every step of the speech construction and delivery. You know a good deal about your classmates so this puts you in a good position to achieve this. But, you will have to conduct a more thorough analysis and make excellent use of it to achieve the successful speech you strive to have. You will have to make sure that what you say is important and useful to them or they may decide to stop listening because their frame of reference is telling them this is not interesting or useful.

You may decide to use both direct and indirect methods to gather information. Direct analysis requires contact with audience members through interviews, surveys or focus groups.

Indirect analysis requires you to analyze the demographic information about your audience, as well as situational factors. Demographic factors you should consider are age, cultural background, gender, memberships, religion, and diversity of sexual orientation. The important situational factors you must examine are the audience size, the physical setting, the audience's disposition toward your topic, the audience's disposition toward you as the speaker and the audience's disposition toward the occasion. The audience's disposition toward the topic requires investigation of their knowledge, their interest and their attitude.

Finally, we addressed adaptation of your speech to your audience based on your research and conclusions. We recommended that you ask a single question at every stage of constructing the speech. That question is, "How will my audience respond?" For example, "How will my audience respond to this introduction?" "How will my audience respond to this first main point?" We also recommended that you pair up with a classmate and share your speech outline. The question here is, "How can I improve my speech?" If you are honest with each other this can be a big step in putting final touches on your speech.

You should be sure to make excellent eye contact when delivering your speech. You should also look for indications of how they are responding to your presentation. Make whatever adjustments you are able to do to help your audience understand your speech.

REFERENCES

Bashi, V. & McDaniel, A. (1997). A theory of immigration and racial stratification. *Journal of Black Studies,* 27, 668–683, p. 6.

Donavan, J. M., Rundle, B. A. (1997). Psychic unity constraints upon successful intercultural communication. *Language and Communication,* 17, 219–236.

Ech, D. L. (2001). *A New Religious America.* New York: HarperCollins, p. 4.

Religious Diversity Data. See "List of Hindu Temples in the U.S.A." *(www.geocities.com/kalyan. geo/temple1.html)*; "Jain Temples in the U.S." (*www.adherents.com/;argecom/templjain_ statesUS.html*); "Gurudwaras in the United States of America" (*http://allaboutsikhs.com/ gurudwaras/gurud_55.htm*); "Muslim Life in America" (*http://usinfo.state.gov/productspubs/ muslinlife/*); and the Pluralism Project's compilation of resources for different religions (*http://www.pluralism.org/resources/tradition/index.php*).

Stewart, John (2012). Constructing ideas. In *Bridges Not Walls* (New York: McGraw-Hill), p. 73–84.

Wilson, G. L. (2014). *Relational Communication.* Boston: Pearson.

Chapter 5
Selecting and Narrowing Your Topic

Courtesy of Dean Bertoncelj/Shutterstock.

SELECTING YOUR TOPIC

One of the most challenging steps of the speech-making process in the public speaking class is for speakers to determine a topic. The task is usually not as challenging for speakers outside the classroom, because those speakers often speak on a topic in which they have a good deal of experience. For example, an investment banker may speak about Roth IRAs and Mutual Funds to a group of students in the College of Business. A relationship expert may speak to a group of newly-weds about effective communication to sustain healthy marriages. The pharmaceutical sales representative may give a presentation to a group of physicians to discuss the latest improvements in the medicines they prescribe.

Your situation will probably be different as a student in the public speaking class. Your instructor will probably give you some guidance about the speech—the overall purpose of the speech (informative persuasive, special occasion/entertaining) and the time limit for the speech. But, you will have to choose the topic. At first glance, this freedom sounds good. But as the speech approaches you may begin to get nervous.

Don't panic. Realize your frustrations in choosing a topic are normal. It is not uncommon for students' thought process to range from "I have nothing important to say" to "I am completely overwhelmed by all the things I would like to say." Get started early considering possible topics for your speeches, no matter what end of the spectrum you fall. Because once you select and narrow your speech topic, you will have completed the first major step in developing your speech.

Hopefully, you will learn how to select and narrow a topic which will be interesting to your listeners by the end of this chapter. The three most common ways students choose their speech topics is to think about their expertise, their experience or things which excite them. Many speakers have also found brainstorming to be an effective technique to generate speech topics. We will say more about this shortly.

What Expertise Do You Have?

You will likely speak best when you speak about a topic with which you are familiar. These speeches can be done without much agony or research. So, this is a great place to start when you are determining a speech topic. If you were asked to stand right now, and speak about a topic of your choice, without any preparation, what would you talk about? Your family? Your favorite vacation spot? Your major? What are some things you know well? We are sure you have some things you know how to do and will be able to present without much preparation. Allow these questions to guide you to develop a list of possible speech topics.

What Experience Do You Have?

What are some things you have hands-on experience doing? What is something you learned how to do and have become pretty good at doing? Think for a moment about some interesting or unusual experiences you've had. Maybe you spent a couple of days with an officer riding around the city in a police patrol car to get an idea of how officers spend their days. Perhaps you learned how to monogram baby clothes a couple of months ago. Or maybe you helped your brother pick out an engagement ring for his girlfriend, so you learned how to judge the value of a diamond. While you may think these subjects are boring, they can be interesting to an audience. We find there are few boring topics. What makes a topic exciting is how you develop it. Don't overlook your experiences. They can make for some of the most interesting speech topics. We will have more to say about developing your speech in Chapters 7 and 9.

What Excites You?

You probably have issues you are excited about and want learn more about. Some of these issues may be things you already know a little about, and you are interested in learning more. Some of these issues may be things you know nothing about, but you are interested in researching. Only consider topics you know nothing about if you have the time to adequately research the topic. Maybe you are interested to know how the university you attend uses funds collected from parking tickets. You could use your speech class as an opportunity to find out, and could present the information to your classmates. Perhaps you are interested to learn about the health benefits of becoming a vegan. You could use your speech to find out more. Maybe you are intrigued about how people are embalmed in a morgue. You could unlock the mystery and present the information through your speech.

WHAT TOPICS SHOULD I AVOID?

Taste and judgment come into play in selecting topics. You should generally avoid topics that your audience may find offensive or embarrassing. Being audience-centered here is a must. There are many topics you, personally, might find interesting. But, will your audience share your enthusiasm for them?

A major problem here is that members of your classroom audience are "captive" in that they cannot simply get up and leave. So, an attempt to convert your audience to your particular religious belief is ill advised. Your audience is likely to be made up of people of various beliefs, so some audience members are more than likely going to be offended.

Perhaps you reason that this speech is an excellent opportunity to test out the persuasive skills you are learning in this course. The truth is that you will have little success in persuading your audience if your purpose is really to convert these members. Changing deep-held beliefs cannot be done with a single speech no matter the logic and passion you display. This same advice can be applied, of course, to most intensely personal beliefs.

BRAINSTORMING YOUR IDEAS

Brainstorming is a timed procedure for generating a large number of ideas quickly. It's important to remember that the goal of brainstorming is quantity, not quality. Before you begin the brainstorming activity, be sure to have the necessary tools at hand—paper, something to write with, and something to time yourself. Set a time limit, and work quickly to jot down as many ideas as occur to you. Don't make any judgments about the quality of your ideas until after your time has elapsed.

On a piece of paper, set up a table similar to the one shown in Figure 5.1 on the next page. Give yourself five minutes to brainstorm a list of possible topics considering your expertise, experience and things which excite you. After your brainstorming activity, take a closer look at the topics. Examine these to discover if the topics are suitable for the occasion and if they can be discussed within the time limits.

Expertise	Experience	Excitement
Topic 1:	Topic 1:	Topic 1:
Topic 2:	Topic 2:	Topic 2:
Topic 3:	Topic 3:	Topic 3:

FIGURE 5.1
Brainstorming Table

NARROWING YOUR TOPIC

To narrow you speech topic, you should identify the general purpose of your speech, determine the specific purpose of your speech and develop your thesis statement. Then, you must ask the question, "Can I cover this topic adequately in the time I have been given to speak?" If the answer is "no," then your topic is too broad. Ask next, "What aspect of the topic might I focus on for my speech?" If this aspect is still too much, you will need to go further in the process. Of course, it is possible that your topic is too narrow, but this does not happen often. If this is the case, it is likely that you are not saying enough when you develop the speech if you think your topic is too narrow.

IDENTIFYING THE GENERAL PURPOSE

The general purpose of your speech will fall into one of three categories: to inform, to persuade, or to entertain for special occasions. The speeches in your speech class will generally be informative or persuasive, but there could very well be an expectation for you to complete a speech to entertain. Students are usually given the general purpose of the speech they will perform in public speaking classes.

Informative Speeches

You should present the information as if you are a teacher when your general purpose is to inform. Your speech should define or describe a person, a place, a thing, a concept or idea, steps in a process or how something functions.

When our nation's president delivers the State of the Union Address, he or she is delivering an informative speech. When tourists visit the Smithsonian Museum in Washington DC, the tour guide gives an informative speech. When a lifeguard demonstrates the steps in the process of administering CPR, this speech is also informative. Although all these examples are different, the one thing they have in common is that all of the speeches are designed to increase the knowledge of their listeners.

Simply put, the primary goal of an informative speech is to enhance the understanding and knowledge of the audience. Listeners should walk away from the speech with more information than they had before hearing the speech. You will need to do more work to dig deeper if what you say does not meet this standard. Your speech must contain news for your audience in order to achieve success. The information presented should be accurate, clear, and interesting.

Persuasive Speeches

Persuasive speeches are different from informative speeches. They do provide information, but the goal of the speech is to espouse a cause. Persuasive speeches attempt to change an audience's convictions and oftentimes to urge the audience members to take some sort of action.

When Dan Savage, author, activist, and creator of the *It Gets Better Project*, speaks to middle school students and urges them to be tolerant of their fellow students who are lesbian, gay and bisexual, he is delivering a persuasive speech. When an Army recruiter talks to graduating seniors about joining the Army branch of the military, he or she is presenting a persuasive speech. When a political candidate speaks at a rally and asks citizens for their vote, he or she is giving a persuasive speech.

The common theme surrounding all these speech examples is that they are all designed to influence how the audience thinks. Undoubtedly, all these speeches will give some information, but the primary goal is to get your audience to believe something, or do something, as a result of hearing your speech.

Special Occasion and Entertainment Speeches

When Ron Reagan, Jr., eulogized his father, former President Ronald Reagan, he delivered a special occasion speech. In an excerpt from the speech, Ron Reagan, Jr. said the following:

> Here's something you may not know, a little Ronald Reagan trivia for you. My dad had an inordinate fondness for earlobes for his entire life. Even as a boy, back in Dixon, IL, hanging out on a street corner with his friends, they knew that if they were standing next to Dutch, that is Ronald Reagan, Sr., sooner or later, he was going to reach over and grab hold of their lobe, give it a workout there.

> Sitting on his lap watching TV as a kid, same story. He would have hold of my earlobe. I'm surprised I have any lobes left after all of that.

When David Gregory, television moderator of *Meet the Press* gives a commencement speech to college graduates, he presents a special occasion speech. When former Secretary of State, General Colin Powell, gave a speech to commemorate the life of Dr. Martin Luther King, Jr., he was presenting a special occasion speech.

Like persuasive speeches, special occasion speeches may inform the audience members. However, providing knowledge is not the primary focus of special occasion speeches. The main focus of special occasion speeches is to make the audience relax, smile, and have a good time.

IDENTIFYING THE SPECIFIC PURPOSE

Now that you have established the general purpose, the next step in narrowing your topic is to identify your specific purpose. Again, in public speaking classes, it is not uncommon for instructors to assign the general purpose to students. Conversely, you alone must determine your specific purpose of your speech because the specific purpose depends directly on the topic you choose. Specific purposes should indicate explicitly what you hope to accomplish with your speech, and it should be stated in a single declarative sentence.

For example, a public university in southern Alabama started an initiative to get students more involved in volunteerism. A university official gave a presentation to faculty members informing them of the university's new department which is solely focused on student service-learning. Considering what we've learned about topics and general purposes, we should find it relatively easy to identify them. Here is an example using the topic, service-learning:

Topic: Service-Learning

General Purpose: To inform

The specific purpose of the speech should evolve from these two elements. What would the speaker explain? Would she give the history of service-learning? Would she explain why their university decided to establish a service-learning department? With only 10 minutes to cover her content, the speaker decided to inform the faculty about the agencies her department supports for service-learning opportunities for students. Her specific purpose was stated as the following:

Consider carefully your specific purpose and central idea.

Specific Purpose: To inform university faculty of the three agencies their classes can use for volunteer and service-learning activities.

Adherence to the following about criteria when developing the specific purpose statement will help you achieve a well-crafted speech.

1. It should be written as a full, simple, declarative sentence. Not a fragment.
2. It should be a single idea.
3. It should not be a question.
4. It should not be too vague or general.

Of course, you must follow these standards to achieve excellence and success.

DEVELOPING THE CENTRAL IDEA

The central idea of the speech is the one-sentence statement you want your audience to understand or accept by the end of your speech. The central idea, sometimes called the thesis statement or the major thought, expands on the specific purpose and reveals exactly what you will say in your speech. The central idea is usually expressed as a simple, declarative sentence.

Consider the example above about the office of service-learning. Suppose a faculty member was not going to be able to make the presentation, but she was interested in knowing more about the topic. The faculty member runs into the presenter in the university library and asks the presenter to give her a quick summary of what she will cover in her presentation. To this, the presenter replies "Service-learning is a growing activity at our university. The three agencies identified by our department for you to use to complete service-learning in your classes include Habitat for Humanity, Mobile Bay Area Food Bank and the Ronald McDonald House for kids." The first sentence of her response is the thesis statement of her speech. The second sentence provides a preview of the main points. It is more detailed than the topic (Service-Learning), or her specific purpose (To inform university faculty of the three agencies their classes can use for volunteer and service-learning activities). By stating what the three agencies are, the speaker gave a synopsis of the speech in one single sentence.

Topic: Service-Learning

General Purpose: To inform

Specific Purpose: To inform university faculty of the three agencies their classes can use for volunteer and service-learning activities.

Central Idea: The three agencies identified by our department for use to complete service-learning in your classes include Habitat for Humanity, Mobile Bay Area Food Bank and the Ronald McDonald House for kids.

From the central idea and summary, we can assume that the body of the speech will be comprised of these three main points: (1) Service-learning with Habitat for Humanity, (2) Service-learning with Mobile Bay Area Food Bank, (3) Service-learning with Ronald McDonald House for kids.

SUMMARY

Selecting and narrowing your speech topic is one of the most important parts of the speech-making process. The three most common ways students choose their speech topics is to think about their expertise, their experience or things which excite them. Many speakers have also found brainstorming to be an effective technique to generate speech topics. Many students find the task overwhelming at first, but once students determine their topic, they are on a launch-pad to developing the remaining parts of the speech. Remember, don't panic. But don't procrastinate. As soon as you get the speech assignment, begin using the strategies mentioned in this chapter to help select your topic.

Chapter 6
Gathering Materials

Courtesy of Lichtmeister/Shutterstock.

WHY GATHER ADDITIONAL MATERIALS?

Seldom will you know enough about your topic to achieve the excellence and success that is your goal. The materials you gather through research of various kinds will significantly add to your knowledge and increase your chance of achieving a well-crafted speech. Of course, you need to have some sense of what kind of additional information you might need and where you should go to get it. But, what level of sophistication do you have with analyzing what you need and knowing where to go to get it? It is the aim of this chapter to sharpen these skills.

There is another reason to gather significant information. A knowledge base of credible material, integrated into your speech, is essential to your success as a speaker. A speech that is based on superficial information will not go far to encourage your audience or your instructor to see you as credible. In fact, in a persuasive speech this can be deadly. A successful outcome to a persuasive speech requires the audience believe you are very knowledgeable.

A significant knowledge base will allow you to support your ideas with a variety of materials—a very good idea. Using a variety of information is a *very* good plan. Why is this so? There are two reasons. First, it adds breadth and depth to your main ideas. Your main points can stand alone, but without a variety of supporting materials it is rare that the audience gets the full appreciation of what is meant. The supporting materials you have gathered from your research provide richness to what is being said. Beyond this, it is the supporting materials that help you hold the audience's attention. The point we make is simple. It is not likely that you can achieve these things without gathering materials to add to what you already know. This is important to your success as a speaker.

Finally, your knowledge base, as revealed in your speech, will add greatly to your credibility with your audience and instructor. Consider yourself as part of an audience. After listening to the speaker for a while, you determine that he or she has no "news" for you. Everything that is being said is general knowledge. The speaker has not gathered the unique materials that allow him or her to provide anything that you consider "news." You are likely, we think, to not be impressed with the speaker because he or she does not seem well informed. Of course, we do not expect a speaker to be an expert. But, we do expect a speaker to have more than general knowledge about the topic. The speaker's poor search for information has tarnished his or her image with you and, probably, the rest of the audience. The credibility of the speaker is in doubt.

The aim of this chapter is to sharpen your skills at gathering materials for your speech. To that end we start with just that—where do you start. Next, we will move to how you add to your knowledge by providing some significant points about using the library to gather materials. Then we will address collecting materials through the Internet and personal interviews. Finally, we will cap off our discussion with some pointers to allow you to do effective data collection and analysis.

WHERE DO YOU START?

We strongly suggest that you talk about topics with which you have some familiarity. You may find an interesting topic, but you know nothing or very little about it. Skip that topic. The effort to collect enough knowledge to be successful would be enormous. If you are like most of us, there is a limit to the time you have to successfully complete your assignment. Beyond this, you will have a difficult memory task in getting just the basics organized and remembered. Resist the urge to talk about an interesting subject that you know very little about.

Your personal experience is vitally important to completing an excellent speech. Consider your personal experience with the topic, that is what do you know about the topic. This is the starting point. Write this down. But, why do we say this is vital?

First, if you have direct experience with the topic it will provide you with excellent examples to illustrate your topic. Suppose you are speaking about diabetes. Illustrating your points with your personal experience will likely have significant impact on your audience.

Second, having a good grasp on what you already know will help you to understand what additional information you will need to gather. Most people seem to get a more thorough understanding when they write things down and examine them. We recommend that you do this and then set this work aside for a short time. Then, come back to it and ask, "What additional information do I need?" Perhaps, you conclude you need some specific data to support an idea or you need more examples to support your ideas. The answer to this question should help you begin your information gathering. Of course, as you get into your research you will discover additional elements that you will want to include.

Here is one piece of advice that requires very little elaboration. Start early because you do not know how long your research may take. It is impossible to know what you will find and how long it will take to get it. The outcome of procrastination is generally not having enough information to craft an excellent speech. And here is the fall out that you may not have imagined. You might still be gathering information when you should be writing the speech and practicing presentation of it. This will surely detract from your success.

LIBRARY AND ONLINE RESEARCH COMPLEMENT EACH OTHER

Why do we say this? Isn't it enough to just go online and get my information? Our answer is, "This practice often does not allow you to get the full picture." Comparing what you find online with what you find in the library reveals gaps in your material that can be filled.

Second, one of these sources can be verified by similar statements or data from the other. Also the Internet materials often do not reveal the source well enough for you to judge how credible it is. Finding a report of similar findings in the library can ensure your accuracy and build your credibility. We will have much more to say about assessing Internet information for its accuracy when we provide pointers at the end of this chapter. So, your research will be more complete and credible if you use online and library materials.

There is a major misconception regarding online research that supports some of what we said, above. The misconception: Web sites have all the basic information I need for my speech. Do you suppose that you can gain the same kind of information from the Internet as you can get by interviewing an expert—perhaps some faculty member—on the topic. The interview allows you to ask your specific question and then follow up with another question to draw out more information that suits your purposes. Consider also how many articles on the Internet will you have to read to gather all the information found in a book written by an expert on the topic? We think we made the point.

DOING LIBRARY RESEARCH

Perhaps you are not a student who has spent a good deal of time in the library doing research. So, some of this will be new and some may be a review, depending on your experience. We will start with some basics to help you understand the library.

Librarians

Do not waste your time wandering around the library trying to find what you need if you are unsure of how to proceed. Ask the expert, the trained librarian. This person is there to help and answer your questions no matter how trivial they may seem.

Librarians are trained in how to help you with your research. If what you want is available only in specialized sections, such as government documents, the person may refer you to the librarian that has intimate knowledge of this complex and enormous holding. This person can help you find what you are looking for and often better information than you would find on your own. He or she may even recommend some databases that address your topic.

Catalogs

The library, believe this or not, used to have something called a card catalog that devoted a single card to each holding, say a book, in its collection. These all were housed in cabinets with numerous drawers filled with alphabetized cards. Because of this conducting research was much more time consuming.

Of course, now we access the list of the library's holdings electronically. This allows you to conduct a computerized search using three categories—the author's name, the title of a book or other holding, and the subject. You will find instructions for using the computer to complete this search posted near a computer or on the help screen. The screen displays the key information about the book, including the publication date. This can be important information because the book may have been written many years ago and not be of much use to you. Notice also if the book is checked out to save you valuable time. Next, jot down the location in the library and call number because this will tell you where to find and identify the book. Ask a librarian to help you if you do not know how to use the call number to find your books. Finally, if you have started on your research early enough you can secure a book article through interlibrary loan. Ask where to find the Interlibrary Loan desk and secure their help.

Perhaps you are thinking that you do not have time to read a book in preparation for your speech. We would guess this is true. You do not necessarily need to read the book to get what you want from it. We recommend that you read the preface and skim through the first chapter to get a sense of the book's focus. Next, go to the table of contents and index to find what is in the book that relates directly to your topic as you will present it. This is how you determine where to go for the material in the book you will want to examine.

Periodical Databases

Periodical databases provide access to articles from newspapers, popular magazines, and scholarly journals. You can access these databases easily. Type your subject in the database's search box. The citations for available materials will appear with their location in the library. You may also find an abstract for the article of interest. An **abstract** of this type is summary of the content of the article written by someone other than the author. Do not make the mistake of citing a quote from the abstract in your speech because this is not the wording in the actual source. Consult the full article. Click on the "Help" button or some other designation that indicates the same thing if you are having difficulty with your search. Consult your librarian if you are still having difficulty.

General Databases

General databases cover a wide range of topics and periodicals. They have information about articles in popular magazines such as Time, Newsweek, Ebony, Sports Illustrated, Scientific American and many more. Here are popular general databases.

Academic Search Complete This database provides text of articles from more than 2,000 periodicals, scholarly and popular.

Lexis/Nexis This indexes over 6,000 legal, news, reference, and business sources. This is a database that provides full-text articles to many periodicals, including broadcast transcripts and both U.S. and international newspapers.

Academic OnFile This is another multidisciplinary database that provides full-text for millions of articles from periodicals, popular and scholarly.

Proquest Newsstand This is a good source for finding newspaper articles. Papers include the *New York Times* and the Wall Street Journal.

Special Databases

You may need specialized information for your speech. Here is where you may need the librarian's help. Tell this person what it is you want and he or she will direct you to a special database. These are examples of common specialized databases:

CQ Researcher

Points of View Reference Center

Opposing Viewpoints

Newspapers

A newspaper article can be a very valuable source of historical and current information. Current issues of several newspapers, including the local newspaper are available for your reading. Back issues will be available on microfilm.

Reference Works

Reference works provide general information about a variety of topics. They are classified as encyclopedias, yearbooks, biographical aids, dictionaries, books of quotations, atlases and gazetteers. Basically, these familiar names tell you what you will find in each. What they do not tell you is where to go for the information you desire. Here again, the names of the works presented under each describe their content. We will briefly discuss each category of reference work and indicate the names and content of frequently used works for each category.

Biographical Aids

Biographical aids are references that provide brief life and career facts about contemporary people. You may or may not need this information, but often will. You will find, however, that it also provides useful background information that will help inform you. Here are ones you will find in the library:

Who's Who in America

International Who's Who

Who's Who of American Women

Who's Who among African Americans

Native American Women

Contemporary Black Biography

Dictionary of Hispanic Biography

Current Biography

Current Biography provides more detailed information than the others listed. Articles found in this reference cover politics, science, the arts, labor, sports, and business for newsworthy people from all over the world.

Encyclopedias

An **encyclopedia** provides general knowledge about your topic so it is a very good place to begin your work. Encyclopedias are of two kinds: general and specialized. Two of the better general encyclopedias are the *Encyclopedia Britannica* and the *Encyclopedia Americana*.

General encyclopedias provide general information about what we know, arranged alphabetically by topic. *Britannica* can be accessed online. You may wish to turn to a specialized encyclopedia once you have gained this general knowledge.

Specialized encyclopedias provide in-depth coverage of a particular field of study. Here are some specialized encyclopedias you may wish to consult:

Dictionary of Art

Encyclopedia of Philosophy

Encyclopedia of Religion

New Grove's Dictionary of Music and Musicians

McGraw-Hill Encyclopedia of Science and Technology

Yearbooks

Of course, **yearbooks** are annual publications that report information from the previous year. These may provide statistics, information about a variety of topics from the most-watched television shows to literacy rates for various countries, and also national and foreign news events. Here some of the most useful yearbooks:

Statistical Abstract of the United States

World Almanac and Book of Facts

Facts on File

Books of Quotations

Most of us probably think of *Bartlett's Familiar Quotations* when we consider this topic since you will find over 25,000 quotations there. You might also consider using the *Oxford Dictionary of Quotations*. These are excellent places to go. But, they might not work as well for you as one of the specialized books of quotations listed below. All of these are indexed by subject and author. Here are the specialized quotation books:

A Treasury of Jewish Quotations

My Soul Looks Back, 'Less I forget: A Collection of Quotations by People of Color

Atlases and Gazetteers

An **atlas** provides maps of the world. The *Rand McNally Cosmopolitan World Atlas* also contains maps of each state of the United States. You may need a map to explain or illustrate some point in your speech. Many atlases will also include a variety of charts, plates, and tables that provide information about the geography of the region of interest.

A **gazetteer** is a geographical dictionary. The *Merriam-Webster's Geographical Dictionary* will certainly suit your needs. This dictionary lists 48,000 places around the world. This work gives facts about countries, regions, cities, islands, mountains, and rivers. This includes facts from the height of mountains to U.S. state flowers.

DOING INTERNET RESEARCH

The **Internet** is a global super network linking thousands of computer networks in order to share information. You are probably familiar with the Internet and its uses, but if you are not you can probably get some pointers from a friend or a librarian. You can also find a tutorial on the Internet by going to dir.yahoo.com (Yahoo Directory), click on "Computers and the Internet," and then click on "Internet," and then on "World Wide Web," and finally on "Beginner's Guides." This will take you to over 20 tutorials.

Internet research is a good place to begin to familiarize yourself with the topic.

The library provides help as we described above. The Internet does not. This means there is no person or group whose duty it is to make sure what is posted is of high quality. Much of what you find on the Internet will be superficial and, perhaps, not directly address your topic in a way that is helpful. Sure, it is fast and convenient. But, it is not necessarily the best way to find credible information. Many experts would suggest that you begin with library research and then turn to the Internet.

We do believe, of course, that the Internet is a valuable source of information.

Search Engines

A **search engine** finds materials on the Internet that you request related to a key word or words based on what you type in the search box. Two commonly used search engines are Google, available at www.google.com and Yahoo, available at www.yahoo.com. There are many useful specialized sites. Some of these are www.academicinfo.net, which is Academic Info online. It is an online educational resource center with a plethora of online degrees, online courses and distance learning information from a selection of online accredited schools. There mission is to provide free, independent and accurate information and resources for prospective and current students (and other researchers); www.allacademic.com is a guide to free online academic resources. All Academic provides a variety of services to organizations wishing to store and archive documents. Public or private archives are available. Finally, if you are looking for pictures for your speech go to http://www.pictures.com.

Key Word Searches

This is where most people start their search for information. Of course, you type a key word in the search box of your search engine. Generally, this word identifies the essence of your topic. The problem with what you will likely find here is thousands of listings—everything about the world that is cataloged by your site. Suppose, for example, you conduct a search on *pregnancy*. Type this word on Google and you will get 233,000,000. Of course, this big number is impossible to deal with. Some of these will deal specifically with your topic, but they may be impossible to find since most of these will not apply.

The question is, "How do I limit the search to find what I need in some reasonable number that I can access to retrieve my information?" The answer to this question is that you will need to narrow your search to reflect your specific topic. Consider again the topic of pregnancy. If you search *teenage pregnancy*, you will narrow this down to 29,800,000. This is still too big, so you will have to narrow your search further. Suppose, now you narrow your search *to teenage pregnancy in Mobile and Alabama*. You will drop the number of listings to 49,700. Many of these are not about Mobile, but are for Alabama. You could go further *to teenage pregnancy in Mobile, Alabama 2011*. You will find that most of the Mobile, Alabama matches that you had for teenage pregnancy in Mobile, Alabama have dropped from the listing. You do have listings for Alabama and that might be helpful for your speech. Back up to the previous search and begin to evaluate these. An important thing for you to know is items that match closest to your key word search are at the top of the list, so they will be the most helpful.

Subject Searches

You may want to conduct a Web search by subject. We recommend that you use Yahoo.com for your search. You will find topic areas like Business and Economy, Education, Government, Health, News and Media, Science, and Society and Culture. You will get a list of subtopics when you click on one of these areas. Each time you click on one of these subtopics you will find your search narrows. Continue until you discover the Web sites you want to visit.

Here is an example of how this works. Suppose you want to find a full text of a legislative bill from the U.S. Congress. Go to Government. Then, click on U.S. Government, then Bills, then Search Full Text of Bills. Pick the bill you want to examine and you have it.

Blogs

Blogs are Web sites or pages that display regular postings by an author or authors—often in the form of a journal. Some allow visitors to comment. These sites can offer unique, credible information when they are created by authorities. Keep in mind, though, that generally blogs will be composed of specific opinions or points of view. Types of blogs include:

- Personal blogs (including Twitter)
- Corporate blogs (used for internal communication or external marketing)
- Subject blogs (fashion, travel, politics, education, law, music, and so forth)
- Media blogs (videos, links, sketches, photos, and the like)

Blogs are useful to you for finding public opinion. If they are kept up to date, they may also provide new developments concerning your topic. (Of course, you will want to verify these with another source.) In addition, the postings may allow you know if your topic is controversial and of current interest.

Keep in mind there are disadvantages to using blogs. The obvious one is a bias toward the topic because the blog represents the opinion of the blogger(s). The use of them can be time consuming if you verify the information and sources. In addition, it may be difficult to identify the sources of the information.

Keeping Track of Promising Web Resources

Web searches can become complicated quickly and you do not want to spend time writing down all the promising sites. All of us who do Internet searches know it can be difficult, if not impossible, if to find a site if you lose track of it. How do you avoid this problem? There are two answers to this question depending on your circumstances.

Internet sites are identified by their URL (Uniform Resource Locator), commonly designated as the site's address. You will be able to access the site through its address. You will also need this address to complete the citation in your bibliography if one is required to go with an outline.

You can use a bookmark to keep track of the URLs by clicking on your browser's "Bookmark" or "Favorites" tab if you are using your own computer. You will see the word "Favorites" at the top of the page if you are using Microsoft Explorer as your browser. Clicking on "Favorites" will result on another tab, "Add to Favorites." This will store the URL of the Web site that is on your screen. You can revisit the site by going to your list of favorites and clicking on the appropriate bookmark and you also have the information for your bibliography.

The second method for keeping track of promising sites is used if you are working on a computer that is not yours. You can either print out the first page of the site or use the copy and paste function to put the site's name and address on a CD or flash drive.

DOING RESEARCH THROUGH INTERVIEWS

Our most common experiences with interviewing tend to be employment interviews and performance appraisal interviews. Of course, you know that information is gathered in interviews, but probably have less experience with this type of interview. The face-to-face interview with an expert can provide just what you need to craft a successful speech. This type of interview can save you time too, since you can get right to the important questions for which you want answers. In addition, if the person really is an expert, the information can be used in a persuasive speech as evidence.

We believe the process will be easier to understand if we divide it into three segments: Preparing for the Interview, Conducting the Interview and Following Up the Interview.

Preparing for the Interview

You will be ready to prepare for an interview after you have collected a good deal of information. It seems unlikely to us that you will know what questions will be productive for you until you are reasonably well informed. Here are three steps that will allow you to be prepared for an interview.

1. Make a list of potential questions that provide information you do not already have.

Then, add to this questions that will allow you to create depth for particularly important areas. This should include quotable information, information about the topic and also personal experiences with it. These personal experiences will be very useful as interesting illustrations. These can add considerable interest to what you say and be very valuable. Next, examine the list and cull those you believe you do not need or are repetitive. Next, develop potential follow-up questions where you can anticipate them. Finally, check for leading questions. A leading question is one that prompts a particular answer that may not reflect the interviewee's opinion. These should be avoided because they may distort your information. These are often stated as a yes or no question, such as, "Don't you agree that teenage pregnancy is a problem in Mobile?"

The answer might be, "I agree." Since you already know this is a problem from your research, it would be better to ask, "What are some of the reasons teenage pregnancy is a problem in Mobile?" (Wilson & Goodall, Jr., 1991, pp. 87–98).

2. Decide whom to interview.

Again, we recommend that you brainstorm to generate a list of possibilities. There may be a number of experts on your topic at your university, since faculty members often share interest. Call and ask a departmental chair. Tell this person what your general area is where you need information. Ask if there is a faculty member in his or her department who could be helpful. Get the name and contact information for this person.

On the other hand, there might be a student group that is organized to address the issue or has experience with the topic. If it is a community issue, you might call the city hall, explain your topic and what information you are looking for, and ask whom to call. Be sure to get a telephone number and location of this person's office while you have this telephone opportunity.

3. Arrange for the interview.

Special attention to how you do this is very important. The problem arises from the fact that most experts are very busy people. Normally, you would call the person, identify yourself, tell your exact purpose, and explain why you especially need to interview this particular person. We do not recommend that you try to set up your interview by email contact. It is too easy to brush off such a contact. You may use an alternative method to arrange an interview if you think the person may say "no." This emphasizes the importance you attribute to the interview. Go to their office and request the interview. You must also indicate approximately how much time you will need for the interview. Stick to what time limit you say, even though this will require careful planning.

Conducting the Interview

1. Dress appropriately.

2. Establish rapport with the interviewee.

3. Get biographical information on the interviewee.

4. Indicate the purpose of the interview.

5. Ask if you may record the interview.

Do so if you are permitted but set up the recorder and ignore it for the remainder of the interview. You must still take notes because sometimes the recorder will not operate properly.

6. Listen carefully to the answer of all questions, but particularly the primary questions.

A **primary question** is the initial question for an area of your topic. You will generally use **follow-up or secondary questions** to discover more in-depth information about the topic.

Although you can and should prepare follow-up questions, you will discover some others if you listen carefully. These will be tailored specifically the way the question was answered and can provide information you did not anticipate getting.

7. End the interview with a clearinghouse question.

A **clearinghouse question** asks the interviewee to talk about something you failed to ask. A general question you might ask is, "Have I missed anything that I ought to know about (name the topic or purpose)?"

8. Thank the interviewee for his or her time and valuable information.

Follow-Up Tasks

1. You should make sure that you have a good audio recording if you were permitted to make one.

You must transcribe the tape or at least the important information from it if you were able to get this. This will take time, so allow for it.

2. You must get to work immediately if you recorded information in note form.

The notes you have from your interview will definitely need your attention. It would be unusual to find that you were able to get everything in your notes that you heard. This is your opportunity to add these things. It is usual that you have incomplete sentences and ideas. Turn these into complete sentences. Contact the interviewee as soon as possible for clarification if you find things you do not understand.

3. Identify the ideas you will want to use and where they will fit into your speech.

Add these ideas using the same method you are using for the rest of the materials you gathered.

4. Send a note thanking interviewee for his or her time.

Tell the person how valuable the information will be for your speech.

EFFECTIVE COLLECTION OF YOUR RESEARCH

Start Early

Do you want to make one of the biggest mistakes made by students that generally ends in a mediocre grade? Put off collecting materials you will need for the speech. Almost everything else you will need to do is dependent on "doing your homework." The "homework" we refer to is getting informed about you topic by gathering excellent materials that will allow you to craft an excellent speech.

Create a Bibliography

You should record the bibliographic information for each source as you go along with your research. Why? This will make the work of creating the list of references you will append to your outline of the speech easier. This will also allow you to include correct citations in your speech.

Efficient Note Taking

Efficient here means systematically and consistently. It also suggests completeness. Many find it efficient to use note cards for each major piece of information or quotation gathered. These need to be complete in that you have indicated from where this information came, where to find it (indicate the library call number or the URL), and page numbers if there are any.

CRITICAL EVALUATION OF INFORMATION

It is absolutely necessary that you carefully evaluate all of the information you collect. In this section we begin by addressing concerns regarding the quality of information, regardless of its source. Then, we will address specifics for evaluating Web information.

Concerns Regarding the Quality of Information

There are five standard concerns you should apply in evaluating the quality of information. Suppose your speech topic is pollution of the water in San Francisco Bay.

1. Is the information you will use relevant?

Does the information relate directly to the issue or point being made? You might argue that spending more money on a pollution problem in San Francisco Bay will produce a greater effect than spending less. Close examination by the audience may suggest, however, that the amount of money spent is not necessarily relevant to solving this particular problem.

2. Is your information current?

When were these data collected? Information that has not been gathered close to the time of your speech may no longer be valid. An audience listening to your speech discussing the pollution problem in San Francisco Bay would want current information. Otherwise, they cannot be certain that your conclusions will be valid.

3. Is your information representative?

You may have a single example or statistic that seems relevant. You would be reasoning from a single example or statistic. You might argue that the bay is polluted because a sample showed bacteria at twice the level considered safe. Your audience and instructor would want to know not only where the sample was taken but also whether that sample would be the same as other samples taken over a period of time in the same area. Be sure to identify the person's credentials.

4. Is the information sufficient?

Important conclusions generally should not be based on a single statement by a single individual. Ask yourself whether other sources are available to examine. Your audience will ask this question if you reason from a single source. If you are forced to use a single source you need to make sure this information is of good quality and from a credible source.

5. Is the information credible?

Two questions will help you tell whether a source is credible. First, ask whether the source is qualified to make the statements. It is not always easy to discover the credentials of a source. If you can discover the person's credentials and use these to assess the qualifications, that is what you should do. When the credentials are not available, you will have to rely on the credibility of the publication where the information was published. A credible publication generally will investigate the credentials of its writers. If the article is an account from another source, you may have to do some checking to evaluate the credibility of the source.

A second issue of credibility is bias that may result from a person's viewpoint or special interest. Ask whether their source has some relationship to what is being reported that might bias the statements. A developer may report his or her testing of San Francisco Bay water shows that it is safe. This information may or may not be true, but it is obvious that a developer might be biased and would have an interest in reporting safe water. You would want reports from other sources before you decide to include this in your speech and claim it is reliable.

Concerns Regarding the Quality of Internet Information

Here are some questions we recommend you ask to help you evaluate Web information:

1. *Is the individual or organization identified on the Web page? Do you recognize this individual or organization as trustworthy?*

2. *Does the author and/or the organization supply credentials or affiliations or supply an "about us" or "who we are" link? Check these out.*

3. *What do you think the motivation is for putting up this page? Does this cause you to see the material differently?*

4. *Does the information appear to have a particular slant or bias?*

5. *Does the author indicate the sources of the information?*

6. *Does the material seem to be factual information and data or mostly opinion?*

7. *Does the page indicate when it was created or updated?*

8. *Regardless of the creation date, can you tell if the information is current?*

9. *Is there some way to contact the author—perhaps an email address or a physical address and telephone number?*

10. *What kind of links, if any, does this page have to other pages? Do these seem credible?*

If our answers to these questions call into question the information's truthfulness or authoritativeness, you will be better off relying on printed library sources.

SUMMARY

We began this chapter by making a strong argument that gathering materials for your speech beyond what you already know will increase your opportunity to craft an excellent speech. We believe you need a significant knowledge base to allow you to support the main ideas of your speech. This provides a richness that you usually cannot draw from the basic knowledge you possess. We did suggest that the place to start this process of collecting additional knowledge is to assess what you already know. This will help you know what you need to collect.

Next we indicated that both a library search and an online research are necessary. They complement each other. We next turned to how to do effective library research and a description of the resources that are available. Reference librarians are an excellent source of advice. Use them. We took you through the process of accessing the libraries holdings by accessing their catalog electronically. Periodicals are newspapers, popular magazines and scholarly journals. We described the databases that will allow you to search them electronically for information that will be useful to you. The library's reference works are also a valuable source of information. These include encyclopedias, yearbooks, biographical aids, dictionaries, books of quotations, atlases and gazetteers.

Internet research is a very useful addition to what you find in the library. We began by discussing search engines. These are Web sites that allow you to access what is on the Internet through entering key words. Two of the most popular are Google and Yahoo. Next, we explained how to do a key word search. The more descriptive you can be, the better chance you have at finding the material you need. This requires that you use several words to describe your topic precisely. You can make the same kind of search using descriptors of you subject.

Some of the information you want may only be available through a face-to-face interview. We lead you through the process of conducting this kind of research. Your preparation should include a list of questions you want answered, identifying the best person for the interview and making arrangements. Next, we provided specific directions for conducting the interview. The initial concerns include dressing appropriately, establishing rapport with the interviewee, getting biographical information on the interviewee and indicating the purpose of the interview. You will also want to gain permission to make an audio recording if you wish to do this. You must also listen carefully and end the interview with a clearinghouse question and thank you. Of course there are follow-up tasks that must be completed. These include revising and adding to your notes, identifying the ideas you want to use and writing a formal thank you note.

Finally, we provided some general pointers on enhancing your research and critical evaluation. Concerns regarding the quality or your research can be answered by asking these five questions. These are, "Is the information relevant?," "Is your information current?," " Is your information representative?," "Is your information sufficient?," and "Is the information credible?" Concerns about the quality of Internet information are numerous. Review the ten point list we provided. If any of the answers call into question the truthfulness or the information's authoritativeness, do not use that material.

REFERENCE
Wilson, G. L., & Goodall, H. L., Jr. (1991). *Interviewing in context*. New York: McGraw-Hill.

Chapter 7
Organizing the Body of the Speech

Courtesy of baranq/Shutterstock.

ELEMENTS OF THE BODY

This chapter examines the elements contained in the body of the speech. You will devote most of your time on structuring the body. The body of the speech brings substance to the speech's thesis. It states the main points of the speech which directly support the thesis statement. You develop your main points with support material or sub points. The support material is more specific than the main points. The supporting points explain, prove and develop the main points. The last element of the body is transitions. Transitions can be in the form of words, phrases or sentences that help with the flow of your ideas.

In Chapter 8, we will discuss the opening and closing of an effective speech. You may be thinking it would make more sense to first discuss the introduction and conclusion of the speech. However, we believe you must fully understand what the body of the speech entails to successfully craft an opening and closing for your speech.

This chapter is divided into three sections: Developing Main Points, Incorporating Supporting Material and Utilizing Transitions.

DEVELOPING MAIN POINTS

Once you select and narrow your topic, you gather research and support material to explore exactly what you want to focus on in your speech. Then you will develop a thesis statement. The **thesis statement** is the key concept of the speech. It is the big idea you want your audience to learn or think from your speech.

Your next step is to write and organize your speech. We suggest you first write and organize the body of the speech. Begin writing and organizing the body of the speech by developing main points. **Main points** express the key ideas of the speech. Main points directly support the thesis statement.

You may be asking yourself, "Where do I start?" "How do I know what my main points should be?" These are good questions. There are several aspects to consider when generating your main points. Let's discuss some of these tips.

Thesis Statement

Sometimes your main points are easy to identify by simply looking at the thesis statement. The thesis statement can reveal obvious divisions of the topic that can be translated into main points. Let's look at some examples in Figure 7.1 of how a thesis statement can be a good indication of what your main points should be in the speech.

Thesis Statement: When the world stopped turning on that September day, great strength, patriotism, and unity were expressed across our nation.

    Main Point 1: On September 11, 2001, America put forth a face of strength and courage toward the rest of the world, showing in times of strife, we will not be afraid. (Strength)

    Main Point 2: Patriotism lends our nation and citizens a unique identity that other nations around the world try to identify with and mimic. (Patriotism)

    Main Point 3: While some may see diversity as a detriment, in this country it is our greatest strength, and it is this unity combined with our diversity that makes us one. (Diversity)

Thesis Statement: Diversity sparks interest, promotes respect, and may lead to unwanted conflict which can be resolved through tolerance and understanding.

    Main Point 1: Diversity sparks interest. (Interest)

    Main Point 2: Diversity promotes respect. (Respect)

    Main Point 3: Diversity paves the way for conflict. (Conflict)

Thesis Statement: The Internet has made life easier by providing endless information, helping businesses grow, and making communication fast and simple.

> Main Point 1: Today's Internet allows its users to have endless amount of information at their fingertips. (Endless Information)
>
> Main Point 2: The Internet has helped businesses get started and grow quickly. (Businesses grow)
>
> Main Point 3: The Internet has made communication very fast and easy. (Fast and Simple)

FIGURE 7.1
Examples of Thesis Statements

You can also brainstorm main points that relate to your thesis statement. Remember the brainstorming techniques you learned in Chapter 5 when choosing and narrowing a topic. You can use these same tips when devising main points. Ask yourself the who, what, when, where or why of your thesis. List quickly and uncritically anything that comes to your mind when reflecting on your thesis statement. Once you have completed the brainstorming session, look at the list you have compiled. Cross out elements that have little or nothing to do with the thesis statement. Combine those items that have a similar focus. Figure 7.2 demonstrates how brainstorming can be an effective way to generate main points.

Thesis Statement: Bells Palsy is a medical condition that affects the nerves and muscles of the face, paralyzing one side.

Brainstorming ideas:

1. Facial weakness - Symptoms

2. Paralysis - Symptoms

3. Recovery - Treatment

4. How long does the condition last? - Treatment

5. How do you get Bells Palsy? - Causes

6. ~~Who has Bells Palsy?~~

7. What part of the body causes this to happen? - Causes

8. Can you take medicine for it? - Treatment

9. Dry eyes or mouth - Symptoms

10. ~~How does it affect daily life?~~

81

11. Drooling - Symptoms

12. Inability to blink - Symptoms

FIGURE 7.2
Using Brainstorming to Generate Main Points

Once you've narrowed down your topic based on the thesis statement, you can develop main points in sentence form. Here is an example of main points that resulted from the brainstorming illustrated in Figure 7.2:

Main Point 1: Its symptoms are defined and they are not hard to recognize. (Symptoms)
Main Point 2: Bells Palsy does not have one specific cause. (Causes)
Main Point 3: There is not a definite treatment for this condition. (Treatment)

Number of Main Points

Limit the number of main points. If you have too few main points, you won't give substance to your thesis statement. The audience will leave unsatisfied. If you have too many main points, the audience will be overwhelmed and confused. You told them a little bit about a lot, which translates into not learning much at all.

Consider your purpose and time limit. For purposes of this class, two to four main points would be appropriate. Let's say you are interested in informing the audience about scuba diving. You are so enthusiastic about it that you wanted to say a whole lot. You want to talk about scuba diving equipment, how to scuba dive, the certification process, safety measures, the cool underwater life you will see and the most popular places to scuba dive. If we used each of these subtopics as a main point, it would be way too much information especially for a 4–6 minute speech. You risk going over time and losing the attention of your audience because your speech lacks focus and won't be valuable for your listeners. A better approach would be to choose one of these subtopics and expand the depth of your speech. This option will allow you to develop a more manageable speech topic.

Sentence Form

Main points should be assertions that support your thesis. They should not be questions or phrases. They should be general ideas about the speech topic in declarative sentence form. Let's look at some options for a main point in regards to a speech topic on the importance of volunteering.

Option 1: Rewards of volunteering (Phrase)

Option 2: Does volunteering make you feel better about yourself? (Question)

Option 3: Volunteering makes you feel good about yourself. (Declarative Statement)

Option 3 is the better alternative; it's clear and direct.

Single Idea

Each main point should focus on a single idea. This helps your audience decipher what you are focusing on in that particular main point. It also enables you to have a more organized approach to revealing the main ideas of the speech. For example, in an informative speech about stress of college students, you would not use the following as a main point: "Stress can be defined in many ways and there are several ways to effectively manage stress." We have two different ideas going on here. One is focusing on the definition of stress and the other is focusing on techniques to manage stress. Instead of combining these two distinct ideas, separate them into two main points. "Stress can be defined in many different ways." "There are countless techniques to use when trying to manage stress."

Balance

Another tip to consider when devising main points is balance. You want to place proper emphasis on all of your main points. In other words, don't play favorites with your main points. If one of your main points only has one supporting point, then it obviously doesn't need to be a main point. If you have two main points, don't spend 75% of your time discussing one main point and 25% the other. Don't dwell on devoting an absolute equal amount of time to each main point but strive for some balance and consistency.

Audience-Centered

It's crucial to maintain an audience-centered approach when constructing main points. In chapter 4, we learned it is necessary to consider your audience if you want your ideas to be received well. Remember our goal is for the audience to listen, understand and remember your message. Tailor your main points to fit your audience's needs, interests and knowledge level.

ORGANIZATIONAL PATTERNS

Never underestimate the importance of organization. You will be a more successful speaker if you present your ideas in a logical, easy-to-follow manner. Remember your goal as a speaker is for the audience to listen, understand and remember your ideas. After listening to your speech, the audience should be able to easily recall your main points. Notice, we didn't say recall your speech topic or what the speech was about but the specific main points.

An organized presentation will enhance your audience's comprehension and
retention of your speech ideas.

It is difficult to listen, understand and remember a speech that is unfocused and presents
information with no clear purpose. Alternatively, if you organize your ideas in a cohesive
manner and utilize repetition and transitions, our ideas will stick with the audience. Another
way you can achieve this goal of organization is by utilizing organizational patterns. There are
five patterns we will discuss in this chapter.

Causal Pattern

A **causal pattern** shows the cause and effect of a situation or phenomena. In short, it looks at
why something happens and the impact of it. Here is an example of causal patterning:

Thesis Statement: Early identification of stroke signs and immediate action will increase
the chance of a better rehabilitation outcome.

Main Point 1: A stroke is caused by a blood clot to an artery or blood vessel interrupt-
ing blood flow to the brain. (Cause)

Main Point 2: A facial droop is the result of a stroke. (Effect)

Main Point 3: Paralysis to one side of the body is also a result of a stroke. (Effect)

Main Point 4: Slurred speech is the last result of a stroke. (Effect)

Chronological Pattern

A **chronological pattern** organizes main points based on time, sequence or steps. This is how a chronological pattern looks:

Thesis Statement: Hopefully, you will never have to provide adult CPR, but if you do, remember to stay calm and the follow the steps of the Hands-Only technique.

Main Point 1: The first thing you need to do before approaching a cardiac arrest victim is making sure the scene is safe. (First step)

Main Point 2: Next, determine if the victim is conscious or not. (Second step)

Main Point 3: Third, locate the center of the chest and place one hand on top of the other pressing down on the chest about two inches. (Third step)

Main Point 4: Provide chest compressions at a rate of 100 per minute (beat of the Bee Gee's song, "Stayin' Alive"). (Fourth Step)

Problem-Solution Pattern

A **problem-solution pattern** establishes a problem or dilemma and offers an answer or fix to the problem or issue. Here is an example:

Thesis Statement: Texting while driving is dangerous and could take your life away in a flash.

Main Point 1: Texting poses a major distraction to drivers. (Problem)

Main Point 2: Individual states are passing laws to ban the use of cell phones while driving. (Solution)

Topical Pattern

A **topical pattern** divides the thesis into subtopics or categories. Here is a topical pattern about stuttering:

Thesis Statement: Stuttering is an age-old communication disorder that occurs in all languages and cultures yet not enough people are aware of the meaning, symptoms or causes.

Main point 1: Stuttering is a complicated, multi-dimensional communication problem. (Meaning)

Main point 2: People who stutter present a wide variety of symptoms both visible and hidden. (Symptoms)

Main point 3: Stuttering is a complex communication disorder and so is the search for its causes. (Causes)

Spatial Pattern

The **spatial pattern** arranges information based on physical space, direction or location. For example, you could arrange your main points based on physical space such as West to East, inside out or top to bottom.

> *Thesis Statement:* Despite the fact Chile is one nation, there are generally three different cultures characterized by the northern, central and southern regions.
>
> > Main point 1: The northern region of Chile is known for its indigenous culture. (North)
> >
> > Main point 2: The central region of Chile is characterized by its Spanish influenced culture. (Central)
> >
> > Main point 3: The southern region of Chile is known for its simple society and German influence. (Southern)

You will learn more about another organizational pattern, the motivated sequence, in a subsequent chapter on persuasion.

INCORPORATING SUPPORTING MATERIAL

The next step in writing a cohesive body is to collect your support material or sub points. We'll discuss specific support options in Chapter 9. **Sub points** provide proof or evidence to bolster your main points. This support may be in the form of examples, narratives, analogies, comparisons, contrasts, statistics or testimony. Your main points are general ideas that support your thesis statement. Your sub points are more specific instances that support your main points. This support brings substance to your thesis statement. Let's look at an example in Figure 7.3 that demonstrates how main points and sub points fit together to formulate a strong body.

Body

I. Main Point 1: Selective mutism is a very rare anxiety disorder.
   A. It prevents people from speaking in certain situations and settings such as a classroom setting but not in others such as at home.
   B. In their book, <u>Understanding and Treating Selective Mutism</u>, Mennuti, Freeman, and Christner say that Selective Mutism occurs in less than one percent of all people, and is usually diagnosed in preschool or kindergarten.
   C. In her article, "Phenomenology and the Treatment of Selective Mutism," Kristi Kumpulainen, says that specific symptoms must be present and others must be absent in order to be diagnosed with Selective Mutism.
      1. For instance, a child must exhibit extreme shyness and anxiety in social situations but not in other situations such as at home for at least one month before diagnosis.

    2. The shyness and anxiety cannot have any relation with a preexisting condition, such as stuttering, that would make the child self-conscious to be considered Selective Mutism.

    3. Finally, the shyness must be severe enough to be having a negative impact on the child's daily life at school and other social situations.

  D. It may seem insignificant, but Selective Mutism is hard to live with.

II. Main Point 2: Because all children are different, and so few have Selective Mutism, a one size fits all treatment for the disorder does not exist, so there are many different options.

  A. According to Pediatric Psychologist, Aimee Kotrba, cognitive behavioral therapy is currently the most common treatment for Selective Mutism patients.

    1. The idea behind cognitive behavioral therapy is that the silence of Selective Mutism patients is a habit that has been learned over time; so it can also be "unlearned."

      a. Treatment involves changing the child's outlook on talking and their surroundings in order to make them more comfortable in speaking situations.

      b. Once again from their book, Understanding and Treating Selective Mutism, Mennuti, Freeman, and Christner wrote that an important aspect of cognitive behavioral therapy is not to focus on making the child talk, but to focus on reducing the child's anxiety level.

    2. Doing so, the child will eventually feel comfortable and confident enough to talk in public.

  B. The newest idea for treatment is drama therapy. Drama therapy uses dramatic elements such as stories, roles, scripted characters.

    1. According to Phei Phei Oon, author of "Playing with Gladys," "drama and materials, and the enactment of these roles and stories help clients explore problems, gain insights, and eventually attain positive changes."

    2. When a child enters drama therapy, he or she enters into a different world where the real world and all of his or her problems and fears are put away.

      a. This new world is called a play space.

      b. In the play space, the child can role-play as anything they want to be from a firefighter to a rock star.

      c. The hope is that through role-playing, the child will become comfortable communicating through the characters, and spontaneous verbalization will result.

      d. Eventually, the child will become comfortable speaking as him or herself.

    3. Naturally, drama therapy doesn't work instantly for a child with a severe anxiety disorder like Selective Mutism, so small steps are necessary.

      a. For example, instead of choosing a role requiring a lot of speech such as a teacher for the first session, the child may choose to begin as a mime which requires no speech.

b. From there he or she may begin to mouth and whisper words to pursue other roles until he or she can eventually speak aloud.

c. Again, there is no perfect solution for this disorder, and each case is treated a little differently.

III. Main Point 3: I had a long, tough battle with the disorder.

A. I attended preschool, and never talked to teachers or any kids other than my two best friends, but at that point everyone thought I was just really shy and would get over it.

1. This continued through kindergarten and first grade.

2. Second grade is when the fun really began.

a. I started begging not to go to school and my dance classes, both of which I had enjoyed going to prior to this point.

3. That was when I was finally diagnosed with Selective Mutism.

a. I began treatment for it that spring, and I finally started talking to other kids in my class in third and fourth grade.

b. However, it wasn't until the beginning of eighth grade that I could talk to my teachers.

B. Until I could talk to the teachers, I couldn't do a lot of basic things such as answer questions (even though I usually knew the answer) or ask for more paint in art class.

1. I had to rely on guessing and relaying questions and answers through kids that I would talk to.

2. I remember every year starting in fifth grade we had to participate in a speech contest, and I couldn't get in front of my class and give my speech.

a. I had to video tape it, and bring it in for everyone to watch, which I also didn't like.

b. So as you can see, I've come a long way since then!

C. One good thing about my experience with the disorder that I am really thankful for is that I could at least talk to my family and best friend, and didn't have to live in total silence.

1. In fact, when I was at home, I would never stop talking.

a. After all, I had to make up for all the lost time at school!

2. In my case, in addition to not talking, I also wouldn't smile for pictures in public, or if I did, it was a very small smile with me looking at the ground.

a. Here is a picture of me in preschool for example, taken by a photographer with a bunch of other dancers watching.

b. Of course though, at home, I was quite the little model.

1). Here is a picture of me at home with just me and my mom in the room. As you can see there is a dramatic difference.

      c. Here's a picture of me on the first day of preschool before we left our house.

         1). As you can see I'm very happy and excited.

      d. And here's one with my best friend once we got there.

D. Through my experience with Selective Mutism, I have learned that barely anyone has ever heard of it.

    1. So when New York Times bestselling author Ellen Hopkins asked for stories of unusual experiences to be used in her books, I figured why not! Here are some of her books. Maybe you have read or seen some of them.

    2. So I emailed her my story, and she wrote me back!

      a. She said that my story was really interesting; one that she might be able to use!

      b. She went to say however, that I write very articulately, and should write a memoir of the experience myself!

    3. I've always loved writing since it was kind of like talking but silent, and one of my major goals is to write and publish a book.

      a. I was ecstatic that someone like Ellen Hopkins believes that I can do it!

      b. So I have begun work on that, and hopefully you'll all see it in bookstores someday!

Works Cited

Kotrba, A., Ph.D., & Psychologist, P. (n.d.). Innovative Treatments for Selective Mutism. *PediaStaff–Pediatric and School-Based Therapy Jobs–Speech Language Pathology, Occupational Therapy, Physical Therapy and School Psychology Jobs*. Retrieved June 14, 2011, from http://www.pediastaff.com/blog/innovative-treatments-for-selective-mutism-1491

Kumpulainen, K. (2002). Phenomenology and the Treatment of Selective Mutism. CNS Drugs, 16(3), 175–180. Retrieved June 14, 2011, from the PsycINFO database.

Mennuti, R. B., Freeman, A., & Christner, R. W. (2006). Understanding and Treating Selective Mutism. *Cognitive-behavioral interventions in educational settings: a handbook for practice* (pp. 107–120). New York: Routledge.

Phei, O. P. (2010). Playing with Gladys: A case study integrating drama therapy with behavioural interventions for the treatment of selective mutism. *Clinical Child Psychology and Psychiatry*, 15(2), 215–230. Retrieved June 14, 2011, from the PsycINFO database.

FIGURE 7.3
How Main Points and Sub Points Work Together to Form a Strong Body

UTILIZING TRANSITIONS

The last element of body is transitions. **Transitions** are words, phrases or sentences that connect one idea to the other. They are beneficial for both the speaker and listeners. As a speaker they will help you stay on track in the hopes of not rambling or going off in unplanned territory. As listeners, it helps us follow you and understand where you have been and where you are going in the speech. Transitions should be included in the following three areas of the speech:

Selecting interesting supporting materials helps hold attention.

1. Between the introduction and body of the speech

2. Between each main point

3. Between the body and conclusion

There are several options to consider when writing transitions for your speech. You can use transitional words or phrases which tell the audience where you are in the speech. Examples of these transitions are: first, second, third, finally, now, then, to begin and in summary. You can also utilize other transitional words or phrases that help connect ideas such as in addition, let's look, however, not only, also, and therefore.

You can create transitional sentences to help connect one idea to the other. These sentences remind the audience of what you just discussed and where you are about to go in your speech. In a speech about the origin and effects of Friday the 13th, a student moves smoothly from main point 1 to main point 2 by utilizing a transition. "Now that we know some of the history, let's look at some of the effects this day has had on society." The student just discussed the origin of Friday the 13th in main point 1 and now he is moving to main point 2 where he will discuss the effects on society. Let's look at more detailed example of how transitions can connect your ideas in Figure 7.4.

In a commemorative speech about the Constitution of the United States, a student uses the transitions in the three critical portions of his speech.

Between the introduction and body: Now I will begin honoring the United States Constitution's ability to establish and protect the great American experiment.

Main point 1: The Constitution provides the foundation for the United States to establish and protect the sanctity of its free nation experiment.

Transition between main point 1 and main point 2: Just as the protection of rights and the establishment of a government for the people were grand achievements for the United States Constitution, so too is its determination for equal protection.

Main Point 2: The Constitution establishes equal protection for all American people, and their natural rights.

Transition between body and conclusion: As I close my presentation, I would like to reiterate the Constitution's impact and importance.

FIGURE 7.4
How Transitions Connect Ideas

Internal Summary

In some instances, you may want to have a more in-depth transition also called an internal summary. An **internal summary** is a transitional device that gives a thorough recap of the main point before moving on to another idea. They are useful when you have just discussed a difficult idea or concept and need to recap in more detail before progressing.

Now that we've discussed all of the elements of a solid body (main points, subpoints and transitions), let's look at Figure 7.5 to learn how these components work together.

Body

I. **Main Point 1:** Music therapy can include a wide range of activities
   A. According to the American Music Therapy Association's website, "Music therapists design music sessions for individuals and groups based on client needs using music improvisation, receptive music listening, song writing, lyric discussion, music and imagery, music performance, and learning through music."
   B. Using dance and exercise to music is a popular application of music therapy, which can encourage fitness, increased range of motion, and elevated mood.
   C. A client or patient may also be encouraged to perform.
      1. The patient may learn a new instrument, for instance, they may learn easy pieces on the piano or guitar.
      2. The patient may learn new songs and vocal techniques.
      3. Songwriting and composition are also popular.

4. The emphasis is not on the mastery of the instrument, but on the benefits gained from the learning.
   a. A sense of accomplishment and self-worth is gained.
   b. The motions of learning an instrument (or singing) are physically therapeutic. For example, learning to play the piano increases coordination and motor skills, according to the Rebecca Institute.
   c. Interactions with the music therapist and other patients, if in group therapy, aid in social interactions and emotional well-being.
D. Passively or receptively listening to music is also encouraged in music therapy.
   1. Brain function increases while simply listening to music.
   2. Patient's mood increases while listening to music, and maintaining a positive attitude and motivation is essential while in therapy. According to their website, Stanford Hospital also uses music to alleviate pain and nausea in cancer patients.
E. To review, music therapy does not employ just one technique. Musical movement, performance, and receptive listening are just some of the ways music therapy is used to help people.

(Transition: Now that you know some of the major techniques used in music therapy, I will tell you about a few of the situations in which it is used.)

II. **Main Point 2:** Music therapy is used to treat a multitude of diverse conditions.
   A. Music therapy can be used to improve many of the symptoms associated with Parkinson's disease.

   1. Parkinson's disease affects muscle movement and often causes choppy motions.
   2. Steady, rhythmic, and upbeat music can help people with PD to initiate movement and move more fluidly, according to music therapist Concetta Tomaino, writing on bethabe.org. They learn to focus on the rhythm in order to keep their own movement steady.
   B. Music can be extremely useful in maintaining cognitive function in patients recovering from a stroke.

   1. In a Finnish study led by Teppo Sarkamo, which I read about in the Washington Post, stroke sufferers were divided into three groups: music listeners, audiobooks listeners, and non-listeners. The music listeners had improved memory and focus, and displayed less depression than the other two groups.
   C. Autistic patients can benefit from music therapists as well.

   1. Autism causes severe social interaction problems.
   2. Music therapy sessions that encourage group musical activities and shared musical experiences help cultivate communication interactions in people with autism, according to the National Autistic Society's (UK) website.

D. Music therapy has been used in the treatment of additional problems as well.

   1. Alzheimer's, schizophrenia, depression, sleep disorders, and chronic pains have all been treated with music therapy.
   2. The social repercussions of illness may be helped by music therapy as well. According to Nordoff-Robbins.org.uk, " . . . for people isolated by illness or disability it can provide a means of socialization, sharing and community."

E. To summarize before I move on, music therapy is used to treat many different problems, including Parkinson's disease, stroke recovery, and Autism.

(Transition: Now I would like to review.)

Works Cited

Frequently Asked Questions. (1999). *American Music Therapy Association.* Retrieved July 8, 2009, from http://www.musictherapy.org/faqs.html.

Frequently Asked Questions. The Rebecca Center for Music Therapy. Retrieved July 8, 2009, from http://www.therebeccacenter.org/faq.html#7.

Music Program. (2009). *Stanford Hospitals and Clinics.* Retrieved July 9, 2009, from http://www.stanfordhospital.org/forPatients/patientServices/-musicprogramGuestServices.html.

Music Therapy. (2008). *The National Autistic Society.* Retrieved July 8, 2009, from http://www.nas.org.uk/nas/jsp/polopoly.jsp?d=528&a=3348.

Music Therapy Improves Stroke Outcomes. (2008, February 20). *The Washington Post.* Retrieved July 8, 2009, from http://www.washingtonpost.com/wpdyn/content/article/2008/02/20/AR2008022001414.html

Tomaino, Concetta M. Music Therapy to Benefit Individuals with Parkinson's Disease. *Institute for Music and Neurologic Function.* Retrieved July 8, 2009, from http://www.betabe.org/MT_Parkinsons_Disease234.html.

What is Music Therapy? (2007). *Nordoff-Robbins Music Therapy.* Retrieved July 9, 2009, from http://www.nordoff-robbins.org.uk/musicTherapy/index.html

Figure 7.5
Main Points, Sub Points and Transitions Work Together

SUMMARY
Students need to follow these steps in writing and organizing a successful speech:

1. Determine purpose

2. Choose and narrow a topic

3. Develop a thesis statement

4. Write and organize the body of the speech

The body of the speech consists of three elements: main points, supporting points and transitions. The main points are the key ideas of the speech. They bring substance to the speech's thesis. You can generate main points by looking at your thesis and seeing if there are evident divisions. You can also use brainstorming techniques. Other tips to adhere to when developing main points are: limit the number of main points, focus on one idea, write a declarative statement, strive for balance and maintain an audience-centered approach. We also urge you to utilize various organizational patterns such as causal pattern, chronological pattern, spatial pattern, problem-solution pattern and topical pattern.

Once you've developed main points, you need to prove, explain or justify them with supporting material or sub points. Supporting material may be in the form of examples, testimony, illustrations, analogies, statistics, narratives, comparisons and contrasts. The sub points are more specific than the main points.

The last element of the body is transitions. Transitions are words, phrases and sentences that help connect your ideas. Transitions need to be in at least three places: between the introduction and body, between each main point and between the body and conclusion.

All of these components work together to formulate a cohesive, organized, well-developed, and interesting speech. If executed well, these elements will help you be successful in this class. In the next chapter, we'll learn how to open and close the speech.

REFERENCES
Beebe, S. A. & Beebe, A. J. (2009). *A concise public speaking handbook,* 2nd ed. New York: Pearson.

DeVito, J. (2009). *The essential elements of public speaking,* 3rd ed. New York: Pearson Education, Inc.

Gregory, H. (2008). *Public speaking for college and career,* 8th ed. New York: McGraw-Hill.

Chapter 8
Developing Introductions and Conclusions

Courtesy of Brett Marty/Corbis Images.

THE OPENING AND CLOSING OF A SPEECH

The introduction and conclusion are vital elements of the speech writing process. The introduction is the foundation of the speech and a key to success or failure. The introduction should set the tone of your speech. You want that tone to be positive so you are on your way to being a successful speaker. Your audience will decide if the topic and the speaker are worth listening to in the first few seconds of the speech. As a speaker, this is a challenge you can meet with proper preparation. The introduction must prepare the audience for what they will hear in the body of the speech. It establishes a purpose and gives the audience a basic structure of the speech. This structure helps them follow better what you are saying and, thereby, enhance their understanding.

The conclusion is equally important. Essentially, you want to end on a good note. In comparison to a successful opening, you also want a successful ending. The purpose of the conclusion is finality and closure. It wraps up the content of the speech in a concise manner and reminds the audience of what was discussed. In addition, you close your speech with a memorable ending.

This chapter is divided into four sections: Essential Elements of an Introduction, Tips for an Effective Introduction, Essential Elements of a Conclusion, and Tips for an Effective Conclusion.

ESSENTIAL ELEMENTS OF THE INTRODUCTION

It is crucial to intrigue your audience from the very beginning of the speech so they will want to continue to listen to your ideas. There are five elements you should address in the introduction:

1. Gain the audience's attention

2. Show relevance to the audience

3. Establish credibility

4. Provide a thesis statement

5. Preview main ideas

Gain the Audience's Attention

The very first item the audience should hear in your speech is an **attention-getter**. An attention-getter is the opening of a speech; its goal is to increase the audience's interest level and encourage them to listen to the rest of the speech. The attention-getter must have an obvious relation to the topic. As a speaker, you need to catch your audience's attention and appeal to their curiosity so they actually listen to your message.

In communication, your goals should be for the audience to listen, understand and retain the message. If the audience is uninterested and bored, they won't be actively listening to the presentation and your success is in doubt. It would not be a good idea to say, "Good morning, my name is Jane Doe and I will be informing you on the life of Abraham Lincoln." You haven't caught the audience's attention; you told them your topic. This is where the attention-getter can be very useful. Imagine the speaker takes a different approach and says,

The person I am discussing today grew up in severe poverty. He persevered through several challenges in his life. His wife died at the age of 26 and he mourned the loss of three children as well. He suffered a nervous breakdown at the age of 27. He lost eight elections before becoming the President of the United States. In January of 1863, he issued the Emancipation Proclamation changing the course of history forever by freeing millions of slaves. Who is this person? Abraham Lincoln. (whitehouse.gov)

Arousing curiosity pertaining to your topic is a better alternative than revealing the topic bluntly. These facts about President Lincoln may be surprising to most people and it awakens the audience because they are curious to know who this person is.

There are several strategies a speaker can utilize to grab the attention of the audience. We will discuss a few of them.

Telling a Story Most people enjoy hearing a story. It can make the topic seem more personal and relatable. It's important to realize the story should be relatively brief. You must stay within your time limit, so your story should not go on and on. It should be clear, direct, interesting and have a point. For instance, a student was discussing a charity, Ronald McDonald House Charities in her commemorative speech. She opened by saying,

For just a minute, I want you to think of a child that you know, maybe a brother, cousin or daughter and then think how you would feel if they were suddenly diagnosed with a serious medical condition. My parents went through a similar situation when I was almost seven-years-old. My mom delivered a baby girl who had a heart defect. She was flown to Mobile, and then to UAB in Birmingham and during the course of their time in Birmingham, my parents stayed in the Ronald McDonald House.

This story accomplishes two goals. The student asks the audience to contemplate and imagine being in this situation. Then she lends a personal story which also gives her some credibility on the topic.

Stories are a powerful way to generate audience interest. A well-selected story will leave the listeners wanting more. Nancy Duarte (2010) stated well the impact of a good story. She sees effective speeches and the power of storytelling as closely joined. Here are her thoughts:

When presentations are packaged in a story framework, your ideas become downright unstoppable. . . . Stories help the audience visualize what you do or what you believe. . . . Sharing experience in the form of a story creates a shared experience and visceral connection [with your audience], pp. xvii, 107.

We add to this, a good story is memorable. Myers and Nix (2011) claim that they are memorable "because of the way that our brains are wired, we will listen with absorbed attention to almost any story, no matter how strange" (p. 113). We agree.

Asking a Question A speaker may ask the audience a question. The question may seek a response or it may be a rhetorical question. A **rhetorical question** does not seek a response. Its purpose is for the audience to reflect about the subject material before the speaker discusses it.

In a speech about the United States Constitution, a student begins with a rhetorical question. "Do you remember the first three words of the *United States Constitution?* Those three simple words, 'We the people' begins one of history's most important and life altering documents and enlightens us to the purpose of the Constitution." His question did not seek a response but rather asked the audience to contemplate the topic he was discussing before he went into detail.

Questions are effective but can also be tricky. Here are some guidelines:

1. Don't pepper your audience with several questions.

2. Be clear and specific.

3. If you ask the audience a question and you depend on them answering but no one answers, it can be awkward.

4. Interaction among a speaker and audience can be beneficial but always consider the situation of speech. The time and place dictates the behavior of both the listener and speaker.

Using a Quote A speaker can also use a quotation to catch the audience's attention. It can be an interesting strategy for beginning a speech and appealing to the audience's curiosity.

In a self-introduction speech, one of the author's of this book began with a quote. She said, "I've been called many names like perfectionist, difficult and obsessive. I think it takes obsession, takes searching for the details for any artist to be good." (Barbara Streisand) This quote is not only interesting but it has the potential of intriguing the audience. The purpose is to bring them into the speech so they want to hear more. Why and how is this quote pertinent to the topic? The answer is: listen and you'll see!

"Shocking" the Audience A speaker can use a statistic or some other astonishing fact to "shock" the audience. This approach leaves the audience member thinking, "This is really interesting and surprising. I had no idea."

If the speaker presents the topic in a manner that surprises the audience, they may be more receptive to listening to the rest of the message for many reasons. The audience members may feel they need to listen to gain more knowledge about the topic or they simply may be interested in hearing more.

You can use statistics as an effective tactic in opening your speech. However, it's important to use numbers and statistics in moderation. They can be overwhelming if used in excess. Also, consider the source. Statistics can be easily manipulated so ensure they are valid and reliable.

When discussing the strategy of shocking the audience, you must apply this rule. The statement that surprises the audience must relate to the actual topic. Don't say something to shock the audience that has no relevance to the speech. A good rule to follow is to avoid gimmicks. A student once opened his speech by walking on his hands and doing a back flip. Did he catch the audience's attention? I would say so. This student was a cheerleader at the University of South Alabama and also served as the mascot, Southpaw. At first glance most people would assume this was a gimmick. However, his topic was gymnastics. Did the attention getter and topic tie in together smoothly? You bet!

Giving an Incentive to Listen The typical audience member wants to know, "Why should I listen to this speech?" Basically, what does this topic have to do with me, the audience member? If you want to be successful, the goal of every speech regardless of the purpose must be an audience-centered approach. You must consider your audience and how they will perceive your message. As a result, you must tie your topic to the audience in the introduction. A brief statement in the introduction that addresses the audience can assist in developing a speech from the viewpoint of the audience. The co-authors of this book practice what they preach. For example, when teaching public speaking, many instructors discuss the benefits of taking the course and specifically address

Courtesy of Louis McNamee/Corbis Images.

Giving your audience incentive to listen is an important function of the introduction.

how it will help students be successful in their academic, professional and personal lives. Let's face it; most students are not looking forward to taking a public speaking class. Similar to an audience, students want to know "Why am I being forced to take this class?" and "What will I get out of this class?" Hence, we discuss the importance of public speaking and the benefits the students will attain by taking the class. By telling the audience, this is what you'll be able to take from my speech, you are giving them a strong incentive to listen.

Using Visual Aids We all learn in different ways. Some of us are auditory learners; others may be visual or tactile. If you appeal to more than one learning style, you'll appeal to a variety of audience members and their interest levels. By displaying a chart, photo, video, model, replica or using a PowerPoint presentation, you are using a visual to complement what you are saying in your speech. In addition, effective visual aids catch the audience's attention. Sometimes we need to not just hear it but see it.

In a speech about tornadoes, it will be helpful to see what a tornado looks like and the aftermath of the damage. The audience will be able to connect with what you are saying because you've shown them. In addition, it may help in retaining what they learned. The audience may not remember everything about the speech but they remember the powerful visual you shared with them.

Relevance to the Audience

The second component of the introduction is relevance to the audience. In some instances, the attention-getter may be the tie to the audience as well. It is imperative to establish relevance. The audience needs to know what this topic has to do with them and their lives. By being sensitive to their needs, you are on your way to maintaining an audience-centered approach to the speech making process.

It sometimes requires creativity depending on the topic but think outside the box. In a speech about clocks, a student simply states that clocks are everywhere. People reference them many times a day. They are in our cars, phones, televisions, laptops, MP3 players and so on. This simple statement relates the topic to the audience.

Establish Credibility

The third component of the introduction is **credibility**. A credibility statement is an explanation as to why the speaker is qualified in regards to the topic. The speaker must answer the question, "Why should we listen to you?" What kind of experience or knowledge does the speaker have in regards to the topic?

Think about it. If you've listened to a speaker introduce another speaker at a conference, meeting or convention, the speaker shares a list of qualifications when introducing the main speaker. Why do we do this? The audience needs to know why this person has been invited to speak to this group. What do they know? Why are they an authority on the topic?

When constructing your own introductions for this class, you need to think along the same lines. You may have personal experience or a unique perspective on the topic. For example, a speaker is discussing a topic in the category of music. The speaker has played the piano since she was five-years-old and is currently majoring in music. This gives the speaker some personal credibility. It would be appropriate to state these qualifications in the introduction.

It is difficult to have personal experience or be an expert in all things. In this case, you do research to show the audience you've done your homework. You may define a term in the introduction to ensure everyone understands the term in the way you intend. By defining a term and giving credit to a source, you are showing the audience you've taken the time to research the topic. You may also use testimony to establish credibility.

In a speech about music therapy, a student uses a quote in the introduction of her speech accessed from Stanford Hospital's website. Oliver Sacks says, "The power of music to integrate and cure is quite fundamental. It is the profoundest non-chemical medication." In an effort to explain the discipline of music therapy, this student accesses a quote from a reliable source proving she has researched the topic.

Thesis Statement

The **thesis statement** is the fourth component of the introduction. The thesis statement is a declarative sentence that explains the key concept of the speech. The thesis statement is central to the speech; everything in the speech supports the thesis statement. Some students write lengthy and wordy thesis statements; this is not effective. It should be clear and concise. Summarize your speech into one sentence. Also, remember you are writing this speech for oral communication. The thesis should be simple yet thorough enough to cover the content of the speech. Attempt to make an assertion about your topic when constructing the thesis statement.

In an informative speech about her home country of Chile, a student's thesis was "Despite the fact that Chile is one nation, there are generally three different cultures characterized by the northern, central and southern regions." Her main points supported her thesis since she described the culture and characteristics of each region in the body of the speech.

Preview of Main Ideas

The last component of the introduction is the **preview statement**. This sentence or sentences alerts the audience of the main points of the speech. The preview statement prepares the audience for what they will hear but also gives them a structure of the speech. In short, it tells the audience where the speaker is going in the speech. It assists listeners in understanding the organizational pattern. In an informative speech regarding tips for finding a job, a student previews the main points of the speech. "I will give you some tips on how to get yourself in the door with a good resume and once in, how to shine in your interview."

Some students decide to combine the thesis and preview together. This is an acceptable option but in doing so make sure the thesis is one sentence that makes an assertion about the topic and includes all of the main points.

An Example of an Introduction

How do all these elements work together to form a smooth, direct, clear and cohesive introduction? Let's view a student's example:

Attention Material: Aristotle, Charles Darwin, Winston Churchill, George Washington, Marilyn Monroe, and James Earl Jones. What do all these famous people have in common? According to the National Stuttering Association, stuttering is what they have in common.

Tie to the Audience: Most of us know or have at least once known someone who stuttered. But, do we really know what stuttering is?

Credibility: I am majoring in Speech and Hearing Sciences. When I tell people about my major they get confused because they don't know exactly what it entails. When I tell them that it has to do with speech and hearing disorders, stuttering is the example I always give.

Thesis Statement/Preview: Stuttering is an age-old communication disorder that occurs in all languages and cultures yet not enough people today are aware of the meaning, symptoms and causes of stuttering.

This example includes all of the pertinent elements of a solid introduction. The student arouses curiosity and catches the audience's attention. She poses a question to the audience and gives the audience an incentive to listen. In addition, she utilizes an outside source to establish credibility. She also highlights personal credibility by mentioning her major, Speech and Hearing Sciences. The thesis is thorough, clear, and direct. She previews her main points in the thesis so we have an idea of what she will be discussing in the body of the speech. This student is on the way to a very successful speech.

Tips for an Effective Introduction

A few tips to follow with creating the introduction of your speech are:

1. Your introduction includes the five elements. You must gain the audience's attention, show relevance to the audience, establish credibility, provide a thesis statement and preview main ideas. It shouldn't be too brief but also not too long. You need to give the audience some time to get in the "groove" of your speech. Avoid excluding the essential elements of an introduction and jumping into the body of the speech. The audience may have a hard time staying on track with you and become confused. The introduction shouldn't be too long either. If the speaker gives too much background information or is "long-winded" in the introduction, the audience may think you've already moved to the body of speech or they may become bored.

2. Start strongly. The audience is going to decide in the first few seconds if your speech is worth their time. Be confident and develop a positive attitude about your speech and your audience. Try to concentrate and focus on the message you are conveying.

3. The introduction should tie in smoothly to the body of the speech. Remember the thesis statement is central to the speech. So everything should support it. The introduction should be the foundation to building a simple, easy to follow speech.

4. Most students assume they should prepare the introduction first since it is the first element the audience will hear in the speech. It's difficult to fully introduce the body of the speech, if you are unsure of what the body entails. It's acceptable to create body of the speech before finalizing the introduction.

ESSENTIAL ELEMENTS OF THE CONCLUSION

A strong conclusion brings closure to the speech and reiterates the ideas you discussed in the body. You also want to leave the audience with something they will remember. Some may compare the conclusion to a finale. Make your speech memorable. There are four elements a speaker should address in the conclusion.

1. Signify closure

2. Summarize the key ideas

3. Reiterate relevance of topic to audience

4. Create memorable ending

Signify the Closure

The speaker should give the audience a hint that he or she is concluding the speech. Some speakers do this with words and others may change the tone of their voice. The speaker should avoid ending abruptly and instead prepare the audience for the ending. The audience should know you are closing the speech before you sit down or walk away from the podium. A speaker may signify closure by using a word, phrase or even a sentence.

Some examples signifying conclusion include, "To summarize," "I want to close by saying," "Today we've discussed," "Let's recap," "Let's review," "Finally," and "Looking back."

Summarize the Key Ideas

In the introduction, the speaker previews the main points. In the body, the speaker discusses the main points. In the conclusion, the speaker recaps the main points and emphasizes the key concept of the speech. In written communication, there is not much repetition. A public speech is different. The audience doesn't have a copy of the speech in front of them. The audience can't refer back to a sentence or word that constituted a main point. In this essence, it's crucial to repeat your ideas in the conclusion so that you will help the audience. As a result, the audience will remember the key ideas and follow the speaker's organizational pattern. A student summarizes his speech about Friday the 13th. He recaps his key ideas by saying:

We know there is really no one origin of this infamous superstition. There are only several speculations and stories from ancient civilizations. Despite this fact however, many people refrain from going out on Friday the 13th. There also are several effects this day has on our current civilization.

A summary should convey finality to the speech and bring everything full circle.

Reiterate the Relevance of Topic to the Audience

In the introduction, the speaker ties the topic to the audience. In the conclusion, it's equally important to remind the audience of the practicality of the topic and why it's important. Some students choose to use the same tie to the audience as in the introduction; some students tweak their approach in the ending.

In a speech about stress, a student ties her topic back to the audience. "Being college students, we all have much more stress to come. We'll all have finals to take. We'll all have papers to write. We'll all have speeches to present." This was a clever way to emphasize a commonality that tied the entire audience together. They were all college students in a speech class.

Create a Memorable Ending

The last element of the conclusion should consist of a **memorable ending**. This is a final statement that emphasizes the overall purpose of the speech. Some students link the introduction to the conclusion. A student opened her speech with the following questions, "What does a person with

Ruth J. Simmons, who was named president of Brown University in 2000, reinforces the purpose of her speech by creating a memorable ending.

diabetes look like? Are they old, overweight or sedentary?" In her speech, one of the topics she discussed was the misconceptions associated with type 1 diabetes. She addressed some of these misconceptions by citing support material from the Juvenile Diabetes Research Foundation.

In her closing statement, she said, "So what does a person with diabetes look like? The answer stands before you right now." Not only was it interesting to connect the introduction with the conclusion, but the ending was a surprise. She had not revealed to us that she had type 1 diabetes and the audience was left intrigued.

Example of Conclusion: How do all these elements work together to create closure and finality of a speech? Let's view a student's ending to her speech on stuttering.

Signal of End/Summary: In conclusion, I have explained to you what stuttering means. I have informed your about the symptoms of stuttering and have told you about the causes.

Tie Back to the Audience/Memorable Ending: I hope you have a better understanding of stuttering. If you know someone who stutters, or meet one in the future, try to be understanding and patient with them. Just remember, the person who is stuttering is ten times more uncomfortable talking to you than you are to him or her.

This conclusion contains the four elements of a solid conclusion. She signals the end to let the audience know she is wrapping up. She reminds us of the main points she discussed in the conclusion. She ties the topic back to the audience by creating a scenario in which her listeners can identify. Her final statement leaves the audience with something to think about, thus creating a memorable ending.

Tips for an Effective Conclusion

A few tips to follow when constructing the conclusion are:

1. Prepare a brief and succinct conclusion. Avoid a long, drawn-out conclusion. The audience will become irritated if they hear "in conclusion" three times. Don't get off track and ramble. Come up with a plan and stick to it.

2. Don't forget to signal the end. It can be confusing to listeners if they have no idea you are closing the speech. Leaving the audience puzzled isn't an effective way to close the speech.

3. Some students make the mistake of bringing in a new main point in the conclusion. The speech is coming to close; don't bring in a new point that needs to be developed. If you forget something in the body of the speech, don't say, "Oh yea, I forgot to say. . . ." This is where practice and preparation work together to create a well-polished speech.

4. This is the end, finish strongly. Don't downgrade your speech and end with "That's it. I guess I am done." or "That's all I have to say. I am glad that is over." You've done your research and worked hard on the speech, don't leave us with "That's it!" Don't blow it in the end. Be confident and give your speech the proper ending it deserves.

SUMMARY

A speech is divided into three major sections: the introduction, the body and the conclusion.

The introduction is the foundation of the speech. It establishes a purpose and tone for the rest of the speech. An effective introduction includes an attention getter, a tie to the audience, credibility, a thesis statement, and a preview.

There are many strategies a speaker can adopt in catching the audience's attention.

- Tell a story
- Use a quote
- Ask a question
- Give the audience an incentive to listen
- Shock the audience with a fact or statistic
- Use a visual aid

The second component of the introduction is relevance to the audience. The speaker needs to establish a connection with the audience. Audience-centered speakers consider their listeners' perspective. They think of the most effective way to get their message across to the audience. Connecting to the audience or relating the topic to the audience is a vital part of audience analysis and the introduction of the speech.

The third component is credibility. How do you know about the topic you are discussing? Do you have experience or qualifications that make you knowledgeable about the topic? Did you do your research? A speaker must establish credibility in the introduction so the audience will trust and believe what you are saying.

The fourth component of the introduction is a thesis statement. A thesis statement is the central focus of the speech. It should be articulated in the introduction because it is so vital to all other parts of the speech. The main points and support material develop the thesis statement. A thesis statement is a one sentence summary of the speech. It's not a question or phrase. It's an assertion that tells the audience what the speech is all about.

The final component of the introduction is a preview statement. A preview statement lets the audience know where you are going in the speech. It specifically highlights the main points of the speech. It keeps the audience on track and gives them a mental structure of the speech.

The conclusion of the speech creates finality and closure. It should be smooth, precise and bring the entire speech full circle. An effective conclusion includes: a signal of the end, summary of ideas, a statement of relevance to the audience and a memorable ending.

The first component signifies the ending of the speech. You must alert the audience that the speech is ending. A speaker can accomplish this by using simple words, phrases and sentences that alert the audience and signal the end of the speech.

The second component of a conclusion is a summary. In the introduction, the speaker previews main points. In the body, the speaker discusses these main points. In the conclusion, the speaker concisely recaps the main points of the speech. This repetition allows the audience to retain the information presented in the speech.

The third component reiterates the relevance to the audience. The speaker emphasizes the importance of the topic and message. Relevance also connects the audience together and may highlight any commonalities that may exist among the listeners. Relevance is key to being an audience-centered speaker. Speakers should strive to be audience-centered throughout the entire speech writing process.

The final component of a conclusion is a memorable ending. A memorable ending should emphasize the thesis statement. It's the final touch on a speech that brings it all together. It's the very last element of the speech; make it count!

REFERENCE

Beebe, S. A. & Beebe, A. J. (2009). *A concise public speaking handbook,* 2nd ed. New York: Pearson.

DeVito, J. (2009). *The essential elements of public speaking,* 3rd ed. New York: Pearson Education, Inc.

Duarte, N. (2010). *Resonate: Present visual stories that transform audiences.* Hoboken, NJ: John Wiley & Sons, pp. xvii, 107.

Gregory, H. (2008). *Public speaking for college and career,* 8th ed. New York: McGraw-Hill.

Chapter 9
Supporting Your Ideas

Courtesy of John Minchillo/Invision/AP Images.

WHY SHOULD YOU USE SUPPORTING MATERIALS?

We will put this question on hold to be answered shortly. This question does, however, prompt another. "What is a speech without supporting materials?" It is nothing but a skeleton of what a speech is meant to be. What you have is a statement of the topic and some ideas about it. The overall purpose of a speech is for some group of people to listen to, understand, and retain your message. The message, of course, is more than the statement of a topic and several ideas about it. If this is all you intend, you should print it on a piece of paper and pass it out or, perhaps, send it in an email to the intended receivers.

It is the supporting material you bring together to develop your main points that can make the difference between the success or failure of your speech. Here are several other reasons to carefully prepare supporting materials:

- Supporting Materials Help to Develop and Illustrate Your Ideas
- Supporting Materials Help to Clarify Ideas
- Supporting Materials Help Hold Your Audience's Attention
- Supporting Materials Help Your Audience Remember Key Ideas
- Supporting Materials Help Prove a Point You Are Making

So, in a broad sense these are the answers to the question, "Why should I use supporting materials?"

107

TYPES OF SUPPORTING MATERIALS

Of course, supporting materials are of various kinds. The major categories are explanation, definition, examples, statistics and testimony.

Explanation

Jack Parker, a very successful debate coach, provided a basic formula for presenting an argument—name the argument, explain the argument and support it. He was right about presenting a successful argument in a debate, but also in how to craft successful presentation of a main point, or even a sub point, in speech. The naming part of this formula would be the actual main or sub point. The explaining and supporting would be what follows the naming of the point. Here is an example.

> *Main Point* I: Most people think wrongly that diet beverages are healthy and will help them avoid the extra intake of calories and carbohydrates and maintain their weight and health.
> Why are they wrong? Let me explain. Drinking diet beverages can contribute to metabolic syndrome. This syndrome is a collection of risk factors for cardiovascular disease and diabetes that include abdominal obesity, high cholesterol and blood glucose levels and elevated blood pressure.
> [The speaker would continue with additional support, evidence, to substantiate this claim.]

The second paragraph is the explanation of the main point. An **explanation** is an elaboration on an idea with the purpose of making it understandable and clear. A specific kind of explanation is definition. A **definition** explains the essential qualities of a word or terminology. It often determines the boundaries of the term—what is in and what is out. In other words, it tells what the term means and what it does not.

A speaker on the topic of hemophilia began her speech with this first main point, "What is Hemophilia?" Here is what she said:

> According to the National Heart, Lung and Blood Institute, hemophilia is a rare, inherited bleeding disorder in which the blood does not clot normally. The bleeding may be internal, especially in the joints, but also external from an injury.

The speaker moved from the definition to sub points that provide a broader explanation of aspects of hemophilia.

Examples

An **example** is a specific case used to represent or illustrate an idea, condition, experience or a group of people. Examples provide clarification for ideas that otherwise might be a bit "fuzzy." They can also personalize the information when you use an example that is tailored to your audience. We also know that vivid, concrete examples will have significant impact on your audience (Tal-Or, et al, 2004).

Here is an example that we think achieves these aims.

Mardi Gras festivities are popular in Mobile, Alabama, where it got its start. You may have had the opportunity to participate in some of these events. The kind of fun connected with Mardi Gras is characterized by the many who have participated over the years. Michael Kraft, for example, organized the first parade. He and a group of other men borrowed some rakes, garden hoes, and cowbells from a local hardware store. They also found costumes somewhere and soon were parading through downtown Mobile streets, making a great deal of noise. Because of the cowbells they called themselves The Cowbellions.

Careful selection of supporting materials helps ensure your success.

There are several types of examples that you will find useful.

Brief Examples A **brief example** is a short, specific instance. These are often used in a series to provide evidence of the wide-spread nature of something—say, the harm of a problem. The series of brief examples may also be used to establish a trend. The speaker might start a series by citing one brief example, followed by, "This is not an isolated incident. Consider these several others that demonstrate that."

Here is a situation where you might use brief examples to serve two purposes: to introduce a topic *and* draw attention to the harmful nature of a problem.

Suppose you believe that skipping breakfast is harmful, especially for children, and decide to do research on the problem to create a persuasive speech. Here is what you might say to accomplish these two aims with brief examples:

Consider these harmful effects of children skipping breakfast as reported in the article, "Ready, Set, Breakfast!," published by kidshealth.org.

- Children who do not eat breakfast tend not to be able to learn and concentrate in school as well as children who eat breakfast.

- Children who skip breakfast tend to be hyper, irritable, anxious and more likely to be disruptive in school than those who eat breakfast.

- Children who skip breakfast may not get enough iron in their bodies and consequently are more likely to develop a higher body mass index which can lead to being overweight than those who eat breakfast.

A brief example might also be used to illustrate. Here are brief examples used to illustrate the point that Mexican Americans have made significant contributions to life and culture in the United States:

Consider these Mexican Americans who have made contributions to our culture:

- Dr. Ellen Ochoa is an astronaut who spent more than 480 hours in space and invented optical methods that have had significant impact on space exploration.

- Ms. Nancy Lopez has won more than 48 tour championships and has had a crucial effect on popularizing women's professional golf.

- Dr. Mario Molina won the Nobel Prize in chemistry for his research on the formation and decomposition of the ozone layer of our atmosphere.

Here is a single example used to illustrate the point that people develop phobias that can be significant enough to affect their behavior.

For example, a person may have an intense fear of dogs. This person may become so anxious when thinking about taking a walk that they do not do so because they may encounter a dog.

Extended Examples An **extended example** is a narrative or story developed at some length with more detail than a brief example. You will find that telling a story is an excellent way to capture and hold your audience's attention. Of course, you must make sure your story is clearly connected to the idea you are illustrating. Your story must explain, illustrate, or reinforce your idea.

Here is an example of an effective story. This is abbreviated from what astronaut Michael Mullane's said in his report. The essence of what he said is still here.

I served as a colonel in the U.S. Air Force as a weapons and navigational systems operator on an F-111 fighter jet. The Air Force has a term, bingo fuel, the point at which the aircraft might not have enough fuel to make it back to the airbase. On one flight, the pilot continued to fly after the plane approached "bingo fuel."

I was on that plane and heard a little voice in the back of my head that told me to speak up and question the pilot's decision to continue flying, but I kept silent because the pilot was a veteran aviator. After all, he had thousands of hours of time in the jet.

Yes, it did happen. The jet ran out of fuel. The crew ejected just short of the runway. The F-111 crashed and became a $20 million pile of rubble (Schwartz, 2006).

Hypothetical Examples A **hypothetical example** is imaginary. This imaginative example must be based on fact and, therefore, plausible. Obviously, a made-up example that seems phony will not be impressive to your audience. You should let your audience know when you are using a hypothetical example. You might say, "Here is a typical experience of a cancer victim." The "real-life" story, a hypothetical example, can help your audience identify with someone or something in your situation. One technique you will want to consider is to follow an example of this type with other evidence, such as testimony or statistics. This will reinforce that your example is realistic.

Here is an example of an excellent hypothetical example that points out the typical effects of hemophilia.

Consider this typical extended family experiencing hemophilia.

Two grown sisters had children who grew up and did everything together. As young children they cried, played, fell and got hurt and *bled*. Yes, I said bled. This is where the children's experiences were different.

When the child who had hemophilia bled, the bleeding was very difficult to control. When the other child fell and bled, she healed normally. When the hemophilic child was three he died because internal bleeding was not controlled. You see the child had not yet been diagnosed with hemophilia. The other child suffered the loss of her friend and finally after years was able to get on with life.

Using Examples Effectively These are several reasons to use examples.

1. *Examples can help clarify your ideas.*

Think of an exceptional teacher, one that is easy to understand. We'll bet this person uses examples often to clarify what he or she is saying.

Notice how this example clarifies the idea.

Main Point:

Hurricanes have a devastating effect on people and communities.
Consider this example. Hurricane Katrina was the most extensive natural disaster in the history of the United States. It is calculated to have cost people and communities approximately $200 billion dollars in destruction. Houses were blown completely away from their foundations, leaving thousands of people homeless. Utility poles were destroyed or damaged, leaving communities without power for days, weeks, or even months. My family did not have power for a week and a half. Many families had to live in crowded FEMA trailers.

111

2. Examples can help personalize your ideas.

Your audience may relate more to a story of your experience with your topic than with the statistics you use to support it (Aronson, 2004). This, of course, does not mean you should omit the statistical data. This type of support, the personal example, adds human interest to your speech.
Here is an example of one that personalizes an idea.

Suppose you have studied to be an elementary school teacher. You were taught to recognize the signs of child abuse. They include physical abuse, such as punching, beating, kicking, burns, and other trauma that are often observable and reportable. But, would you be able to recognize the signs of child neglect? These are more difficult to detect. Listen carefully to my speech and you will know what the warning signs are and, also, be able to recognize them.

Of course, maybe most of you are saying, 'I have no intention of becoming an elementary school teacher.' True. But you could see these signs when observing a child in your neighborhood and know to take action.

3. Examples can help reinforce your ideas.

Here is an example of reinforcement of an idea.

> *Main Point:*
>
> Music therapy is used successfully to treat several diverse medical conditions.
> 1. Music therapy is used to improve many of the problems associated with Parkinson's disease.
> 2. Music can be extremely useful in maintaining cognitive functions in patients recovering from a stroke.
> 3. Autistic people can develop communicative interaction skills through music therapy.

Of course, each of these ideas would be explained.

4. Examples, even if brief, can give you the vivid detail that brings the topic "to life."

Contrast just saying one of the signs of a stroke is facial drooping vs. saying it with a word picture.

Often a person will experience facial drooping as a result of a stroke. Here is what facial drooping is like.
If you ask a normal, healthy person to smile, you will see both cheeks perk up with both eyes in equal sizes and shapes.
However, if you ask a person with a stroke to smile, one side is paralyzed making the cheek look wrinkled and the eye appearing to be much smaller than its normal size.

A caution is in order here. You should avoid reading your example to your audience if possible. The impact is increased significantly if you can maintain eye contact. Practice talking through your example until you can present it without your notes.

Comparison

Comparison is a process of examining two items by pointing out their similarities. Perhaps, the speaker uses a familiar object, person, place or concept to help the audience understand an unknown object, person, place or concept. Comparisons are frequently used to make a difficult or abstract concept more concrete and therefore more understandable.

An excellent example of comparison, and also contrast, came from a presidential debate with Ross Perot, an independent candidate for president, and Bill Clinton, as described by Goldman, et al. (1994). Clinton asserted that his clearly successful leadership as governor of the state of Arkansas showed that he could lead and would make a great president. Perot fired back saying that such a claim was very much like comparing the successful management of a mom-and-pop grocery store with managing a Walmart Super Store.

We now turn to brief discussion of contrasts.

Contrast

A **contrast** shows the difference between two or more things, ideas, factors, or issues. A familiar item is used to show something about the unfamiliar item. Here is an example from a speech by Paul Starbuck (2007). Paul presented this contrast in a speech that sought to point out the significant danger of exercise anorexia. **Exercise anorexia** takes exercise to the extreme that it becomes dangerous to the person's health. Here is what he said:

> According to Psychology Today, June 2005, this disorder can affect 35 percent of those who work out three to five times a week for more than an hour each time. Specific symptoms can be when someone exercises even when ill, or withdraws from others to exercise, or becomes upset if unable to work out. Just like alcoholics, exercise anorexics are literally addicted to their behavior. But unlike alcoholics, exercise anorexia is an even bigger epidemic because people don't recognize that there is a problem (Starbuck, 2007).

In this illustration, Paul dramatically explained the danger of exercise anorexia by contrasting it with alcoholism.

Statistics

Statistics are numerical ways of summarizing information or facts. Our most familiar experience with statistics is in the advertising we find on the television. Undoubtedly you have heard, "Eat this cereal because it contains 100% of the recommended daily allowance of essential vitamins."

"Purchase this soup which is 97% fat free." In these cases, the statistics are used to make a point and persuade you to buy the product.

Statistics are used to describe quantities, show trends, or infer relationships. They are calculated to appeal to the audience's rationality. Perhaps you want to talk about daycare in Mobile, Alabama. You might say that [some percent] of children under the age of 5 participate in daycare to describe quantity. You might go further and identify the percentage of infants, toddlers, and other preschoolers who attend. If this turned out to be an increasing percentage you would be showing a trend. Finally, if you were to show that a certain kind of daycare situation yielded better academic achievement for those who attended it than other kinds; you would be showing a relationship.

Compare a well-supported idea with a statement.

Of course, your purpose of using several statistics is to increase the overall impact on your audience, not for them to remember the specific statistics.

A speaker who is arguing that the U.S. Electoral College system is biased used statistics to support her claim. Here is how she did it.

> The number of Electoral College votes each state gets is not distributed evenly, that is according to population, among all the states. California gets one electoral vote for every 407,000 voting aged people. In Wyoming they get one electoral vote for every 106,000 voting aged people. So, simple arithmetic makes it clear. If you live in Wyoming, your vote is worth more—three times as much as if you live in California.

Here are two tests of the quality of statistics you will want to consider if you use statistics for proof. First, are the statistics representative? Statistics are supposed to represent something. If this is the opinion of a group of people, we want to say the statistic is typical of the whole group. It is often impractical to collect opinions from all members of the group. So, instead, we ask a sample of this group to respond to our questions. Say, you want to know the thoughts about parking at Northern Illinois University. You could stand outside of the chemistry building and collect data. Of course, you probably would not get the opinion of the basic population of students. This would require collecting data at a number of locations and at a number of different times each day.

Second, are the statistics from a reliable source? One way to determine this is to examine the credentials of the researcher or the credentials of the organization or news reporting source. You may not be able to verify the reliability of the source completing, but this should give you a sense of the reliability.

Using Statistics Effectively Here is some help in making sure you use statistics effectively.

1. *Use statistics to give your audience a sense of what your ideas mean.*

For example, your audience will want to know "how many" or "how much" if you are describing some problem people are experiencing. How many means how many are affected, how wide-spread is the problem, how much is this costing. One student reported credit card debt for students this way:

> According to the latest issue of Money magazine, the average credit-card debt of for graduating students is $3,700. Recent graduates often have a number of other expenses in getting situated in a new living space and job so their income for debt reduction is limited.

> The solution to this is to make minimum monthly payments on this credit-card debt. What does this mean in real costs? There will be about $4,200 in interest charges paid before repaying of their original $3,700 debt. What is one implication of this problem? The number of people under 25 years old who filed for bankruptcy has increased by over 50 percent.

2. *Explain your statistics in terms your audience will understand.*

You will need to interpret your statistics in such a way that your audience understands. You might say,

> Ten percent of the population is affected by this problem. Since there are roughly 20 people in this room, two of you are likely to be effected. Are you one of those two people?

> Perhaps a number is large, say 100,000. You might point out; this number is about the size of the entire city of Mobile, Alabama.

3. *Use statistics sparingly.*

If you use too many statistics, your audience may not remember any of them. This is self-defeating in that you are not actually achieving the goal of presenting statistics. But, this situation could get worse. Your audience may be totally lost and just tune out in response. In this case, they may not even remember the point you are making. Our best advice to avoid this is to only use the statistics that are important to establishing your point.

4. *Identify the sources of your statistics.*

Careful listeners are likely to want to know where you gathered the numbers. But, even if they don't wonder, they will be impressed by impressive sources. You are likely to have impressive sources if you have done careful research. If the statistics came from the *New York Times*, say so. There is ample support for the importance of citing the source if you are to be persuasive (Reynolds & Reynolds, 2002).

5. *Round off complicated statistics.*

You should round off large numbers unless there is some reason to give exact numbers. Why would you say that the population of Saudi Arabia is 23,513,300 when you could say it is about 23½ million? You can see why this could get confusing and particularly if you have several large numbers to report.

6. *Finally, you should consider using visuals to show your statistics.*

This is particularly important if your statistics are complicated, used as comparison with each other, or used to show trends.

You will find statistics in *The World Almanac and Book of Facts*, the United Nations' *Statistical Yearbook*, and *Guinness World Records*.

Testimony

Testimony is the statement or declaration of a witness, often used in support of a fact or statement. Testimonies can come from peers or experts. You might, for example, inquire of a friend who is the best teacher of CA 275, Small Group Discussion. Your friend might reply, "Take Professor Bush. She is the best they have at teaching small groups. I'd take it from her for sure if she is available." This is just one case of the many we experience as we interact with our friends in an attempt to make the right decisions. We trust our friends because of the relationship we have with them and their experience with the issue.

An excellent speaker will understand that this is also true of their audience. Audiences tend to make decisions based on their respect for the opinions of people who have special experience and/or knowledge about the topic. Your ideas will have greater impact and strength when you can quote or paraphrase those who know. Now, let's turn to the topic of peer testimony.

Peer Testimony **Peer testimony** is support of a fact or statement that is given by ordinary

No amount of statistical data would help your audience understand the impact of deafness as well as the testimony of a hard-of-hearing individual.

people like us. Of course, we may have credentials in some area to warrant expert status. Yet, most of us would have wisdom to offer about things from our experience even though we would not classify as experts. Peer testimony can be very important in helping you audience understand your problem. Suppose you wish to talk about hearing impairment. No amount of statistical data would help your audience understand its impact as well as the testimony of a hard of hearing individual describing what a day is like for her. This kind of testimony is so valuable because it gives a personal, firsthand view on your issue. There is richness in peer testimony because it provides feelings, and knowledge from the voice of genuine experience.

We believe this example will help you see the value of peer testimony. A student came to one of your authors with an excellent speech on attention deficit disorder (ADD), but it was lacking in one thing. It did not seem to give the audience a sense of the effect that ADD can have in a learning situation and the effect it can have on success. The professor arranged for the student to talk to a person who could tell him what this was like as a child who was trying to do well in school. Here is the testimony given.

> I remember how frustrating ADD can be. You see it is often difficult to direct your attention on a task because any little distraction will pull you attention away from what you are doing.

> Here is a situation that may help you know what I mean and how difficult paying attention can be. I recall trying to take a test, but the person next to me kept tapping his pencil on the desk. Every time he did this, it drew my attention away from my test. This simple act kept me from giving my best effort.

Expert Testimony **Expert testimony** is a quotation or paraphrase of a statement by an acknowledged authority in their field. You may be absolutely right in your particular view regarding your topic, but not be an expert. In this case, you will want to rely also on the credentials and testimony of a recognized expert on your topic. Citing the view of an expert is a good way to lend credibility to your own position. Expert testimony is especially important if you have a skeptical audience or the topic is controversial.

Here is an example of expert testimony. A speaker who was trying to persuade her audience to be healthy in their eating habits surprised them by saying that pizza can be a healthy food. Here is what she said from her reading of the article, "7 Healthy Foods:"

> Pizza can be good for you because the tomato sauce is packed with beta carotene, lycopene and vitamin C. If the pie is made with real mozzarella cheese, you get a healthy dose of calcium. A whole wheat crust with extra veggies on top can also be a plus. So, pizzas can be a great base to add highly nutritious vegetables, including red peppers, mushrooms, onions, broccoli and spinach.

Should I Quote Directly or Paraphrase? There are some general rules about this. Quote when the testimony is brief and it conveys the meaning in a way that will have more impact than paraphrase. This is, of course, a judgment call. Perhaps the quotation is eloquent, compelling, or witty. Paraphrase when the wording is long or difficult to understand. Use your own words, but be sure to be faithful to the text.

Using Testimony Effectively Here is some help to ensure you use testimony effectively.

1. *Check the credentials of your sources to ensure that they are qualified.*

There must be a direct connection between the source and the topic of the source. Just because a person is an authority in one area does not make the person an authority on your topic. The exception to this advice is the person who has direct experience with your topic and is reporting that experience.

2. *Ask yourself if the person has a particular bias in saying what they have said.*

If there is an obvious bias, discover it. If you do not, someone in your audience is likely to notice it.

3. *Identify the credentials of the person testifying.*

Give the name of the person and his or her connection to your topic. For example, "Secretary of State Colin Powell identified the impact of AIDS using this concrete language and these statistics in a speech to the United Nations General Assembly during a special session on the international AIDS crisis."

4. *Finally, quote or paraphrase accurately.*

This advice may seem silly, but it is not. Make sure you understand the quotation, the context in which the words were uttered. Be sure to represent the words and ideas of the person with complete accuracy. This is a matter of ethics.

SUMMARY

We began this chapter by answering the question, "Why should you use supporting materials? Without supporting materials the speech is just a skeleton of what it is meant to be. Supporting material develops, illustrates and clarifies your ideas. It also helps hold your audience's attention and remember key ideas. Further, in a persuasive speech, it helps you prove the point you are making.

Of course, supporting materials are of various kinds. The major categories are explanation, definition, examples, statistics and testimony. Explanation is the elaboration on an idea with the purpose of making it understandable and clear. A definition explains the essential qualities of a word or terminology. Examples provide a specific case to represent or illustrate an idea, condition, experience or group of people. They may be brief, extended or hypothetical. A brief example is a short, specific instance. They are often used in a series to s how the nature of the harm of a problem. Extended examples are a narrative or story developed at some length with more detail than a brief example. These are an excellent way to capture and hold your audience's attention. A hypothetical example is an imagined extended example based on fact and, therefore, plausible. Examples are useful to clarify ideas, personalize ideas, reinforce ideas and give vivid detail to bring your topic "to life."

Statistics are numerical ways of summarizing information or facts. Statistics must be from a reliable source that you will need to reveal within the text of your speech. Statistics are used to give your audience a sense of what your ideas mean. They often answer the questions how much and how many to describe some problem. They are also used as proof. You will want to explain your statistics in terms your audience will understand and round off complicated statistics. Often you will want to display your statistics by creating a visual representation of them.

Testimony is the final type of support. It is the statement or declaration of a witness that is often used to support a fact or statement. You may obtain the statement from a peer or expert. Peer testimony is support of a fact or statement that is given by ordinary people who direct experience with your topic. Expert testimony is a quotation or paraphrase of a statement by an acknowledged authority. Expert testimony is especially important if you have a skeptical audience. Should you quote or paraphrase the expert testimony? Use a quotation when the testimony is brief and it conveys the meaning in a way that will have more impact than paraphrase. There are two tests to be applied to judge the effectiveness of testimony. Do the credentials of the person qualify them to speak on the issue? Does the person have a particular bias in saying whatever was said? Likewise, there are two rules for use of testimony in your speech. Identify the credentials of the person testifying and quote or paraphrase accurately.

REFERENCES

Aronson, Elliot (2004). *The social animal,* 9th ed. (pp. 73–74). New York: Worth Publishers.

Gavin, Mary L. Ready, Set, Breakfast! March 2007 12/Nov./2007. Retrieved November 14, 2007 from kidshealth.org/kid/stay_healthy/food/breakfast.html.

Goldman, P., DeFrank, T. M., Miller, M., & Murr, A. (1994). *Quest for the presidency 1992.* College Station, TX: Texas A&M Press.

Moores, S. R. MSNBC.com/7 Healthy Foods. Retrieved November 17, 2007, from MSNBC. http://ww.msnbc.msn.com/id/20610558/?pg=4#Secretly_healthy_foods

Reynolds, R. A. & Reynolds, J. L. Evidence. In J. P. Dillard & M. Pfau (eds.). *Persuasion handbook: Developments in theory and practice* (pp. 429–430). (Thousand Oaks, CA: Sage.)

Schwartz, J. (January 24, 2006). A wide-eyed astronaut becomes a NASA critic. *New York Times*.

Starbuck, P. (2007). "Exercise Anorexia: The Deadly Regimen." Winning orations, 2007. Mankato, MN: Interstate Oratorical Association.

Tal-Or, N., Boninger, D. S., Poran, A., & Gleicher, F. (204). Counterfactual thinking as a mechanism in narrative persuasion. *Human Communication Research,* 30, 301–328.

Chapter 10
Outlining the Speech

Courtesy of Lucky Business/Shutterstock.

WHY SHOULD YOU CREATE AN OUTLINE?

In previous chapters, you've learned about the components of a solid speech. Here are a series of steps we have recommended: You first begin with clear objectives to pave a successful path in preparing a speech. You then support your thesis statement with main points and develop them to bring substance to your ideas. You also learned how to generate interest in your topic and open your speech. Finally, you learned how to summarize your ideas and reemphasize your thesis statement with a memorable ending. Following all these steps will help you achieve success, but they are not enough. You will need a well-crafted outline.

All of these elements will work together to allow you to formulate an effective outline. The purpose of this outline is to organize your thoughts in a logical, cohesive manner. A well-prepared outline can maximize your success in this class.

This chapter will be divided into four sections: Benefits of an outline, Format for formal outline, Preparing an effective outline, and Speaking notes.

BENEFITS OF AN OUTLINE

For each speech, you should prepare an outline. Outlines in a public speaking class are probably very different than the outlines you are accustomed to preparing. You may think of an outline as a series of short sentences or phrases with some numerical system to show relationships among them. This is a streamlined approach to organizing your thoughts. For your purposes you will find a formal outline more useful. **A formal outline** is a full-sentence, content plan of your speech ideas.

So, how do you create a full-sentence outline? Basically, you type out everything you plan to say in your speech. Students may wonder why this is necessary. (We will provide an example shortly.) While this approach does take some effort on your part, in the long-run it is an essential stepping block in preparing a successful speech. The formal outline has many benefits that increase the likelihood that you will craft an excellent speech. Some of these benefits include:

- You can see the structure and relationship between ideas.

- It helps you reflect and "think out" the way you'll present your speech prior to the speaking date. This negates the just "wing it" approach that will definitely hinder your success.

- This type of outline will make it obvious if you have a main point that is underdeveloped or if you have over-emphasized a particular main point.

- It can serve as a check and balance to ensure you have all the vital components for a successful speech.

- You will want to refine your speech. It can make editing more efficient.

- Your outline will also provide an excellent guide in preparing speaking notes or a delivery outline to present your speech.

You can see that a well-crafted outline will be very useful in helping you achieve success in your speech assignment.

FORMAT FOR A FORMAL OUTLINE

In order for you to prepare an effective outline, it's crucial to understand the format and items that need to be included in it.

Standard subdivisions are used in outlining your ideas. Use numbers and letters to organize your thoughts. Each time you subdivide use a standard indentation. Here in Figure 10.1 is a brief sketch of how a formal outline should be formatted.

I. Main Point 1
   A. Support for main point 1
   B. Support for main point 1
      1. Sub-point for support B
   C. Support for main point 1
      1. Sub-point for support C
      2. Sub-point for support C
         a. Sub-subpoint for C

Transition

II. Main Point 2

FIGURE 10.1
Format for a Formal Outline

The formal outline includes the three sections of a speech: introduction, body and conclusion. These components are labeled and developed fully in the outline. Recall the introduction includes the attention-getter, thesis statement, preview, tie-to-audience and credibility statement in whatever order the speaker desires with one exception. The attention-getter must be listed first in the introduction.

The body of the outline includes each main point, subpoints, sub-subpoints and transitions. Each main point is labeled as well as transitions. Transitions are found in three places: between the introduction and body, between each main point and between the body and conclusion.

The conclusion of the outline includes a signal of the end of your speech, a summary, a tie-back to audience and a memorable ending.

Constructing an effective outline has many benefits.

In addition to the introduction, body and conclusion, the outline encompasses the objectives and reference page as well as a brief summary of any visual aids used in the presentation. The objectives contain the general purpose, specific purpose and thesis statement. The reference page includes all the sources used in the speech. These sources are also included within the outline adhering to the standards of APA (American Psychological Association) style in-text citation. If you utilize a visual aid in your presentation, include a brief synopsis of the visual at the end of the outline after the conclusion.

Once you've prepared a formal outline, cross-reference it with this check-list to ensure it's correct.

1. Is your name and title of speech on the outline?
2. Is the outline in complete sentences?
3. Did you include objectives (general purpose, specific purpose and thesis statement)?
4. Does the outline label and include 2–4 main points? These main points should be declarative sentences that support the thesis statement.
5. Did you state the support material for each main point?
6. Do you use standard subdivisions?
7. Are transitions included in the proper places?
8. Do you have a reference page?
9. Did you include in-text citation?
10. Did you label the three sections of a speech (introduction, body and conclusion)?
11. Did you label and include the elements of the introduction (attention-getter, tie-to-audience, thesis, preview and credibility)?
12. Did you label and include the elements of a conclusion (signal of end, summary, tie-back to audience and memorable ending)?

Figure 10.2
Outline Checklist

Here is an example of a speech formatted as a formal outline.

Title of Speech:	Protect Your Skin
General Purpose:	To persuade
Specific Purpose:	To persuade my audience to protect their skin from harmful effects of UV damage (both natural and artificial).
Central Idea/Thesis Statement:	One should proactively protect their skin from the harmful effects of daily UV damage.

Introduction
I. Attention Material
  A. Look around the room; according to current statistics from melanomafoundation. org, 20% of us, which is approximately four of us in this room, will have skin cancer at some point in our lives.
II. Orienting Material
  A. Tie to the audience: We all have different shades of skin, all beautiful in its own way. Despite all the good differences, one of the things we have in common is that we are all susceptible to the damaging effects of UV exposure (though some more than others).
  B. Establish credibility: Having been so fair-skinned throughout my entire life, I have learned important lessons on UV exposure.
  C. Central Idea/Thesis Statement: One should proactively protect their skin from the harmful effects of daily UV damage.
  D. Preview statement: I will begin by telling you why you should protect your skin to prevent both skin cancer and premature aging. Then I will end by telling you easy ways in which to protect yourself from the damaging effect of UV exposure.

(Transition) Let's begin by looking at the most important reason you should protect skin.

Body

I. Main point 1: Protecting your skin helps to prevent skin cancer, the most common form of cancer.
  A. According to World Health Organization's website, "skin cancer is caused primarily by exposure to ultraviolet (UV) radiation—either from the sun or from artificial sources such as sunbeds." (who.int).
    1. This means that one should not only be cautious of the sun, but should avoid tanning beds as well.
      a. For those who enjoy the look of being tanner, there are many self-tanning products available that will give you the golden look of tanned skin, but without the risk of skin cancer.
  B. According to playsmartsun.org, an educational resource from the American Academy of Dermatology, skin cancer is the most preventable form of cancer.
    1. With so many unpredictable things that can occur to us, skin cancer is the one cancer we have most control over.
    2. We should make the wise choice to protect our skin from cancerous dangers from the sun.
  C. According to AAD.org, the official website for the American Academy of Dermatology, everyone is at risk for skin cancer, no matter your ethnicity or color of skin.

1. We tend to associate those with lighter skin to be the only ones who get skin cancer, when in actuality, everyone is susceptible.
2. Skincancer.org states because of this misconception, those who have darker skin are often unaware of their skin cancer until the later, more fatal stages.
   a. Such was the case of Bob Marley, who died as a result of an aggressive form of melanoma, a deadly type of skin cancer.
3. According to the mayoclinic.com, those with naturally darker complexions are less likely to get sunburns because of the extra melanin in their skin. However, they are still not protected against UV damage.

(Transition) Now that we know the major reason for protecting your skin, let's look at another, if not more vain reason.

II. Main point 2: Protecting your skin helps to protect premature aging.
   A. We will all age eventually.
   B. However, increased exposure to the sun can cause premature aging such as age spots and discolorations.
   C. Sun exposure can also cause dryness of the skin which will lead to premature wrinkles and an overall leathery look and feel to skin.

(Transition) Now that we've seen reasons why we should protect our skin, let's look at a few ways in which to do so.

III. Main point 3: There are several ways to protect your skin from the damaging effects of UV exposure.
   A. Apply sunscreen daily to prevent UV damage that will add up over time.
      1. The Center for Disease Control suggests a sunscreen of at least SPF 15 that has both UVA and UVB protection (cdc.gov)
      2. There are products available to make this easy.
         a. Some daily moisturizers now have sunscreen in them so you can combine some of your daily regime.
         b. Also, for the ladies, there are some makeup items that have sunscreen in them as well.
   B. Try not to go outside during the sun's peak times (10 am-4 pm).
      1. If you go out during these times, try to seek shade when possible.
      2. Be sure to reapply sunscreen every couple of hours, sooner if you have been swimming, sweating or if you are in an area with high humidity.
      3. Don't forget to apply sunscreen on your face and head area, which is most likely to be affected by the sun.
   C. Try to wear sun-protective clothing.

1. Although many of the websites I have already mentioned suggest that you wear clothes that cover up as much skin as you can, this is not usually practical for those who live in hotter climates like we do.
2. However, when you can, try to wear loose-fitting but tightly-knit fabric that will be more protective from the sun.

(Transition/Signal of end) So, let's review.

IV. Conclusion
   A. Signal of end: Today we learned why you should protect your skin from UV damage.
   B. Summary: First we learned that UV damage is the leading cause of skin cancer. Then we learned UV exposure can lead to premature aging. Finally, we learned some simple steps in which to prevent those problems by learning to protect our skin.
   C. Clincher: At the beginning of my speech, I mentioned approximately 4 people in the room will get skin cancer. What will you do to make sure it's not you?

References

Skin cancer | AAD. (n.d.). *Home Page | http://www.aad.org*. Retrieved July 21, 2010, from http://www.aad.org/public/publications/pamphlets/sun_skin.html

American Melanoma Foundation > Statistics. (n.d.). *American Melanoma Foundation*. Retrieved July 22, 2010, from http://www.melanomafoundation.org/facts/statistics.htm

Be sun smart: Protect yourself from the sun. (n.d.). *Play Sun Smart of the American Academy of Dermatology*. Retrieved July 21, 2010, from www.playsmartsun.org/sun_safety.html

CDC–Skin Cancer Prevention. (2010, April 6). *Centers for Disease Control and Prevention*. Retrieved July 21, 2010, from http://www.cdc.gov/cancer/skin/basic_info/prevention.htm

Sunburn: Risk factors–MayoClinic.com. (2009, May 19). *Mayo Clinic*. Retrieved July 21, 2010, from http://www.mayoclinic.com/health/sunburn/DS00964/DSECTION=Risk factors

The Skin Cancer Foundation–Skin Cancer Facts. (n.d.). *The Skin Cancer Foundation*. Retrieved July 21, 2010, from http://www.skincancer.org/skin-cancer-facts/

The Skin Cancer Foundation–Skin Cancer and Skin of Color | Skin Cancer and Skin of Color. (n.d.). *The Skin Cancer Foundation*. Retrieved July 21, 2010, from http://www.skincancer.org/skin-cancer-and-skin-of-color.html

Figure 10.2
An Example of a Formal Outline

PREPARING AN EFFECTIVE OUTLINE

You may be overwhelmed by the concept of a full-sentence, content outline. Usually, the response we get is "this is a lot." The outline is detailed and very organized. Although, this isn't an easy or fast task to complete, it's advantageous for you. Think about it! If you have an organized speech, your listeners will not only be able to follow your thoughts, they are more likely to remember your ideas. It's much easier to listen to a speaker that is organized than a speaker that rambles and has little direction.

There are many different ways to approach writing a formal outline. You must figure out which approach or system works best for you. One option you have is to type out the entire formal outline beginning with the body and then work on the introduction and conclusion.

Another way is to develop a preparation outline and then polish the speech into a more complete, formal outline. A **preparation outline** consists of short sentences and phrases to help guide you in developing a formal outline. A preparation outline is much like a rough draft.

A final way is to create a template or worksheet and build the speech from beginning to end. This **template** lists all the components of the speech from the introduction to the conclusion and then the speaker fills in the missing pieces. The template can be used for different types of speeches. Even if the purpose changes, the format and major components of the speech stay the same.

PREPARING SPEAKING NOTES

When the formal outline is complete, you can use it to develop speaking notes or a delivery outline. A **delivery outline** is a more condensed version of the formal outline using short words and phrases to guide the speaker during his or her presentation.

These speaking notes are prepared on 4 x 6 note cards. You will use these during your presentation. There's not one way to prepare speaking notes. Here again, you will have to figure out a system that works well for you. Some tips to consider when preparing speaking notes include:

1. Don't write the entire speech on note cards.

You will be tempted to read to your audience. Eye contact will be limited and you won't be successful in your delivery.

2. Use shorts words and phrases.

They should prompt you and guide you in remembering your speech. It will aid you in speaking in a more natural, conversational manner since you won't be reading each sentence.

3. Number your note cards.

If you drop your note cards or get confused, you can easily put your note cards back in order.

4. Make sure your note cards are legible.

If you can't read them, they won't be helpful to you. Some students type their note cards to ensure they can easily read them.

5. Avoid fumbling and shuffling through your note cards.

This can be very distracting.

6. Practice with your note cards.

7. Don't wait until the day of your speech to write your note cards.

8. Incorporate speaker's cues on note cards.

Courtesy of Ventura County Star/The Image Works.

Speakers often use delivery outlines to guide them through their speech. Text included on a teleprompter can also be in outline form.

Figure 10.3 presents an example of the delivery outline using the speech, Protect Your Skin.

Pause! Be confident!

Introduction
  I. Attention
      A. 20% (1 in 4 in room) skin cancer (melanomafoundation.org)
  II. Familiarize Audience
      A. All different shades of skin
      B. Fair-skinned myself
      C. THESIS: One should proactively protect their skin from harmful effects of UV.
      D. Why protect, how to protect
PAUSE
Transition: Most important reason you should protect skin.
PAUSE

Page 1

BODY *Look at audience!*
  III. **Main point 1:** Protection helps prevent skin cancer.
      A. **World Health Organ.** – it is caused by UV radiation. Cautious of sun and tanning beds.
      B. **Playsmartsun.org** – Most preventable form of cancer. We have control.
      C. **AAD (American Academy of Dermatology)** – everyone is at risk no matter ethnicity.
          1. **Skin cancer.org** – misconception, those with darker skin are unaware of risks. Bob Marley example.
          2. **Mayoclinic.com** – darker complexions less likely to get sunburns but still need to protect against UV damage.
  Pause: Transition: Let's look at more vain reason.

Page 2

Look at audience! Watch UMS!
  IV. **Main point 2:** Premature Aging.
      A. All age eventually.
      B. Increased exposure leads to age spots and discoloration.
      C. Cause dryness – premature wrinkles and leathery look and feel of skin.
  Pause: Transition: We know why we should protect, how to do so.
  V. **Main point 3:** Several ways to protect
      A. Apply sunscreen daily.
          1. **CDC** at least SPF 15. Use moisturizers that have sunscreen. Even some make-up has sunscreen.

Page 3

      B. Avoid outside at peak times (10 am–4 pm)
          1. Seek shade outdoors during time frame. Reapply every couple of hours. Apply to face and hand area.
      C. Sun-protective clothing.
          1. Cover as much skin as possible. Wear loose-fitting but tightly-knit fabric.
  Pause: Transition: So let's review. *Almost done!*
  VI. **Summary**
      A. UV leading cause of cancer. Exposure leads to premature aging. Learned simple steps to prevent problems by protecting skin.
  VII. **Clincher**
      A. Stat (20% or 1 in 4) What will you do to make sure it's not you?

Page 4

Figure 10.3

SUMMARY

The formal outline has many benefits. It encourages you to organize your ideas in a logical manner and reflect on the best way to construct the message. If you are organized, you will be easier to understand. If the message is easier to understand, the audience is more likely to remember the message. As a result, you will be less likely to ramble leaving the audience confused. It also ensures that you have all the essential elements of a speech. If the speech includes all of the important pieces that make it whole and flow well, the speech will have substance. You will be on your way to being a successful speaker if you have a solid formal outline.

The formal outline contains all parts of the speech in a full-sentence, content format. The objectives, introduction, body, and conclusion are dissected in the outline using standard subdivisions. In addition, sources are cited within the outline and on the reference page. Students utilize a variety of approaches when developing a formal outline. Students construct templates and build the speech from beginning to end. Others create a preparation outline with short words and phrases and then go back and develop their ideas more fully.

Once the formal outline is complete, students use it to write speaking notes. These speaking notes are used during the actual presentation and help keep the speaker on track. The note cards should include short words and phrases that jog the speaker's memory. The goal is for the speaker to glance at the speaking notes keeping them on track while speaking in a natural, conversational manner.

REFERENCES

Beebe, S. A. & Beebe, A. J. (2009). *A concise public speaking handbook,* 2nd ed. New York: Pearson.

DeVito, J. (2009). *The essential elements of public speaking,* 3rd ed. New York: Pearson Education, Inc.

Gregory, H. (2008). *Public speaking for college and career,* 8th ed. New York: McGraw-Hill.

Chapter 11
Wording the Speech

Courtesy of Jim Watson/AFP/Getty Images.

USING WORDS WELL

In previous chapters, we discussed how to organize your ideas and examined types of support to bolster those ideas. Now we will consider what words to use when we communicate those ideas and to make your speech come to life.

History is filled with memorable examples of individuals using words well. John F. Kennedy's famous words, ". . . ask not what your country can do for you; ask what you can do for your country" made tremendous impact in his 1961 inaugural address. When Franklin Delano Roosevelt addressed the nation regarding the attack on Pearl Harbor in 1941, he used the memorable words to describe the event as, ". . . a date which will live in infamy." Abraham Lincoln closed his Gettysburg Address in 1863 with these words, "God shall have a new birth of freedom, and that government of the people, by the people, for the people shall not perish from the earth." These examples show words can make your ideas thought-provoking and captivating.

We have also witnessed examples of words used inaccurately, inappropriately and unclearly. Words are powerful. If they are used incorrectly they can severely inhibit you from getting your message to your listeners and being successful in this class.

We'll look closely at the distinction of writing for the eye and writing for the ear. We'll also explore other principles of good speech writing. This chapter will be divided into five parts: writing for the eye and ear, using words accurately, using words appropriately, audience-centered language and being memorable.

WRITING FOR THE EYE AND THE EAR

Most students approach writing a speech similarly to writing a research paper or essay in an English class. Writing for the eye and writing for the ear require different approaches. Writing for the eye incorporates longer words and sentences. If the reader doesn't understand a word, he or she can consult a dictionary or thesaurus. If the reader is having difficulty comprehending a sentence he or she can reread the material until it clicks. In oral communication, the audience doesn't have this luxury. So, what can the speaker do to meet this challenge?

Simplicity and Clarity

One manageable solution to this challenge is using simple words and sentences. It's not necessary to use long, fancy words to impress your audience. It's impressive when you combine a series of simple, clear and concrete words to communicate your message. Long drawn out sentences are hard to follow and confuse your listeners. Instead, use short, concise, straight-forward sentences that can be interpreted easily.

Remember to translate jargon in using simple language. **Jargon** is technical language of a group of people. If you ignore this advice, your audience will most likely not understand a word of what you are saying. Speaking above your audience's level of understanding can divert their attention and they may stop listening to your message. You should translate unfamiliar language so the average person in your audience can understand its meaning.

You can also enhance clarity by using active voice opposed to passive voice. An example of active voice is, "The supervisor scheduled a meeting for Monday." The subject, the supervisor, is performing the action verb, scheduled. An example of passive voice would be, "A meeting was scheduled by the supervisor for Monday." The latter example is less direct and less clear than the first example since the subject is the receiver of the action rather than the performer of the action. You should also take advantage of frequent transitions and organizational patterns. These items increase comprehension and retention among your listeners.

Personal Style

It's also more common to use personal language when writing for the ear rather than writing for the eye. Remember you are delivering these words in a natural, conversational manner. It's appropriate to use words such as "I," "we," "you," "us" and "our." These words make your speech more practical and relatable. In this instance, writing for the eye is more formal than writing for the ear. It's not that writing for the ear is informal because we know it involves preparation and practice. However, it's less formal than writing for the eye. In a sense, we write more like we talk in oral communication.

Repetition

Additionally, we see more repetition and restatement in oral communication versus written communication. In written communication the reader has more control and can reread material as necessary. In oral communication, as the speaker you have to ensure the audience understands your message when they hear it.

Repetition can place emphasis on certain ideas. **Repetition** is articulating words, phrases or sentences the exact same way in different instances to make impact and enhance communication.

Reflect on the textbooks you've read in your academic career. How would you describe the writing style of a textbook in contrast to the writing style of a speech?

Restatement is similar to repetition. **Restatement** reinforces ideas using different words that communicate a similar message.

Vivid Language

This message will be more memorable and clear if you use vivid words. Concrete language is preferred over abstract language in oral communication. Words we can "see," "touch," "smell," and "hear" will make more of an impact on your audience. Abstract language is not as clear and can be interpreted in many different ways. There's too much room for miscommunication. You can also use specific, interesting examples and "paint" a picture with words.

A student was commemorating his grandfather and explained how he was a successful musician. He described to his audience how he discovered this part of his grandfather's life by saying: "When I opened the case, I was greeted with many years worth of dust. As I wiped away some of the dust off the body, the shine became very apparent. Colors of many shades appeared under the clear lacquer finish. The neck was long and sleek, a solid piece of wood having a shine

Writing for the Eye	Writing for the Ear
Words with many syllables	Shorter words
Long sentences	Shorter sentences
More abstract language	Concrete words
Formal language	Less formal language
	Repetition
	Personal words

FIGURE 11.1
Distinction between Writing for the Eye and Writing for the Ear

that matched that of the body." This colorful description helps the audience "see" what the speaker was experiencing. Figure 11.1 summarizes the characteristics of writing for the eye and ear.

Let's see how all these elements formulate a well-written speech. In 1939, Lou Gehrig delivered a "Farewell to Baseball Address" at Yankee Stadium after being diagnosed with Amyotrophic Lateral Sclerosis (ALS, also known as Lou Gehrig's Disease). Figure 11.2 is a script of his speech. As you read this speech look for the qualities of good speech writing we've discussed so far in this chapter.

Fans, for the past two weeks you have been reading about a bad break I got. Yet today I consider myself the luckiest man on the face of the earth.

I have been in ballparks for seventeen years and have never received anything but kindness and encouragement from you fans. Look at these grand men. Which of you wouldn't consider it the highlight of his career just to associate with them for even one day?

Sure I'm lucky.

Who wouldn't consider it an honor to have known Jacob Ruppert? Also, the builder of baseball's greatest empire, Ed Barrow? To have spent six years with that wonderful little fellow, Miller Huggins? Then to have spent the next nine years with that outstanding leader, that smart student of psychology, the best manager in baseball today, Joe McCarthy?

Sure I'm lucky.

When the New York Giants, a team you would give your right arm to beat, and vice versa, sends you a gift–that's something. When everybody down to the groundskeepers and those boys in white coats remember you with trophies—that's something.

When you have a wonderful mother-in-law who takes sides with you in squabbles with her own daughter—that's something.

When you have a father and a mother who work all their lives so you can have an education and build your body—it's a blessing.

When you have a wife who has been a tower of strength and shown more courage than you dreamed existed—that's the finest I know.

So, I close in saying that I might have been given a bad break, but I've got an awful lot to live for.

FIGURE 11.2
Lou Gehrig's Farewell to Baseball Address

USING WORDS ACCURATELY

In addition to using simple, vivid language, it's crucial to use words accurately. Ensure you choose the correct words in the proper context. In other words, be aware of the meaning of the words you are using in your speech so you communicate effectively.

Using words inaccurately can damage your credibility. For example, "She misunderestimated the scope of the assignment." The problem with this statement is "misunderestimated" is not a word so the language used is not accurate. It's also a problem when a word is not used in the right context. For example, "It's ironic that the productive employee was awarded a raise." The word ironic is not used accurately. It's logical, not strange or inappropriate, that a productive employee would be recognized for his or her hard work.

Be mindful of the denotative and connotative meanings of words. The **denotation** is the literal meaning or dictionary meaning of a word. The **connotation** is the emotional overtones that an individual associates with the word. It's pertinent that you know the denotative meaning of words so you can have shared meaning and communicate your message accurately.

Comparatively, the connotation of a word should also be considered. Always think of the consequences of the words you use. Know that words arouse different feelings for different people. Some words have positive connotations. Others have neutral or negative connotations. Think about the word "disagreement" and "altercation." These words are similar in meaning but altercation has a stronger impact than disagreement.

People also interpret and filter the meaning of words based on their own experiences. The word "baby" might mean something different to a mother opposed to a person who has not experienced parenthood. A mother could associate baby with her own experience of having a

Incorrect	Correct
She don't	She doesn't
They was	They were
I ain't	I am not
We be	We are

FIGURE 11.3
Common Grammatical Mistakes

baby and the bond she shares with her child. In contrast, an individual who has not experienced having a baby may think in more literal terms of a baby being a very young child.

When speaking to your audience, you must use correct grammar. If you dismiss the rules of grammar, you will appear unknowledgeable. Your listeners are less likely to believe and trust what you are saying if you use incorrect grammar. Figure 11.3 shows some of the common grammatical mistakes made by speakers.

USING WORDS APPROPRIATELY

Not only should your language be accurate but it should be appropriate. Your language should be appropriate for your topic, occasion and audience.

Make sure your language is suitable for your topic and occasion. If you are presenting an informative speech you would need to be careful and stay away from persuasive language. You would avoid words and phrases such as "should adopt," "better alternative," "it's a major problem" and "you must act."

Consider the reason your audience is gathered and the environment of the speaking engagement. If you are presenting to a small group of sorority sisters or fraternity brothers, your language will most likely be less formal since they are your close friends. If you have been asked to speak to a professional association about a current trend in your industry, you'll use more formal language and jargon. If you are teaching a night class to a group of nontraditional students, you may use different words and examples to relate to them more effectively.

When a professional in the newspaper industry was asked to speak with college students regarding his career, he used language that was appropriate to the occasion. When asked a question regarding the importance of prior work experience when seeking employment, his response was, "Yes on steroids!" This may not have been his typical response to his boss if asked a question but his response was interesting, humorous and appropriate for the occasion.

Avoid using words that may offend your audience. Of course, some listeners can be ultra sensitive and unreasonable. You can't always control how people will react to your speech but you can control your intentions and your message. Avoid words that may alienate or offend someone in your audience. Areas of heightened sensitivity include: political, religious, racial, ethnic and sexual remarks. Steer clear of stereotypes or generalizations of a group of people. If you question yourself, "Is this going to offend someone in my audience?" It most likely will.

AUDIENCE-CENTERED WORDING
In Chapter 4, we discussed how important it is to relate to your listeners. Your audience will interpret your message based on their own beliefs, attitudes and experiences. Take time to analyze your audience so you can communicate your message in the most effective way possible. Your goal is to get your message to your listeners but also relate to them on some level so they will be receptive to your ideas. The words you choose for your speech can help you be an audience-centered speaker. Here are some ways you can relate to your audience.

Use Language They Can Understand
Try to assess knowledge levels. Don't use language that is too complex resulting in your listeners not comprehending what you're saying. You also don't want to be too simplistic; your audience will be bored. Translate jargon or technical language of a group in straightforward manner.

Use language they can relate to on some level. Think about the purpose, audience and occasion. How can you get on the audience's level and show them you've taken the time to learn about them and their needs? This makes them feel important and gives them an incentive to listen to you.

Use Personal Language
It's acceptable to use inclusive words such as "we," "our," "us" and "you" when constructing words for your speech. This makes your speech more natural, intimate and conversational. It's more interesting and easier to listen to a personable speaker.

Consider Special Circumstances
Always be aware of the environment and circumstances of the audience and occasion. Use language that shows you are empathic and conscious of the situation. This will make you more real, believable and trustworthy.

Use Words that are Interesting
Take advantage of the techniques we've discussed. Use vivid, concrete words. Give intriguing examples. Incorporate figures of speech. If you include interesting language in your speech, your listeners will be more engaged.

Figure 11.4 is a portion of Robert F. Kennedy's speech regarding the assassination of Martin Luther King, Jr. on April 4, 1968. As your read, notice the words he uses to empathize and connect with his audience.

Martin Luther King dedicated his life to love and to justice between fellow human beings. He died in the cause of that effort. In this difficult day, in this difficult time for the United States, it's perhaps well to ask what kind of a nation we are and what direction we want to move in. For those of you who are black—considering the evidence, evidently there were white people who were responsible—you can be filled with bitterness, and with hatred, and a desire for revenge.

We can move in that direction as a country, in greater polarization—black people amongst blacks, and white amongst whites, filled with hatred toward one another. Or we can make an effort, as Martin Luther King did, to understand, and to comprehend, and replace that violence, that stain of bloodshed that has spread across our land, with an effort to understand, compassion, and love.

For those of you who are black and are tempted to fill with—be filled with hatred and mistrust of the injustice of such an act, against all white people, I would only say that I can also feel in my own heart the same kind of feeling. I had a member of my family killed, but he was killed by a white man.

But we have to make an effort in the United States. We have to make an effort to understand, to get beyond, or go beyond these rather difficult times.

FIGURE 11.4
Excerpt of Robert F. Kennedy's Reaction to the Assassination of Martin Luther King, Jr.

Adapt Your Language to Audience Diversity

Although there are a number of diversity characteristics that may be present in your audience, we focus on the three that most commonly cause difficulties for the speaker's relationship with the audience. These are gender bias, cultural bias, and exclusionary language. We understand that our culture is evolving in directions that attempts to avoid these biases that reveal themselves in the way we use language. So, this may serve as a reminder for you.

Avoid Gender Bias in Your Language A frequent form of language that was found in printed text is the use of *he* to refer to an unspecified individual, who might be female. So, you would read something like, "Every speaker should pay attention to *his* words." Today this same idea might be expressed in a sentence like this, "Speakers should pay attention to *their* words."

Here are the three techniques you can use to avoid gender bias:

1. *Use plural forms.* Instead of saying, "Every speaker should pay attention to his words," substitute "All speakers should pay attention to their words."

2. *Avoid the use of pronouns.* Frequently, you can rephrase a sentence by removing the pronoun, as in "Good speakers pay careful attention to language."

3. *Avoid gender bias in job titles.* Use actor instead of actress; mail carrier instead of mailman; soldier instead of female soldier; people or human beings instead of mankind.

Avoid Cultural Bias in Your Language This bias is most easily understood in terms of international students. As a speaker, how would you help a person who speaks English as their second language understand more fully? Some non-native speakers translate what they hear into their language as they are trying to understand. Fast talkers make this translation process difficult. Also, some non-native speakers do not have the sophisticated vocabulary in their second language that the native speaker has.

Here are four suggestions to help you be a better communicator with these audience members:

1. *Speak clearly and somewhat slowly.* This delivery style gives the listeners time to translate into their own language.

2. *Adapt your visual aids.* Key word aids, something we often recommend, are difficult for some non-native speakers. Use full sentences when you can. And, give your listeners time to read and take notes.

3. *Avoid U.S. clichés and colloquial expressions.* A **cliché** is an expression whose effectiveness has been lost due to overuse. Examples are: "One person's garbage is another person's treasure," "Absence makes the heart grow fonder," "Absolute power corrupts absolutely," and "Actions speak louder than words."

   A **colloquialism** is an expression that is appropriate to everyday speech, but not to formal speaking or writing. Here are some examples: "You better get on the stick," "Go around the barn at high noon," "If that don't beat all," "On December 12, 2013, Ms. kicked the bucket (died)," and "The officer tore up the stairs in search of the big enchilada (leader of the crime syndicate)."

4. *Use the racial or ethnic names people prefer.* Common examples of these are: African American, Asians, Native Americans, Latino, Hispanic.

Avoid Exclusionary Language **Exclusionary language** uses words that reinforce stereotypes, belittle other people, or exclude them from understanding an in-group's message. The effect of this kind of language is to separate people. There are people like you and others who are not like you. The people who aren't like you become the *these* and *those* people.

Exclusionary language alienates others. Use language that includes others, thus avoiding this problem. A good general rule is to avoid referring to anything about age, health, abilities, sexual orientation, race, and ethnicity unless these characteristics are relevant to the topic being discussed.

Here are four specific suggestions to help you avoid exclusionary language:

1. *Avoid reference to age.* If you are referring to an *older lady*, do not say *old lady*. Say, instead *older woman* or just *woman*.

2. *Avoid stereotypical references to health and abilities.* Instead of using terms such as *cripple* or *head case*, use *physically disabled* and *person with emotional illness.*

3. *Be sensitive in reference to a person whose sexual orientation is not heterosexual.* Refer to these people as *gay* or *lesbian.*

4. *Use names people prefer to make reference to their racial or ethnic group as indicated above.*

Perhaps you are thinking we, as an American culture, are above using biased language in public. It appears that we are not.

In the 2010 election, the National Republican Senatorial Committee put out a casting call for people to be used for a political advertisement. They sought "hicky-looking" blue-collar actors to play everyday West Virginians. The Democratic Senatorial opponent, Joe Manchin, pointed out the Republican candidate John Raese "thinks we're hicks." The Republican Committee pulled the ad calling for actors (Diemer, 2010).

BEING MEMORABLE

One of the goals of a successful speaker is to be memorable. You can achieve this through the language you use in your speech. One of most memorable speakers in history was Martin Luther King, Jr. His speeches were filled with vivid imagery and powerful language that left a lasting impression on his listeners. One of his most notable speeches was his "I Have a Dream" speech delivered in 1963 at the Lincoln Memorial in Washington, DC. Figure 11.5 is a portion of this famous speech.

Let us not wallow in the valley of despair, I say to you today, my friends.

And so even though we face the difficulties of today and tomorrow, I still have a dream. It is a dream deeply rooted in the American dream.

I have a dream that one day this nation will rise up and live out the true meaning of its creed: "We hold these truths to be self-evident, that all men are created equal."

I have a dream that one day on the red hills of Georgia, the sons of former slaves and the sons of former slave owners will be able to sit down together at the table of brotherhood.

I have a dream that one day even the state of Mississippi, a state sweltering with the heat of injustice, sweltering with the heat of oppression, will be transformed into an oasis of freedom and justice.

I have a dream that my four little children will one day live in a nation where they will not be judged by the color of their skin but by the content of their character.

I have a *dream* today!

I have a dream that one day, down in Alabama, with its vicious racists, with its governor having his lips dripping with the words of "interposition" and "nullification"—one day right there in Alabama little black boys and black girls will be able to join hands with little white boys and white girls as sisters and brothers.

I have a *dream* today!

I have a dream that one day every valley shall be exalted, and every hill and mountain shall be made low, the rough places will be made plain, and the crooked places will be made straight; "and the glory of the Lord shall be revealed and all flesh shall see it together."

FIGURE 11.5
Excerpt of Martin Luther King, Jr.'s "I Have a Dream Speech"

This speech demonstrates the use of vivid language along with repetition. Repetition highlights certain words or phrases. By placing emphasis on words and phrases, the audience is more likely to be aware of the point you are trying to communicate and more likely to retain the information they learn. Repetition is an effective strategy in making your words memorable. Use repetition carefully though so it doesn't become too redundant. If you are utilizing repetition too frequently, everything will blend together and nothing will be significant.

Another way to make your speech memorable is to incorporate figures of speech. Although it's unrealistic to create a student speech filled with these rhetorical devices, it is certain that using them can make your language unique and memorable. Listed below are some options you can incorporate in your speech.

- **Alliteration** is the use of consecutive words that start with the same consonant sound. An example is "cash cow."

- **Antithesis** is the use of words or phrases that contradict each other to create a well-balanced outcome. An example is in Charles Dickens's *A Tale of Two Cities*, "It was the best of times, it was the worse of times."

- **Parallel Structure** is the arrangement of words, phrases or sentences in a similar form. An example is in Lincoln's Gettysburg Address, ". . . government of the people, by the people, for the people shall not perish from the earth."

- **Personification** is the attribution of human characteristics to nonliving objects. An example is "My computer is tired."

- **Rhetorical questions** are questions that are used to make a point rather than obtain a response. "Do you know how many children are obese in the United States of America?"

- An **oxymoron** joins two opposite qualities. An example is "jumbo shrimp."

- A **simile** compares one thing to another using like or as. An example is "Her personality is like a watermelon. It is hard on the exterior but soft and sweet inside."

- A **metaphor** compares two things by stating one item is the other. An example is "The United States is a melting pot."

- An **analogy** compares an unfamiliar concept to a more familiar one. An example is "In his position at work, he wore many hats."

SUMMARY

Words convey meaning. These meanings convey a message. If we want our message to be effective, we must give careful consideration to word choice when writing our speeches.

We must first understand that writing for the ear requires a different approach than writing for the eye. Writing for the ear involves simplicity, clarity, self-reference words, repetition and vividness.

Other elements of good speech writing include using accurate, appropriate, audience-centered and memorable language.

Always ensure your words are accurate. Know the denotative meanings of the words you use and be aware of the connotative meanings that can be associated with it. Also avoid grammatical mistakes. Using inaccurate words can damage your credibility.

Also use appropriate language in your speeches. Your language should be appropriate for your topic, occasion and audience. Ensure your language is appropriate for your purpose, your audience's knowledge and interest levels, and speaking situation.

We should all strive to be audience-centered speakers. By using language that relates to our listeners, they are more likely to understand and retain our message. You can relate to your listeners by using language they understand, personal words and interesting words. Address any special circumstances affecting the audience. Incorporating these tips will give your listeners an incentive to listen.

Finally, make your language memorable. The last thing your want is for your speech to be forgettable. Be unique with your word choice so your audience wants to listen to your message. Paint a picture with words. Integrate repetition and figures of speech.

If you incorporate these guidelines, you'll be on your way to using words well and being successful in this class!

REFERENCES

American Rhetoric: Abraham Lincoln—Gettysburg Address. (n.d.). *American Rhetoric: The Power of Oratory in the United States*. Retrieved April 19, 2012, from http://www.americanrhetoric.com/speeches/gettysburgaddress.htm.

American Rhetoric: Franklin Delano Roosevelt—Pearl Harbor Address to the Nation (12-08-41). (n.d.). *American Rhetoric: The Power of Oratory in the United States*. Retrieved April 19, 2012, from http://www.americanrhetoric.com/speeches/fdrpearlharbor.htm.

American Rhetoric: Lou Gehrig—Farewell to Baseball Address. (n.d.). *American Rhetoric: The Power of Oratory in the United States*. Retrieved April 19, 2012, from http://www.americanrhetoric.com/speeches/lougehrigfarewelltobaseball.htm.

American Rhetoric: Martin Luther King, Jr.—I Have a Dream. (n.d.). *American Rhetoric: The Power of Oratory in the United States*. Retrieved April 19, 2012, from http://www.americanrhetoric.com/speeches/mlkihaveadream.htm.

American Rhetoric: Robert F. Kennedy—Statement on the Assassination of Martin Luther King, Jr. (n.d.). *American Rhetoric: The Power of Oratory in the United States*. Retrieved April 19, 2012, from http://www.americanrhetoric.com/speeches/rfkonmlkdeath.html.

Beebe, S. A. & Beebe, A. J. (2009). *A concise public speaking handbook,* 2nd ed. New York: Pearson.

DeVito, J. (2009). *The essential elements of public speaking,* 3rd ed. New York: Pearson Education, Inc.

Dickens, C. (1932). *A Tale of Two Cities . . . Illustrations by "Phiz."* London: Thomas Nelson & Sons.

Diemer, T. (2010). "West Virginia Democrat Strikes Back at GOP "Hick" Ad: 'It's Insulting.'" Politics/AOL News, October 10, 2010. Retrieved February 13, 2014, from http://politics-dailycom/2010/10/19/west-virginia-democratic-strikes-back-at-gop-hick-ad-its-insu/.

Gregory, H. (2008). *Public speaking for college and career,* 8th ed. New York: McGraw-Hill.

John F. Kennedy's Inaugural Address. (n.d.). *American Rhetoric: The Power of Oratory in the United States*. Retrieved April 19, 2012, from http://www.americanrhetoric.com/speeches/jfkinaugural.htm.

Chapter 12
Constructing and Using Visual Aids

Courtesy of Andresr/Shutterstock.

WE ARE SURROUNDED BY VISUALS

Think of how many visual messages you are exposed to in one day. Lawyers, teachers, doctors, and advertisers use visuals. Why? They can be powerful, informative and persuasive but they also can enhance communication. A **visual aid** is any item that reinforces the speaker's ideas visually. There are many benefits to using visuals. You appeal to another sense so your audience is not only hearing your speech ideas but you are translating those words into something they can see. The addition of visual aids allows you to appeal to various learning styles, your audience is more likely to receive, understand and remember your message.

Speakers have various options when choosing a visual. You can use graphs, charts, pictures, videos, objects, replicas, drawings, text, PowerPoint presentations, brochures and much more. These visuals can be shown via poster boards, televisions and projectors. There are several items to consider when designing and displaying visual aids. If visuals are used correctly, they can enhance understanding and add value to your speech. If used incorrectly, they can be confusing and distract from your message.

This chapter will be divided into five sections: benefits of using visual aids, disadvantages of visual aids, types of visual aids, media for visual aids and guidelines for designing and displaying visual aids.

BENEFITS OF VISUAL AIDS

Visuals can add a dynamic dimension to your speech. Your audience may not remember everything about your speech but your visuals are ingrained in their head. There are many benefits to using visual aids.

Visual Aids Strengthen Communication

Visuals can make your ideas more clear. By reinforcing the content of your speech with a visual, the audience has more time to grasp and understand the concept. So if a listener didn't understand the information verbally, they may have a better understanding once they are exposed to the idea in a visual format.

Visual Aids Clarify Difficult Ideas

A visual can be very useful if the speaker is discussing a complex topic. For example, if a student was informing the audience of a genetic disorder such as alpha-1 antitrypsin deficiency, a visual aid can help explain what it is and how it works. In the speech the student used pictures to explain how the abnormal shaped AAT proteins in the liver can't exit into the bloodstream causing serious complications.

Visual Aids Make Speech Ideas Memorable

Visuals can make your speech more interesting and memorable. In a face-to-face public speaking class, students were asked to introduce themselves to the class during the second week of the semester through the use of an object. The purpose of the object was to explain some aspect of the speaker's personality, interests, hobbies, background and experiences. One student brought a hat rack to explain the many "hats" he wore. Almost three years later his teacher still remembers the object he chose in his icebreaker speech. His visual made his speech memorable.

Visual Aids Enhance Credibility

Is the speaker trustworthy? Why should we believe the speaker? Think of the presentations you've listened to in your academic career. When a speaker puts effort and time in their visual it can enhance their credibility. Visuals can make a speech more impressive which reflects positively on the speaker.

Visual Aids Reduce Apprehension

Most students get the jitters when presenting a speech. A visual can help reduce this anxiety. For a few seconds, the audience is not entirely focused on the speaker. Their attention is directed toward the visual. This may seem insignificant but it can definitely boost the confidence of the speaker.

DISADVANTAGES OF VISUAL AIDS

Although visual aids can be advantageous, they can also have drawbacks if not used properly. The following is a list of challenges posed by the use of visual aids in your presentation.

Visual Aids Can Distract

Visual aids can be distracting if not used properly. If the speaker shows a pie chart with 15 slices and numbers to the side, it won't clarify a concept. It will confuse your audience and they'll think, "What did all those numbers mean?" Similarly, if you circulate visual aids or handouts and students begin to whisper to one another, the audience and speaker can become distracted. Further, it takes time to circulate a visual aid throughout your audience. So doing this violates the principle of displaying the aid when you are actually speaking about the point. Obviously, you will have completed talking about the topic and many members of you audience will not have seen it.

Visual Aids Can Negatively Affect Delivery

It's crucial that you practice with your visual aid so your delivery is smooth and natural when you incorporate it in your speech. Presentation aids can reduce your eye contact. Many speakers focus so much on presenting their visual, they forget about engaging the audience. The speaker appears to be too dependent on the visual and their delivery is not as strong as it needs to be.

Technology Failure May Interfere

Technology is wonderful and awful all at the same time. When it's working correctly, we love it. When it is not functioning properly, we loathe it. Many of your visuals will be shown with some use of technology. Some students will use the Internet to access a YouTube video. You may utilize PowerPoint to incorporate a slideshow in your speech. You may save your visual on a jump drive. What happens if any of these items fail? You're dependent on your visual and you are being graded on the visual. Always visit the room in advance to ensure everything is working properly. If this isn't possible, at the very least contact the person who asked you to talk and inquire about the technology available in the presentation room.

Remember, these last minute problems will increase your anxiety and affect your credibility. Even when you have taken the proper precautions, circumstances still may not work in your favor. Don't place too much emphasis on the problem. Proceed with your speech and focus on your message. Avoid saying negative comments such as, "Well, I wanted to show you this video but it's not working." Make the best of the situation.

Visual Aids Can Reduce Credibility

If you are unprepared or fumble through your visual aid, your audience will question your credibility on the topic. We've seen students forget to show their visual aid and try to throw it in the conclusion of the speech. It's misplaced and doesn't make sense. Practice with your visual aid so it flows well. Additionally, if your visual aid is sloppy or inaccurate, your credibility will suffer.

Visual Aids Can Offend Your Audience

Some visuals may offend your audience. If your visual is controversial, inappropriate or gruesome, it can be a turn-off to your audience members. Try to think in advance how others may perceive your visual message. If you think someone may be offended by it or take it the wrong way, reconsider your approach. Go back to the drawing board and think of a safer visual aid that can equally get the message across.

TYPES OF VISUAL AIDS

For students who don't know where to start in choosing a visual aid, there is good news. You have a variety of options that serve many purposes.

Graphs and Charts

Graphs can be especially helpful when communicating numerical data in visual form. Some examples include a bar chart, a line graph or pie graph. These visuals can be easily constructed utilizing programs such as Microsoft Office, PowerPoint and Excel.

A **bar graph** consists of horizontal or vertical bars that contrast two or more variables.

A **line graph** uses a horizontal and a vertical scale to show trends and the relationship between two variables.

A **pie chart** is a circle representing 100 percent and divided into segments of various sizes.

FIGURE 12.1
LT Commander Dale Taylor

Pictures

Most of us have heard the saying, "A picture can be worth a thousand words." For example, Andrea Parker, a student at the University of South Alabama, took a picture (Figure 12.1) of Coach Dale Taylor during the final Upward basketball game of the 2011–2012 season. The picture showed Coach Dale Taylor gathered with his team praying center court. Three days later after the picture, LT. Commander Dale Taylor was the instructor pilot aboard the Coast Guard HH-65c helicopter, 6535, that crashed into Mobile Bay. A picture can tell a story and can impact your message dramatically.

Videos

A short video clip can also be a simple but effective presentation aid. Always keep in the mind the clip will count toward your overall time. So your video clip needs to be relatively brief. Video clips can be captivating and really catch your audience's attention.

Text

Visuals can appear in many forms. In addition to graphics and pictures, text can be used as a visual. Some speakers create a list of text. Many of your teachers may do this when lecturing. It helps the audience know the highlights of the presentation and it keeps the speaker on track. For example, in a lecture on visual aids, the instructor may put the following list of key ideas on a slide:

Types of Visuals:

Graphs or Charts	Objects or Replicas
Pictures	Drawings
Videos	Handouts and Brochures
Text	PowerPoint Presentations

Students may also use a single word or phrase on a presentation aid to place emphasis. For example, in a persuasive speech about living a healthy lifestyle, a student showed a website link on his presentation aid so students could calculate their daily calorie needs to ensure proper health.

Objects or Replicas

Sometimes it is helpful to show the audience an object or a replica of the object that is being explained or discussed. For example in a speech about the different types of tennis rackets, the speaker would show the audience the actual object. A **replica** is a representation of an object. It's not the actual object but it's a look-alike or model of the actual object. For example, in a speech about the titanic, the speaker may bring a replica of the British passenger liner to show the audience.

Courtesy of Cayton Photography/The Image Works.

Drawings

Drawings that explain what something looks like or how it works are also an option when considering visuals for a speech. When explaining directions to a friend, sometimes it's helpful to "draw" it out. Similarly, the same approach applies to visuals in a speech. A prepared drawing can improve clarity in a speech.

It can be effective to show the actual object.

Handouts and Brochures

Handouts and brochures can supplement what's being said in the speech. They also give listeners something they can take with them when the presentation is complete. Handouts and brochures can be very informational and are easy to put together. In a speech about organ donation, a student gave her audience a handout regarding the misconceptions associated with the process. Be cautious of when you will be distributing handouts during a speech because they can be distracting if listeners are reading ahead.

PowerPoint Presentations

PowerPoint slides have become a standard when giving presentations. They are easy to read and simple to design. The slides can include text, pictures, audio, links to web sites, video and the graphics. Figure 12.2 shows two slides used in a persuasive speech regarding the need to control lobbying groups. Information was accessed from the official website of the Center of Responsive Politics. We'll discuss some tips when designing these presentation aids later in the chapter.

In another speech, a student utilized PowerPoint slides to persuade her audience to read more. In her speech she was convincing the audience of how reading can be rewarding and adventurous. She said, "I have had many adventures in my 12 years of reading." She proceeds by showing several slides. Each slide displayed a picture of the cover of each book she highlighted. "I read my first chapter book at age 6. My first adventure consisted of me solving mysteries and living in a boxcar with my brothers and sisters. At age 8, I had a magical cupboard with an Indian inside it. At age 10, I lived through a plane crash with just a hatchet to survive. At age 12, I enrolled at Hogwarts and began the age-old battle of 'good vs. evil.' At age 15, I moved to Forks,

Total Lobbying Spending In Billions

Year	Amount Spent
2001	$1.65 Billion
2002	$1.82 Billion
2003	$2.04 Billion
2004	$2.18 Billion
2005	$2.42 Billion
2006	$2.62 Billion
2007	$2.85 Billion
2008	$3.30 Billion
2009	$3.50 Billion
2010	$3.51 Billion
2011	$3.30 Billion

Number of Lobbyists

Year	Number of Lobbyists
2001	11,840
2002	12,125
2003	12,920
2004	13,168
2005	14,071
2006	14,526
2007	14,847
2008	14,168
2009	13,677
2010	12,929
2011	12,633

FIGURE 12.2
Example of Two PowerPoint Slides

Washington and fell in love with a vampire. However, my adventures have taken a more sad and serious turn as I am currently trying to survive the holocaust in Auschwitz-Birkenau."

Not only was this a creative way to get her message across to her audience, but it helped listeners connect and identify with her speech.

People and Other Living Things

Some students choose to be creative and incorporate themselves in their visual aid. For example, in a speech about the culture of Saudi Arabia, a student wore an ankle-length shirt known as a thawb and ghutra on his head. The audience was able to witness the dress of a male in Saudi Arabian culture first hand. Consequently, we always ask that you dress professionally, since you are always a visual aid for your speech!

When presenting on topics such as animals students always want to know, "Can I bring my dog, cat or snake to my speech?" The answer is no! Some people in your audience may have severe anxiety regarding the animal. The situation would be extremely scary and uncomfortable for them. Also, some students may have health issues such as allergies that are not conducive to being around the animal. A better alternative would be to bring in a picture (enlarged) or display the picture via projector.

MEDIA FOR VISUAL AIDS

There are a variety of types of visuals and media available to display them. This media includes: posters, whiteboards, flipcharts, chalkboards and projectors.

Posters

Before computer-generated media, many students created visuals with the help of posters. Students can still use posters to display their visuals but need to make sure they follow a couple of guidelines.

Remember, visuals should be prepared, neat and professional. We suggest that you use cut out letters instead of your own handwriting. This will give your visual a more polished and professional look. You need to also ensure the poster can be seen by everyone in the room.

One student gave an informative speech about the voting process. He utilized several different posters throughout his speech. One poster showed an enlarged voting ballot. Another poster displayed photos of the two presidential candidates. The last poster revealed an enlarged voter registration card. He incorporated the visuals at different times in the speech. After he revealed the poster, he briefly explained it and then put it away.

Students who lack comfort with computer technology choose to take advantage of this media. In addition, some students rather not use technology because of fear of malfunction.

Flipcharts

A **flipchart** consists of large pieces of paper that are bound together at the top. It's very similar to a notepad but on a larger scale. The purpose is to be able to flip one piece of paper on top of the other so you can present the information in sequential order.

Flipcharts are very helpful in a small group situation or even a brainstorming session. However, we do not recommend them for a speech class because they are informal and lack a professional touch.

Projectors

A **projector** uses lenses and light to project an enlarged image on to a screen. Students can utilize projectors to display videos, pictures, web sites, graphs, charts, slides and more.

In a persuasive speech convincing the audience to adopt pets, a student opens her speech with pictures of cuddly cats and dogs that are homeless and are ready to be adopted. She does this with the help of a projector.

Before you decide on utilizing a projector, ensure the room has one available. Also, arrive to the presentation a little early to double-check that everything is working properly.

Chalkboards, Whiteboards, and Smartboards

Many of your teachers may use chalkboards, whiteboards, or smartboards when lecturing to the class. In classes where you are working out a problem or have many insertions or erasures, it would be appropriate to take advantage of a chalkboard or whiteboard. However, we do not recommend the use of a chalkboard for drawings in a speech class. Although chalkboards are appropriate for some occasions, the end product lacks neatness and polish. Presentation aids should always add a professional touch to your speech which can be difficult to do when using a chalkboard or whiteboard. We also suggest you prepare your visual aids in advance. In addition,

Whiteboards can be used in a small group situation where members brainstorm for ideas.

Courtesy of Yuri Arcurs/Shutterstock.

to write on either one of these items, the speaker has to turn his or her back to the audience. Some will even keep conversing with the class while writing on the board which affects clarity and overall effectiveness of delivery.

GUIDELINES FOR DESIGNING VISUAL AIDS

The purpose of using a visual aid is to enhance or strengthen your message. However, if visuals are used incorrectly or awkwardly they will distract the speaker and audience. There are a few tips you should consider when designing a visual aid so you can maximize your effectiveness.

Preparation

One of the most important guidelines to follow is to prepare your visuals in advance. Don't wait until the last minute. Your visuals should be neat, polished and professional.

If given a choice we would rather you not have a visual at all rather than putting forth little effort in your presentation aid. A poorly crafted visual will not have a positive impact on your message and will have a negative effect on your credibility. Preparation will also give you the opportunity to practice with your visual aid. This will be difficult to do if you give yourself little time to prepare.

Visibility

A mistake we see too often is the visual can't be seen. When designing your visual aid, make sure you adhere to the element of visibility. How big is the room? Can the back row see the visual aid? In a speech about Nelson Mandela, you could show the audience a picture of him. The problem is the printed picture is so small the audience cannot see it. The visual has not enhanced the message. A better alternative would be to enlarge the picture so everyone in the room can enjoy it or display the visual with a projector.

In addition, ornate fonts are difficult to read. The audience won't be impressed by the visual and they may even be frustrated with the speaker if it's hard to read.

Color
Use color consistently across all of your visual aids. Avoid using too bright of colors that might overwhelm the audience. When using text and color, make sure the colors contrast rather than blend into the background. For example, if the base color of your visual is black, you would not choose a navy blue color for the text. Navy blue has some black in it. So navy blue on top of black would blend together. The text would not stand out and the audience would not be able to comprehend the message. You also want to somewhat limit the number of colors and fonts you use in a presentation aid. Using more than four colors would be excessive. Use of more than two fonts would also be excessive.

Simplicity
Visuals should be relatively simple. They should be easy to understand once you explain them. In a speech class, the time limit will not allow you to utilize a visual that requires extensive explanation. Some students ignore this warning and include an extremely detailed visual such as a graph with many numbers. Then the speaker rushes over the visual with minimal explanation. The audience is confused and the visual did not enhance the message. It would have been more advantageous if the speaker approached the visual with simplicity in mind.

Consistency
When designing several visual aids for one presentation, always consider the element of consistency. The visuals should be consistent to bring unity and balance to your speech. Consider color, typeface, styles, fonts, and layout when creating consistency across your visual aids. The result will be a more unified, complete and polished presentation.

Designing PowerPoint Slides
As stated earlier in the chapter, PowerPoint has become a norm in a professional setting. However, we know if visuals are not used correctly, they can be detrimental to the speaker's message and credibility. Here are a few tips to consider when using PowerPoint:

- Make sure your pictures and graphics are not distorted
- Don't use too many slides

- Simplify text—"key" phrases, not whole sentences
- Use custom animation in moderation
- If you use a dark background, use a light font
- Leave first and last slides blank
- Have a title slide and an end slide
- Practice your speech with the equipment you will be using
- Check for compatibility of equipment
- Back up slides onto a jump drive or e-mail it to yourself (anticipate technical problems)
- Use spell check

GUIDELINES FOR DISPLAYING VISUAL AIDS

Once you have designed and prepared your visual aid, you then must execute it in your speech. You've put a great deal of effort and energy into the visual so you want to make sure you implement it appropriately. These are a few tips you should consider when displaying visuals during your speech.

Reveal, Discuss and Remove

Students should follow a three step strategy when utilizing visual aids. First, display and introduce your visual aid. Then you should explain your visual. Don't assume your audience will immediately understand your visual aid. It's necessary for you to briefly explain it so everyone is on the same page. The last step is to put your visual away. There's no reason to keep the visual exposed when you are done explaining it. If the visual remains visible, it will be distracting to the audience. You have moved onto other material in your speech and yet you still have this visual in the open. You want the audience focused on your message not the visual you've already covered.

We also recommend that you cue yourself in your speaking notes. Delivering a speech can be challenging especially when you are nervous. Some students forget to reference their visual aid in the speech due to a couple of reasons. Many students don't practice with their visual aid so they lack a conscious effort of communicating it. Students can become distracted by anxiety they may feel when delivering a speech. This distraction can lead to the student simply forgetting to introduce and discuss the purpose of the visual aid. We suggest you practice and remind yourself of the presentation aid in your speaking notes.

Don't Talk to Your Visual Aid

It's very tempting to talk to your visual aid. You must remember to maintain strong eye contact with your audience. It's appropriate to glance at your visual aid especially when you introduce it.

This signals to your audience that they should pay attention to it. It's also acceptable to look at the visual occasionally when you are explaining it. However, it becomes a problem when you are so focused on the visual that you are talking to it and ignoring your audience.

Avoid Circulating Visual Aids

Some students will choose an object as his or her presentation aid. Do not circulate your visual aid. We understand that you may want to share your visual aid up close with your audience members. However, circulating your visual aids can be very noisy and distracting. You want to maintain as much control as possible. This will be difficult to achieve if your listeners are passing around an item and focusing on it instead of your message. You can always invite your listeners to view your objects more closely at the end of the presentation.

Technology Malfunction

Technology is a part of our daily lives. It would be impossible for us to teach our classes without the help of technology. We've also heard of Murphy's Law. If it can go wrong, it will. So be aware that technology can fail you. Do everything you can in the preparation stages of the speech process to ensure success when using technology. Practice with the technology. Visit the room in advance to make sure everything is working properly.

Sometimes we can do everything right in the preparation stages but technology does not live up to our expectations. In this case, don't dwell on it. Improvise and move forward. It can be distracting to your listeners if you place too much emphasis on the problem.

Cite Sources

Don't forget to let us know where you accessed the information you are using to construct your visual aid. Where did you get those statistics? Whose pictures are you displaying? Remember to always give credit to the source of your information. We refer to this as verbal citation. It's ethical to attribute your sources.

SUMMARY

The nickname for the state of Missouri is the "Show Me State." According to the Missouri Secretary of State home page, although it's not the official slogan, it is associated often with the state and included on Missouri's license plates. There are many speculations as to why the state has been coined with this phrase. One of the most popular explanations is based on Congressman Willard Duncan Vandiver, a member of the United States House of Representatives from 1897–1903, who gave a speech in 1899 at a naval banquet in Philadelphia. He said, "I come from a state that raises corn and cotton and cockleburs and Democrats, and frothy eloquence neither convinces nor satisfies me. I am from Missouri. You have got to show me."

We can adopt this same philosophy to our speeches. "Show me" a concept, idea, issue, process, person, place, concept, situation, phenomena or thing. Visuals can have various benefits. They clarify difficult concepts, enhance credibility, make ideas memorable, and reduce speech apprehension. In contrast, if they are not used correctly they can have a negative affect on your speech. Visuals can distract, negatively affect delivery, make apparent technological malfunctions and reduce credibility.

There are many options people can choose from when incorporating visuals into a presentation. You can use graphs, charts, pictures, videos, text, objects, replicas, drawings, handouts, slides and people. These types of visuals can be displayed though the use of posters, flip charts, chalkboards, whiteboards and projectors.

In designing visual aids adhere to the principles of preparation, visibility, color, simplicity and consistency. In addition, there are several elements to consider when utilizing PowerPoint slides which have become a standard in presentations. These tips include: don't use too many slides, use short words and phrases, limit custom animation, edit your slides, practice your speech with slides and equipment, and use colors that contrast rather than blend together.

Once you've prepared, designed and practiced with your visual, it's time to display the visual aid during the actual speech. Follow the three step model: reveal, discuss, and remove. This will help your audience remain focused on your message and will reduce distraction. Avoid turning your back and talking to your visual aid. Maintain strong eye contact with your audience. Be aware of the technology you'll be using and remember Murphy's Law! Avoid circulating your visual aids since it can be noisy and can divert your audience's attention. Always cite sources and give credit where credit is due.

REFERENCES

Beebe, S. A., & Beebe, S. J. (2006). *Public speaking: An audience centered approach,* 6th ed. Boston: Pearson.

Beebe, S. A. & Beebe, A. J. (2009). *A concise public speaking handbook,* 2nd ed. New York: Pearson.

DeVito, J. (2009). *The essential elements of public speaking,* 3rd ed. New York: Pearson Education, Inc.

Gregory, H. (2008). *Public speaking for college and career,* 8th ed. New York: McGraw-Hill.

Lobbying Database | OpenSecrets. (n.d.). *OpenSecrets.org: Money in Politics—See Who's Giving & Who's Getting.* Retrieved March 28, 2012, from http://www.opensecrets.org/lobby/

Osborn, M., Osborn, S., & Osborn, R. (2012). *Public speaking,* 9th ed. Boston: Pearson.

SOS, Missouri–State Archives Missouri History FAQ–Origin of "Show-Me" Slogan. (n.d.). *Missouri Secretary of State Home Page.* Retrieved March 28, 2012, from http://www.sos.mo.gov/archives/history/slogan.asp

Chapter 13
Delivering the Speech

Courtesy of Julie Dermansky/Corbis Images.

WHO ARE THE BEST SPEAKERS?

Who are some the best speakers you've ever heard speak? Dr. Martin Luther King, Jr.? President Ronald Reagan? President Bill Clinton? Your 12th grade English teacher? The pastor of your church? Who? Chances are, the people you consider to be a great speakers have one thing in common: their speech delivery is captivating.

This chapter focuses on delivering your speech. **Delivery** is the vehicle speakers use to transmit ideas to listeners and it is both verbal and nonverbal. We will begin the chapter by discussing the qualities of good delivery. Next the chapter will identify and present effective ways to use verbal and nonverbal strategies to improve delivery. Finally, we will address the four most common methods of delivery.

GOOD DELIVERY CAN MAKE OR BREAK A SPEECH

President Barack Obama rose from obscurity to a household name, mostly because of a wonderfully delivered speech. In 2004, Illinois Senator Barack Obama gave the keynote address at the Democratic National Convention. Senator Obama's 17-minute speech electrified a nationwide television audience and captured the nation's attention.

Before the speech, the idea of the state senator from Chicago running for president in 2008 would have been laughable. However, after the speech, Democratic and Republican observers began to view the senator as a star in the Democratic Party. Many argue this was the speech that opened the way for a run at the presidency. In the most commanding portion of the speech, Obama declared the following:

Now even as we speak, there are those who are preparing to divide us—the spin masters, the negative ad peddlers who embrace the politics of 'anything goes.' Well, I say to them tonight, there is not a liberal America and a conservative America—there is the United States of America. There is not a Black America and a White America and Latino America and Asian America—there's the United States of America.

The pundits like to slice-and-dice our country into Red States and Blue States; Red States for Republicans, Blue States for Democrats. But I've got news for them, too. We worship an 'awesome God' in the Blue States, and we don't like federal agents poking around in our libraries in the Red States. We coach Little League in the Blue States and yes, we've got some gay friends in the Red States. There are patriots who opposed the war in Iraq and there are patriots who supported the war in Iraq. We are one people, all of us pledging allegiance to the stars and stripes, all of us defending the United States of America.

The video of the speech better illustrates how Obama used delivery to enhance the content of his address.

C-Span has stored the speech on YouTube. To view the speech in its entirety, enter the following web address in your browser: http://www.youtube.com/watch?v=eWynt87PaJ0.

Just as really good delivery can improve your image, poor delivery can damage your image. In 2008, Louisiana Governor Bobby Jindal was seen as a rising star in the Republican Party. Governor Jindal was elected by an overwhelming majority after the devastation of Hurricane Katrina. Because he was one of the most popular governors in the United States in 2008, Governor Jindal was an obvious choice to deliver the Republican response to President Obama's first State of the Union Address. Much to the surprise of observers, Jindal's rebuttal came up short. Democrats and Republicans alike described Jindal's rebuttal in terms that were decidedly harsh: "amateurish," "laughable" and, most commonly, "a missed opportunity." Much of the critique of Jindal's address focused on his hokey, folksy, seemingly-forced tone and vernacular.

All said, Jindal's speech was received with disappointment by conservatives who had looked to the governor as the Republican Party's next star. In an interview on CNN, Governor Jindal conceded his delivery was not as good as it could have been. In a moment of sheer candidness Jindal said "Let me take responsibility—it's so easy to blame others, blame consultants, blame advisers— I delivered the speech, it's my fault, clearly it was awful." Jindal's good-nature was refreshing. And it spoke to the undeniable effect a poorly delivered speech can have on one's image.

To view a full video of the speech, enter the following web address in your browser: http://www.huffingtonpost.com/2009/02/24/bobby-jindal-respone-to-o_n_169704.html.

Anyone who has listened to people speak probably can come up with a list of boring, uninspiring speakers. Chances are, most of the people on your "boring speaker" list had a good speech on paper but could not get it across to the audience. Fairly or unfairly, delivery significantly influences how audiences receive messages, including how persuasive they are. The manner in which you present your speech, using your voice, body and language, forms your style of delivery. So, while the content of your speech is extremely important, your audience will agree both content and delivery contribute to the effectiveness of your speech. You may not have the extensive speaking experience of people you might list as great speakers, but you do have a unique voice, unique body movements and a unique wording of ideas. Use your uniqueness to aid in your delivery.

As you read this chapter, please remember, delivery cannot improve the ideas included in the speech, but a good delivery can make the most of the ideas you have. Your delivery can either be an asset or a liability to your speech performance. In short, *how* you say something is often as important as *what* you say. *What* you say is your speech content. *How* you say it is your speech delivery.

Note also, because you want to do an excellent job, you will be keenly aware of any deficiencies in your voice. These are normal. In fact, they are present in everyday conversations. People are used to hearing them so people don't pay much attention to them. What does this mean for you as a speaker? It means you are probably doing better than you may think you are. Perhaps, if you remember this, it will help.

QUALITIES OF GOOD DELIVERY

There are three basic qualities of good speech delivery:
1. Good delivery is natural
2. Good delivery is comfortable
3. Good delivery is spontaneous

Courtesy of Michael Brennan/Corbis Images.

Good delivery is natural, comfortable and spontaneous.

Good Delivery is Natural

Natural delivery is delivery that does not call attention to itself. Think about it: any aspect of a speaker's voice or body movement that causes the audience to attend to it rather than to the speaker's message is unnatural.

Most of us use natural delivery in our everyday talk with friends, relatives and co-workers, so we are accustomed to what natural delivery "looks" and sounds like. When you complete your speaking assignments, view the experience as a conversation instead of a speech. This will help foster a more natural delivery.

Good Delivery Looks Comfortable

In addition to looking natural, effective speakers also look comfortable. We understand it may be difficult for you to be totally relaxed as you deliver your speeches. However, you should really try to relax. Again, the most effective speakers are those who look comfortable speaking to their audience.

Research has found that speakers who are more familiar with their speech context look more comfortable delivering the speech. Schedule multiple practice sessions before you present your speech, allow a little space in time between sessions and practice until you are comfortable.

Good Delivery is Spontaneous

When we communicate with people with whom we are familiar, we speak spontaneously. We are not artificial and we are more likely to be enthused. We are more natural in these speaking situations because we are being ourselves. As you emerge into a public speaker, it is important for you to interject your personality into your speeches. Respond to the feedback the audience members give you as you speak. Authenticity and spontaneity will be wonderful assets to your speech.

USING THE VOICE FOR EFFECTIVE DELIVERY

Your voice is a powerful instrument to enhance public speaking delivery, because it can be varied to get almost any effect you desire from your speech. You can use your voice to speak loudly one second then drop to a whisper the next second. You can vary your speaking speed to either rush through unimportant details quickly or slow down to emphasize key ideas. You can also alter your voice pitch to indicate differences in word meanings. One of the keys to having a good speech delivery is to maximize the effectiveness of your voice.

Speaking Rate

Audiences can make assumptions about us based on the rate at which we speak. You may be aware of the stereotype of the "fast talker" who talks fast to put something over on us. There is a widely held belief that people who speak really fast do so to keep the listener from fully processing what is being said. Similarly, when speakers talk too slowly, there is an assumption that the speaker is too deliberative—weighing the words carefully in an attempt to manipulate the audience to get the desired response.

Research has found that delivery which is too fast (195 words or more) or too slow (120 or fewer words) is ineffective. The happy medium falls between 120 and 195 words per minute. At this speed, listening is comfortable for the audience, and talking is comfortable for the speaker. Your goal should be to find a speaking rate that is comfortable for you, but also for you to vary your speaking rate throughout your speech. For example, if you are expressing excitement or surprise, you might consider speaking a bit faster than your normal rate. On the other hand, if you are expressing sadness or concern you should speak a bit slower than your normal rate. Pauses can also be advantageous to your speaking rate if they are used correctly.

Pauses

Pauses are the silence between words and are important to effective speech delivery. Oftentimes, speakers fear pauses. To some, pauses are seen as silence which should be avoided at all costs. But silences are a part of all talk. So, try not to focus too much on this. You have probably seen the speaker who talks continuously, blending all of their words together, until they run out of breath. This, of course, is not effective delivery. The audience may not bother to keep up with you if you do this. So, it is possible they will "tune out."

Amy was asked to lead the audience in the Pledge of Allegiance at her high school assembly. Amy was determined to get through the speech as quickly as possible, so she recited the Pledge like this:

"IpledgeallegiancetotheflagoftheUnitedStatesofAmerica (gasp), andtotherepublicforwhichitstands (gasp), onenationunderGod,indivisible,withlibertyandjusticeforall."

Other times, speakers try to avoid pauses by inserting verbal fillers into their speeches. These verbal fillers, vocalized pauses, are sometimes used when speakers need time to think about or formulate their next idea. Too many of these verbal fillers will likely annoy your audience.

Justin used verbal fillers in his speech as he recited the Gettysburg Address in a competition at the Evening Optimist Club. When Justin made it to the podium, he began by saying "Uh, mm. Four score and seven years ago—er,—our fathers brought forth—umm—on this continent, a new nation. . . ." We doubt anyone would see this as effective speaking.

I'm sure you've heard a speaker interject similar verbal fillers in speeches. You may agree these pauses or fillers disrupt the smoothness of a speech. The good news is verbal pauses can be eliminated once you realize you have a habit of using them. Generally speaking, verbal fillers are used to take up time while a speaker decides what he or she wants to say next. Carefully planning purposeful pauses can help most speakers overcome the habit of inserting verbal fillers.

Justin's speech would have been much better if he had presented it in this manner:

> (Pause) Four score and seven years ago (pause) our fathers brought forth (pause) on this continent (pause) a new nation . . ."

Brief pauses can be useful for adding emphasis and effect and also to give listeners a second or two to reflect upon the meaning you are trying to convey. We encourage you to strategically plan pauses in your speech delivery.

Volume

Volume refers to the loudness or softness of your speaking voice. You can manipulate the volume of your voice to add variety to your delivery. Simply raising your voice slightly can help you stress key ideas, making key ideas stand out in addition to helping cut down the monotony of your delivery.

In your public speaking class, volume is critical. As you deliver your speech, make sure to project your voice loud enough for everyone in the room to hear you without straining. Take note of the size of the room, the number of people who will be in the room and other artifacts which may have competing noises (like the hum of a computer). Taking these characteristics of your speaking environment into consideration will give you a good sense of how loudly you will need to project your voice.

Pitch

Pitch is described as the highness or lowness of the tone of our voices. Every speaker has an optimal pitch range. Your optimal pitch range is the range in which you are most comfortable speaking. However, like your speaking rate and your volume, you should vary your pitch in your speech. Speakers often shift their pitch downward to indicate confidence, decisiveness or determination. Upward shifts in a speaker's pitch can suggest surprise, questioning, or suspense. Pitch variations in a single word can totally change the meaning of a sentence. Take, for example, the simple sentence "She is my friend." This sentence can have four different meanings if you change the pitch of one word:

> "**She** is my friend." (Not the other woman standing with her.)
> "She **is** my friend." (Don't try to tell me she isn't!)
> "She is **my** friend." (Not yours.)
> "She is my **friend**." (There's nothing more to our relationship than that.)

As you practice your speech delivery, be sure to incorporate variations in your pitch to the words or expressions you want your audience to notice and remember.

Enunciation

Enunciation refers to how we articulate and pronounce words. **Articulation** is the degree to which we pronounce letters in words correctly and clearly. Most articulation errors are made from habit. For example, you may tell your roommate you are going to the "libary," when what you really intend to say is "library." Chances are, you know how to spell the word—and you would say it correctly if you were pressed to do so—but you have fallen into a habit of misarticulating it. Further, articulation errors are often reinforced by people around us who make the same mistakes.

Pronunciation, in contrast to articulation, refers to how the letters of a word sound and where the stress falls when the word is spoken. You may have heard someone pronounce the word "accessory" as "ass-ess-or-y" (omitting the first C as a "hard" sound). If so, this is an example of a mispronunciation. Most speakers do not have major problems with mispronunciation. However, many of us do that which give us trouble and work to pronounce them correctly. As you prepare your speech, think about words which have been difficult for you to pronounce. If any of those appear in your speech, spend a little extra time practicing those words so that you are comfortable with them when you present your speech.

USING NONVERBAL BEHAVIOR FOR EFFECTIVE DELIVERY

In public speaking settings, nonverbal communication is as important as verbal communication. There are four kinds of nonverbal behavior which impact public speaking: eye contact, posture, body movements and clothing choices.

Eye Contact

Good **eye contact** is defined as direct, visual contact with another's eyes. Eye contact is one of the most important nonverbal behaviors a speaker should utilize for their speaking performances. As a novice speaker, you may think making eye contact with your audience members will cause you to feel more apprehensive. However, research suggests effective eye contact usually makes a speaker feel more at ease. Speakers often comment that making eye contact with their audience members shifts the experience from feeling like a speech, to feeling like a conversation.

A good way to maintain eye contact is to slowly scan the audience and look directly into the eyes of a handful of listeners. As a general rule, you should aim for making eye contact with your audience members approximately 90 percent of the time you are delivering your speech. Frequently scanning the room, being careful to actually make eye contact, will also encourage members of your audience to stay focused on your speech.

Posture

When you deliver public speeches, your posture is a nonverbal behavior your audience will notice. **Posture** refers to the position or bearing of your body. There are two extremes with posture—rigidity and sloppiness. A speaker who has good delivery avoids both extremes. It is imperative for you to stand erect while delivering your speech. Don't hang on to or "drape" yourself across the podium.

Be careful to avoid a nervous swaying motion because this will be very annoying to your audience. Rather, keep your weight balanced on both legs. It often helps to place one foot slightly in front of the other. It is very difficult to sway in this position. Posture may not appear to be important in speech delivery, but it is. Good posture communicates your confidence, poise and improves your overall delivery.

Movements and Gestures

When used skillfully, purposeful movements are a very effective form of nonverbal communication. In the public speaking setting, confident speakers are more likely to move away from the podium during their speech. In contrast, the uncertain speaker tends to stay in one place for the duration of the speech.

In public speaking settings, nonverbal communication is as important as verbal communication.

Courtesy of Alex Wong/Getty Images.

As you progress through your public speaking class, consider adding movement to your delivery. Just remember, your movement should have purpose and should add to your speech. An excellent speaker, one who is not standing behind the podium, will use movement to help signal a transition between points.

Personal Appearance

Personal appearance is the impression you make on your audience through your clothing, jewelry, hairstyle and grooming. When you deliver a public speech, personal appearance matters for two reasons. First, members of your audience will form initial impressions of you, based on your personal appearance, before you say anything. People will make an assessment about you based on how you look. So, it's important for you to make sure your appearance communicates the right message about you. Second, studies indicate the initial impression based on appearance can be long lasting and very significant. If you make a negative first impression because of an unappealing appearance, you will need to expend a lot of time and effort to rebuild credibility.

Your instructor will give you specific guidelines as to what constitutes appropriate personal appearance for your speaking assignments. But in any speaking situation you should take special care to look presentable through professional appearance and good grooming.

TYPES OF DELIVERY

The four primary types of delivery are manuscript speaking, memorized speaking, impromptu speaking and extemporaneous speaking.

Manuscript Speaking

Manuscript speaking is defined as speaking from a text which has been prepared in advance. There are some occasions when speaking from a manuscript is essential. Speaking situations which require precise, accurate, well-worded content are appropriate for manuscript delivery. The State of the Union addresses delivered by US Presidents are always delivered from manuscript. Presidents understand when they address Congress and the American citizens the focus is not only on being understood but on *not* being misunderstood. Delivering a manuscript speech ensures listeners hear *exactly* what you want them to hear.

For inexperienced speakers, manuscript speeches may appear to be the easiest type of speeches to deliver. After all, with a manuscript speech you will have every word of your speech in front of you. For many speakers, having every word of your speech scripted is likely to boost your confidence. However, written speeches are not ideal for your public speaking class. In theory, manuscript speeches sound easy to pull-off successfully. But in practice, they may cause special problems.

Problems with Manuscript Speaking First, manuscript speaking often lack eye contact and spontaneity. The more you read, the less time you will spend looking at the audience. Most audiences do not like to have a speaker read to them. Reading to an audience could cause the listeners to lose interest in you and your message.

Second, manuscript speeches give you less opportunity to move around. If you read your speech from a manuscript, you will either have to hold your text, or place it on a podium. Either option will restrict your ability to be mobile and possibly to use gestures. With the manuscript as restriction, you will not be able to move as freely as you would if you did not have to rely on the manuscript.

Finally, manuscript speeches usually lack a conversational tone. They usually don't sound like something you would say in conversation. We have all heard speakers who sound like they are reading. Their inflection is flat, they are less animated than they are in normal speaking, and they may sound "sing-song."

Taken together the reasons listed are reasons why we will not perform manuscript delivery in your public speaking course. Manuscript speaking is useful a times. However, is it is not the desired delivery method for your speaking assignments in your public speaking course.

Memorized Speaking

We **speak from memory** when we prepare a written text and then memorize it word for word. The memory method is like the manuscript method in all ways except that the speech is not read aloud. Rather, the speech is committed to memory and then given from memory at the time of delivery. The speech is planned, written out completely, and then memorized. Memorized speeches require speakers who are excellent at memorizing and remembering what is committed to memory.

Like speeches delivered from manuscript, there are a few situations when memorizing a speech is a preferred option. An example of a speech where memorized delivery is accepted is an oratorical speaking contest. Some speaking contests, such as the American Legion's Oratorical Contest, are required to memorize speeches. Also, very short speeches for formal ceremonies may be appropriate for memorized delivery. You may not want to speak from note cards or a manuscript to propose a toast at a wedding. So, in these instances, a memorized speech might be appropriate.

Even though there are some situations which are appropriate for memorized speeches, you will not be expected to use memorized delivery in your public speaking class. There are many disadvantages to memorized delivery which may become more troublesome for novice speakers. We will not use memorized speaking in our public speaking class.

Problems with Memorized Speeches First, under the pressure of the speaking situation, a speaker could forget several parts of the speech and ruin the entire presentation. Forgetting can lead to an odd silence, which is often embarrassing to the speaker and the audience.

A second disadvantage of memorized speaking is adaptive feedback is almost impossible. Therefore, delivering a memorized speech in a natural, conversational mode is difficult. The end result is that your speech is likely to sound and appear artificial.

Impromptu Speaking

Impromptu speaking is speaking "off the cuff," casual, and delivered with little or no time for preparation. There will be times when you will be called upon to speak on the spur-of-the-moment. This can happen at school, on your job, or in community organizations. For example, your English professor may call on you, without warning, to come to the front of the classroom and discuss the symbolism you noticed in your reading assignment, "To Kill a Mockingbird." Or, at one of your sorority or fraternity meetings, your president could turn to you and ask "Alex, you attended the national conference this summer. Can you give the chapter a brief synopsis of the new membership intake guidelines?"

In impromptu speaking, you have minimal control over what you say and how well you say it, because you will not have had time to practice for it. However, these speeches do provide you a great opportunity to practice your delivery. For this reason, impromptu speech activities are common in public speaking classes. Your speech instructor may choose to include an impromptu speech activity in your public speaking class. The purpose of doing the impromptu speech in the public speaking class is to get you up and speaking in front of the class without having to worry about a formal evaluation. Impromptu speech activities also give you a chance to try to "think on your feet." So, if you are given the opportunity to deliver an impromptu speech, be creative and have fun.

Extemporaneous Speaking

In most public speaking situations, extemporaneous speaking is best. **Extemporaneous delivery** is when a speaker carefully plans and practices a speech and delivers the speech from speaking notes.

Extemporaneous delivery has several advantages. First, extemporaneous speaking allows you to be flexible and more responsive to your audience's feedback. For example, if you notice members of your audience looking puzzled during your speech, you can further explain the portion of the speech which is confusing and try to clear up the

Courtesy of Mark Ludak/The Image Works.

Flexibility and spontaneity are qualities of an extemporaneous speaker.

misunderstandings. Extemporaneous speaking gives you the flexibility to repeat the message, explain the message using other words, or give a better example to clarify the concept. Also, if you notice the listeners appear to be bored during your speech, extemporaneous delivery gives you the flexibility to interject a short entertaining story or joke to help engage the audience again.

A second advantage of extemporaneous delivery is you will probably feel more confident as a speaker. You won't have to worry about one specific way of forming your ideas, because you will not have scripted the speech. Neither will you have to worry about forgetting something you have memorized. Your speaking notes will be in front of you, so you will be free to interact with the audience in a natural, conversational tone.

A common mistake speakers often make when they deliver extemporaneous speeches is a lack of practice. Speakers sometimes think, "I'll have my notes with me while I speak, so there really is no need to practice." This thought could not be further from the truth.

The following is a list of suggestions which are helpful for success in extemporaneous delivery:

1. *Number your note cards.*

In the unfortunate event your note cards are disheveled before (or during) your speech performance, you will have less trouble getting back on track if your note cards are numbered in the correct order.

2. *Practice with the notes you will actually use in your speech.*

Practicing with the notes you will use in the speech will help you become more familiar with the content of your note cards, enabling you to only need to glance down briefly.

3. *Determine when you should, and should not, look at your notes.*

You should not need to refer to your note cards for every "a," and "the" in your speech. Instead, glance at your notes for direct quotes or statistics.

4. *Rehearse aloud.*

Silent practice is not adequate. Practicing aloud will enable you to time your speech, decide when pauses are appropriate, and allow you to actually hear how the speech will sound to your audience.

5. *Practice in front of others, if possible.*

Whenever possible, find someone who will offer suggestions to improve your speech content and delivery.

6. *Practice often, but do not over-rehearse.*

Practicing a speech too much may eliminate spontaneous expression. We suggest you devote about two-thirds of the preparation time to developing the speech content and about one-third of the time to rehearsing the speech. Space your practice of the speech by taking a break and coming back to it. This can be very helpful.

Extemporaneous speaking is the most effective method of delivery for the average person. Extemporaneous delivery encourages a natural, conversational tone while also allowing for flexibility when needed. As such, the speech activities in your public speaking course should be delivered extemporaneously, unless otherwise stated.

SUMMARY

Most people will judge your speech based on your delivery, no matter how brilliant your ideas are. If you are lively and fluent, your audience will be more likely to think highly of your speech than if you are monotonous and stumble through your speech. Well-delivered speeches are easier to listen to, and since ideas can't be conveyed in speeches unless the audience listens, good delivery is important. In some ways that is unfortunate because it tends to emphasize style over substance. However, that is reality.

In this chapter, we discussed the importance of a good speech delivery. We established that good delivery is natural, comfortable and spontaneous. We also suggested strategies you could use to make your voice aid in better delivery. These strategies include altering your speaking rate, altering your volume, altering your pitch and enunciating your words well.

The chapter further outlined nonverbal behavior which enhances delivery. Good eye contact, erect posture, purposeful body movements and professional personal appearance are effective nonverbal behaviors.

Finally, this chapter explained the four types of delivery. These are manuscript, memorized, impromptu and extemporaneous. We discussed the advantages and disadvantages of each type of delivery and discussed the type we would use most often in your public speaking class.

REFERENCES

Beebe, S. A., & Beebe, S. J. (2006). *Public speaking: An audience-centered approach,* 6th ed. New York: Pearson.

Fraleigh, D. M., & Tuman, J. S. (2009). *Speak up! An illustrated guide to public speaking.* New York: Bedford/St. Martins.

Hanna, M. S., Gibson, J. W. (2002*). Public speaking for personal success,* 6th ed. Boston, MA: Pearson Custom Publishing.

Taylor, J. (2010). *Bobby Jindal Reflects Upon His Disastrous State of the Union Response.* Retrieved February 10, 2012, from http://www.aoltv.com/2010/11/17/bobby-jindal-reflects-upon-his-disastrous-state-of-the-union-res/.

Smith, L. J. & Malandro. (1990). Personal appearance factors which influence perceptions of credibility and approachability of men and women. In J. A. DeVito and M. L. Hecht (eds.). *The nonverbal communication reader*, (p. 163). Prospect Heights, IL: Waveland Press.

Obama, B. Address to the Democratic National Convention (2004). http://www.youtube.com/watch?v=eWynt87PaJ0.

Jindal, B. Address in response to Barack Obama's address to the Democratic National Convention (2004). http://www.huffingtonpost.com/2009/02/24/bobby-jindal-respone-to-o_n_169704.html.

Chapter 14
Speeches to Inform

Courtesy of Gallo Images/Alamy.

WHAT IS AN INFORMATIVE SPEECH?

An **informative speech** is a presentation intended to help an audience gain understanding. Organizing and presenting informative messages is one of the most valuable skills you will learn in this public speaking class. We believe you will find this skill useful well after you have completed the public speaking class. The most important function of informative speeches is to provide information or to present ideas.

Unlike the persuasive speech, the goal of the informative speech is not to convince the audience to do anything. The goal of the informative speech is to provide insight and understanding. For example, a student, Taylor, gave an informative speech on the advantages and disadvantages of the state of Alabama legalizing gambling. In his speech, he did not urge listeners to sign a petition or call their member of the legislature. Rather, his specific purpose was stated like this: "I want my audience to know the pros and cons of legalizing gambling in the state of Alabama." Taylor ensured the speech was balanced by presenting three advantages of legalized gambling and three disadvantages of legalized gambling.

When developing informative speeches, it is important to remember you must be very knowledgeable about the subject for which you inform. You must have an excellent command of the concepts.

In this chapter, we will discuss the primary types of informative speeches. The four types of informative speeches are definition speeches, explanation speeches, description speeches and demonstration speeches. The chapter also discusses the qualities of informative speeches. The essential qualities of informative speeches we will discuss include clarity, associating new ideas with familiar ideas, coherence and motivating the audience.

TYPES OF INFORMATIVE SPEECHES

The most common types of informative speeches are definition speeches, explanation speeches, description speeches and demonstration speeches.

Speeches of Definition

Speeches of definition are useful when speakers need to clarify the meaning of a word, phrase or idiom. Definition type informative speeches usually focus on an object, an event, or an idea. If you decide to present an informative speech focusing on definitions, you will probably present one of the following types: dictionary, etymological, negation, or functional.

Dictionary Definitions Dictionary definitions present a formal and concise statement of the meaning of a word. For example, if you were defining a Roth IRA to your audience, you might use the following definition, "A Roth IRA stands for Roth Individual Retirement Arrangement. It is a special type of retirement plan under U.S. law that is generally not taxed, provided certain conditions are met."

Etymology Etymologies define a word by telling the history of the word. For example, the word *propel* comes from the Latin prefix *pro* (which means forward) and the verb *pellere* (which means to drive). Therefore, a propeller is an instrument which drives something forward.

Negation Definition by negation clarifies a meaning of a word by telling what something is not. For example, if you were doing a speech to define socialism, you might explain, "By 'socialism,' I don't mean 'communism,' which believes in the common ownership of property. Instead, I mean. . . ."

Functional One of the best ways to define a word is to use the word in context. Patricia, a phlebotomist, gave a speech to a group of middle school students. She started her speech by defining what she does: "I am a phlebotomist. I draw blood from living people for tests, transfusions, donations, or research."

The table below, Table 14.1, demonstrates how you could prepare a speech, using each type of definition speech, to define the word "euthanasia."

Type	Explanation	Example
Dictionary	A speech outlining the meaning of a word as the word appears in the dictionary	According to *Merriam-Webster's Collegiate Dictionary*, euthanasia is defined as "the act or practice of killing or permitting the death of hopelessly sick or injured individuals (as persons or domestic animals) in a relatively painless way for reasons of mercy"
Etymology	A speech which defines a word by explaining the root of the word	The word 'euthanasia' comes from the Greek roots eu (good) and thanatos (death)
Negation	A speech which defines a word be explaining what something is not	Some people consider euthanasia to be murder, but it is not. Murder is defined as unlawful killing, with malice aforethought, of another human, whereas, euthanasia is defined as….
Functional	A speech which defines a word by using the word in context	In 2005, there was a controversial court case involving a woman named Terri Schiavo. For years Schiavo had been kept alive via the use of a feeding tube. Schiavo's family was divided over allowing her to be euthanized, or be kept alive with a feeding tube.

TABLE 14.1
Speeches of Definitions with Examples

Speeches of Explanation

Speeches of explanation are useful when your goal is to clarify complicated concepts, abstract concepts, or unfamiliar concepts. Your professors often give explanation speeches with their lectures by effectively explaining abstract or difficult concepts to students.

Explanation speeches work well when you are giving a speech about how something happens (the stages of meiosis), the emergence of a historical event (how Google was founded) or how an interesting object works (such as hybrid cars). If you decide to present a speech of explanation, you should be extremely knowledgeable about your topic and you should be able to explain the topic clearly to your audience. You also should consider using visual aids to enhance your speech, especially if you are explaining a concept that has several main points. For example, for his informative speech, Chandler decided to explain how a bill becomes a law in the United States Congress. In the body of his speech, Chandler explained the stages of the process as follows:

I. A member of Congress introduces a bill.
   a. The bill sent to the clerk of the Senate or House.
   b. The bill is given a number and title.
II. The bill goes to the appropriate committee.
   a. Committees are made up of small groups of senators or representatives.
   b. Committees specialize in different areas, such as foreign relations or agriculture.
   c. The committee may reject the bill and "table" it, meaning it is never discussed again.
   d. Committee may hold hearings to listen to facts and opinions, make changes in the bill and cast votes.
   e. If most committee members vote in favor of the bill, it is sent back to the Senate and the House for debate.
III. Senate and the House debate and vote on the bill.
   a. Separately, the Senate and the House debate the bill.
   b. Senate and House offer amendments to the bill and cast votes.
IV Differences are settled between the House and Senate.
   a. The bill goes before all of Congress for a vote.
   b. If a majority of both the Senate and the House votes for the bill, it goes to the President for approval.
V. The President signs the bill
   a. If the President approves the bill, he or she signs it.
   b. The bill becomes a law.

To further explain these steps, Chandler used the visual aid in Figure 14.1.

Speeches of explanation are among the most important speeches to make. These types of speeches have the potential to make a significant contribution to the listeners' learning.

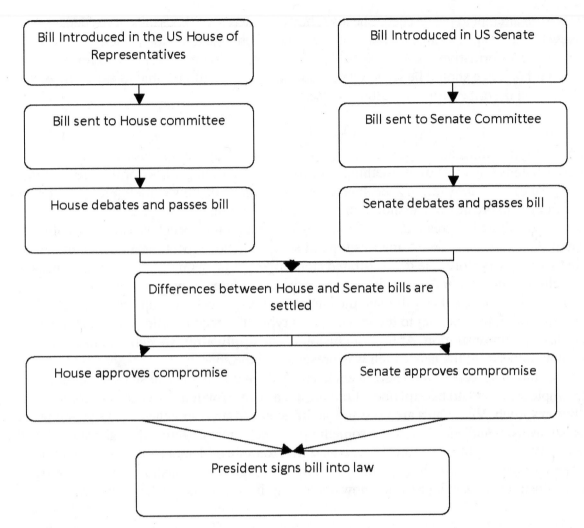

FIGURE 14.1
Diagram or How a Bill becomes a Law

Speeches of Description

The **description speech** is an informative speech designed to provide a clear picture of a person, place or event. You should put a major focus on your language if you decide to use a speech of description. Your language should be full of descriptive words, color and clarity to help bring a concept to life. Like speeches of explanation, visual aids can be very useful with description speeches.

For example, Linda, a student from New Orleans, Louisiana, decided to give a description of the condition of New Orleans immediately after Hurricane Katrina. In addition to her vivid language, Linda showed images of New Orleans residents standing on the rooftops of their houses waving white shirts in an attempt to get rescued. She also showed a picture of thousands of residents packed into the New Orleans Super Dome, because there was no where else to go for shelter.

Description informative speeches should paint a mental picture of your topic for your listeners. Your language should be so detailed; your audience should be able to experience, vividly, what you describe through multiple senses.

Speeches of Demonstration

Demonstration type informative speeches are popular in public speaking classes. To **demonstrate** means to show how something is done, how something works or how something is made. The goal of a demonstration speech is to teach the audience how something works or how to do something—to create understanding or provide application.

Speeches designed to create understanding by demonstration speeches usually involve complicated steps. Speakers delivering this type of speech do not expect the audience members to be able to actually perform the demonstrated steps after the presentation. Rather, the speaker's goal is to help the audience members simply grasp the procedures or processes involved.

In some cases, the speaker will want the audience to apply certain steps or to actually learn how to do something by listening to the speech. This type of speech is called an application speech, a class of demonstration. At the conclusion of the **application speech**, the listeners should be able to perform the task which was presented in the speech.

Demonstration speeches require speakers to carefully and fully explain steps in a process. Even the simple steps should be explained. Oftentimes, a speaker will use a visual aid for a demonstration speech. Visual aids are good to use for demonstration speeches, because in most instances, *showing* an audience how to do something is much more effective than simply *telling* the audience how to do something. Figure 14.2 gives some example of demonstration speech topics.

Notice all these examples begin with the word *how*. Again, demonstration speeches are intended to illustrate steps in a process—how something is done or how something works.

ESSENTIAL QUALITIES OF INFORMATIVE SPEECHES

There are four basic qualities which characterize informative speeches: clarity, association of new ideas with familiar ones, coherence and the motivation of the audience.

Clarity

The quality of your speech is largely the result of effective organization and the careful selection of words. In Chapter 7, we discussed methods you can use to organize your speech. In Chapter 11, we discussed the importance of wording your speech. You should review Chapters 7 and 11 as you began to prepare your informative speech. These chapters should serve as a foundation for your informative speech, because good organization and a good selection of language will help you maximize clarity in your speech. You will achieve the success you deserve only if your listeners can follow you and understand what you are saying.

Examples of Demonstration Speeches

How to change a flat tire

How to use the software, Photoshop

How to set a formal dining table

How to make vegetarian lasagna

How to perform CPR

How to plant an organic garden

How wireless routers work

FIGURE 14.2
Demonstration Speeches Examples

Speech Organization There are three rules you should follow regarding your informative speech organization. First, limit the number of main points. Confine your speech to three or four principle ideas. Even if you know a tremendous amount about your subject, remember you probably cannot make audience members an expert on the subject in a single speech. Second, word your transitions carefully. Plan the transitions in a manner in which your audience members can follow you from point to point. Finally, make sure your speech is forward-moving. In our everyday talk, it is not uncommon for us to jump back and forth between ideas. However, in your informative speech, it is imperative for you to organize your speech in a manner which keeps you from backtracking and repeating ideas. Speakers who jump back and forth between ideas—especially in an informative speech—tend to cause their audience to become more confused than informed.

Courtesy of Wally McNamee/Corbis Images.

The goal of the informative speech is to provide insight and understanding.

Selection of Words Informative speeches require you to pay special attention to your choice of language. You should keep three things in mind as you select words for your informative speech. First, use specific, accurate language. Second, simplify your language, when possible. Include technical language only when you have no other option, because an audience bogged down in unnecessary details and complicated language can become confused and bored. Be sure to define the terms when you use technical language. Finally, if you must use complex ideas, use reiteration. **Reiteration** simply means to repeat over and over again. If you decide you do need to use reiteration, don't use the same word. Instead, use rephrasing to help simplify ideas for listeners who may have trouble with complicated language.

Links New Ideas with Familiar Ideas

Most people grasp new ideas more rapidly when they can associate them with what they already know. You should try to connect new information with the listeners' prior knowledge in your informative speech. Helping your audience relate new information to something they already know, or can visualize, will assist in making your information clear. In Chapter 4, we discussed the importance of conducting an audience analysis before you prepare your speeches. You should use your analysis of the audience to guide you in determining how much or how little you think your audience knows about your topic.

Chip Heath, a professor of business and Dan Heath, a communication consultant, developed a teaching principle called "using what's there." This principle suggests the most effective strategy to teach new information is to relate the new information to something more familiar.

Based on Heath's and Heath's theory, the authors Beebe and Beebe provided an exercise to illustrate the principle. We have developed an exercise similar to the Beebe and Beebe example:

Take 15 seconds to memorize the following group of letters. After 15 seconds, close the book and write the letters exactly as they appear.

IJU   LU   ALBA   FSBF   SOL   PS   PUOA

Chances are, you remembered about half the letters in the group. However, if the same letters are organized differently, into acronyms that make more sense to you, you would remember more letters. Take a look at the letters below:

LBJ   IOU   ASAP   BFF   LOL   UPS   USA

The point here is, we are more likely to make sense of, and remember, things we already have a mental category for.

Coherence

As we discussed in Chapter 7, choosing an organizational pattern is an important part of good speech preparation. Coherence is, in part, a matter of organization. **Coherence** is the process of finding a pattern which fits your main points together in a meaningful manner. For some topics, it's very easy to establish coherence in your speech. For example, if you decided to give an informative speech on the three branches of government, the element of coherence is basically already established. There are only three branches of government, executive, legislative and judicial. Organizing a discussion around these three points would be pretty straight-forward.

Other times, however, you may need to do a bit more work in order to make your speech coherent. Suppose you decide to give a speech on the Academy Awards. To do this, you might decide to discuss three aspects of the Academy Awards: the nominating process, the notification and announcement of the nominees, and the final ballot voting process. To give this speech coherence, you could use a chronological pattern. You could begin your speech by saying something similar to this: "Year after year millions of Americans tune in to watch the Academy Awards. Have you ever wondered 'What is the process for nominating a film or actor for an Oscar? When are the nominees notified? How is voting done?' In my speech, I will answer these questions. I will explain the 'what, when and how' of the Academy Awards." Using a common trio of words (like what, when, and how) as an organizing principle can help to give coherence to a speech which is not naturally coherent.

Motivating the Audience

Finally, and perhaps most importantly, you must be able to motivate the audience to listen to your speech. Motivating the audience to listen is vital for good informative speeches, but many speakers ignore this criterion. Many speakers assume because they are interested in a topic, the audience will also want to hear about it. For you, coin-collecting may be an interesting hobby, but your audience members may find it totally boring.

When preparing your informative speeches, keep in mind what we have previously discussed about gaining your audience's attention and interest. If you need a refresher, refer to Chapter 8. Once you have captured the audience's attention, focus on the reasons they should want to know what you are about to tell them. In short, make you speech relevant to your listeners.

SUMMARY

Your informative speech is one of the most important speeches you will deliver as a student in the public speaking class. But, the importance of informative speeches does not diminish when you complete your public speaking class. When you graduate from college and become a working professional, the ability to deliver an effective informative speech will be equally important.

In this chapter, we discussed the various types of informative speeches: definition, explanation, description and demonstration. Speeches of definition teach listeners what something means by using dictionary definitions, etymology, negation or functional definitions. Explanation speeches interpret how something happens, the emergence of a historical event, or how an interesting object works. Description speeches use vivid, colorful language to inform about a person, place, or event. Demonstration speeches show how something works, how something is done, or how something is made.

Whichever type of informative speech you choose, your speech should have four fundamental qualities. First, your speech should have clarity. Your speech should have a limited number of main points, carefully worded transitions and be forward-moving. Your speech should have specific, simple language. And when possible, you should use reiteration. Second, your informative speech should link new ideas with familiar ideas by employing the "use what's there" principle. Third, your informative speech should have coherence. You should find an organizational pattern to present your main points in a logical, systematic manner. Sometimes finding an organizational pattern will be easy. Other times it may take a bit of work. Finally, your informative speech should motivate the audience to listen to and remember your speech.

REFERENCES

Beebe, S.A. & Beebe, S. J. (2012). *Public speaking: An audience-centered approach,* 8th ed. Boston: Pearson.

Beebe, S. A., & Beebe, S. J. (2006). *Public speaking: An audience-centered approach,* 6th ed. New York: Pearson.

Fraleigh, D. M., & Tuman, J. S. (2009). *Speak up! An illustrated guide to public speaking.* New York: Bedford/St. Martins.

Hanna, M. S. & Gibson, J. W. (2002). *Public speaking for personal success,* 6th ed. Boston: Pearson.

Heath, C. & Heath, D. (2007). *Made to stick*, pp. 63–64. New York: Random House.

Chapter 15
Speeches to Persuade

Courtesy of Mary Altaffer/AP Images.

WHAT IS A PERSUASIVE SPEECH?

Consider the messages you hear throughout the day. Chances are many of these messages are persuasive in nature. Think about it: the preacher in your church persuades sinners to become saved; politicians persuade citizens to vote for them; the waitress in a restaurant persuades you to try the soup of the day.

Obviously we will focus on the more formal kind of persuasion found in a speech. A **persuasive speech** is a designed to influence your audiences' beliefs, attitudes or actions. Persuasion usually seeks to accomplish one or more of the following three goals: (1) to strengthen your audiences' commitment, (2) to weaken your audiences' commitment, and (3) to advocate an action from your audience.

Many rhetoricians believe learning to persuade is one of the most important skills an individual can learn. You may find your persuasive speech easier to prepare than your previous speeches, because this speech allows you to advocate ideas that are important to you.

In this chapter, we will discuss seven principles specifically related to persuasive speaking. These principles are designed to help increase the likelihood of you persuading your audience.

PRINCIPLES OF PERSUASIVE SPEECHES

Principle 1: Believe in Your Goal

You have a better chance of persuading your audience when they are convinced you believe in the goal of the speech and that your goal in is their best interest.

By nature, we are often skeptical of persuasive messages. Chances are you've gone to a repair person to get work done on your car. As the repair person gives you the litany of work you need done on your car, you may begin to question how ethical is the repair person's message. As a persuasive speaker, your aim should be sure to lead your audience toward choices that are in the best interest of the audience and society—not just you, the speaker. If your audience members are convinced you are ethical in your persuasion, you will be more likely to persuade them.

Principle 2: Align Your Goal with Your Audience

You have a better chance of persuading your audience when your goal is aligned with their attitudes.

Much of the success of a speech depends on determining how an audience is likely to react to your goal. In persuasive speeches, especially, you must find out your audiences' attitudes about your topic. As we discussed in Chapter 4, you can conduct an audience analysis to help you make judgments about your audience. The more data you have about your audience, the better you will be at judging your audiences' attitudes accurately.

Audience attitudes often are distributed along a continuum from highly favorable to your view to hostile to your view (see Figure 15.1).

It's likely your audience will have at least one individual at nearly every point along the continuum distribution. However, most audiences will have a majority of listeners whose overall opinion will cluster at one particular point. You should classify your audiences' attitude at the point of the continuum where you believe the majority of your listeners' positions are. Generally speaking, your audiences' attitudes will be predominantly "in favor" (already holding a particular

Hostile	Opposed	Mildly Opposed	Neither in favor nor opposed	Mildly in favor	In favor	Highly in favor

FIGURE 15.1
Continuum of Audience Attitudes

belief), "no opinion" (uninformed, neutral or apathetic), or "opposed" (holding an opposite point of view). Being aware of the general attitude of your audience will help you develop persuasion strategies to adapt to their attitude.

Your Audience Is In Favor Of Your View Some audiences will include people who already accept and agree with all or most of what you plan to say. You may have heard the phrase "preaching to the choir." This phrase is often used to describe what can happen when we speak to an audience who is in favor of our position. It is often believed that speaking to a favorable audience is relatively easy, because there will be little to no resistance to the ideas. However, speaking to a favorable audience may be more complicated than you think, especially if you don't do something to engage the audience. If the audience members already accept your position, it's likely they know a good deal about the topic and have considered the alternatives. This could be the perfect formula for the listeners to tune out much of what you say. So, if your audience is in favor of your position, you may have to work even harder to hold their attention.

If you have determined the majority of your audience already favors your belief, you should consider making your goal a focus on a specific course of action. Usually, lack of motivation keeps people who have a favorable attitude from acting. So, as a persuasive speaker, your job is to provide a call to action—something specific your audience can do as a result of hearing your speech. The call to action should be something practical. Otherwise, your audience is likely to ignore your appeal regardless of the merits. For example, if your audience members already favor organ donation, you might crystallize their attitudes by rallying them to complete organ donor cards that you provide. You could also go one step further by encouraging your audience to urge their family members to donate their organs.

Your Audience Has No Opinion Of Your View Some audiences won't have strong feelings for or against your speech topic. The "no opinion" status could be because your listeners are uninformed, neutral or apathetic.

If your audience has no opinion because they are *uninformed*, you should give enough information to help them understand the subject before you introduce persuasive appeals or try to establish beliefs or actions. For example, if you believe your audience is uninformed about organ donation, you should define organ donation, talk about how organs are donated, and share evidence of how lives are saved by organ donations. Giving a brief amount of information is imperative when your audience is uninformed. However, you should be cautious about how much time you spend informing. If your subject takes more than half of your allotted speaking time to explain, you may not have enough time to persuade.

If your audience has no opinion because they are *neutral*, it is very likely you will be able to reason with them and they will be open to accepting sound reasoning. If your audience is neutral, you should focus your speech on why the topic matters to them. Once you make the topic relevant to the listeners, you will be more likely to persuade them to accept your position.

If your audience has no opinion because they are *apathetic*, your effort may be solely dedicated to moving them out of apathy. For example, your audience may be familiar with organ donation, how organ donations are performed, and even be aware of the lives saved because of organ donations. But, they may not seem to care. Instead of focusing on information with this audience, you should emphasize motivation. You should present less information that proves the logic of your positions and more content that is directed towards your audiences' personal needs.

Your Audience Is Opposed To Your View Some audiences will be opposed to your topic before you even begin to speak. The strategy you use to persuade them will depend on whether their attitude is slightly negative or totally hostile.

If your listeners are *slightly opposed* to your positions, you can approach them directly with your argument. Sometimes, a forthright argument will swing listeners to your side. While being forthright, you should also be objective with your material.

The most difficult audience to persuade is a *hostile* audience. These audiences have a predisposition to disagree with you; and usually, they are against you even before you start speaking. If your audience is hostile, your goal is to try to neutralize the hostility. You can begin to neutralize the hostility by approaching the topic indirectly. With hostile audiences, it is unrealistic to expect a complete shift in attitudes or behaviors as a result of one speech. However, if you present a modest proposal which seeks a slight change in attitudes, you may be able to convince your audience to, at least, consider the values of your ideas. Persuading a hostile audience to change must be accomplished through a series of speeches. The idea is to move them toward your position a little each time.

Principle 3: Focus on One Specific Claim

Your audience is more likely to be persuaded when your speech focuses on one specific claim.

In persuasive speeches, you will make one of three types of claims: claims of fact, claims of value or claims of policy or claims of action.

Claims of Fact Claims of fact assert that something is true or false or is so or is not so. For example if you were trying to persuade your audience that "Breast cancer survival rates are higher when the cancer is detected early," you would be presenting a factual claim.

Claims of Value Claims of value assert that something is good or bad, desirable or undesirable, justified or unjustified. For example, if you were advocating support for Planned Parenthood, you could persuade your audience that "Planned Parenthood is a worthwhile organization which administers thousands of free breast exams to women every year. Without the organization many women would not be able to get the breast exams."

Claims of Policy Claims of policies recommend a course of action for which you want the audience to approve. These types of claims usually contain "should" statements. For example, as a claim of policy, you could persuade your audience that "The Susan G. Komen foundation should continue to make contributions to Planned Parenthood to ensure women can continue to receive free beast exams."

Claims of Action Claims of action go a step father than seeking the audiences' approval. Claims of action specify the actions the audience should take. For example, your speech could be designed to persuade your audience to "make a contribution of any amount to Planned Parenthood."

Principle 4: Present Good Reasons and Evidence

Your audience is more likely to be persuaded when you present good reasons and evidence to support your claims.

Reasons are statements why your audience should believe something or do something. In persuasive speeches, it is essential to do research to explain reasons why you are soliciting a particular action. For example, if your speech goal was "I want to convince my audience that corporal punishment laws should be repealed and outlawed in every state," you could present the following four reasons:

I. Executions have resulted in innocent people being killed.
II. Execution is more expensive than life in prison without the possibility of parole.
III. Capital punishment is often considered barbaric.
IV. Racial biases often pervade death penalty cases.

After you have established the reasons, you should evaluate each to ensure they can be supported, they are relevant to your goal and that they will have an impact on your audience.

Principle 5: Organize Your Speech to Persuade

You have a better chance of persuading your audience when your speech is organized in a way which is most persuasive to your audience.

A persuasive speech is designed to influence your audience's beliefs, attitudes or actions.

In Chapter 7 we discussed organizational patterns which can be used to structure your speech. Presumably, any of the patterns discussed in Chapter 7 could be used to organize your persuasive speech. However, you may have greater success persuading if you use a problem to solution pattern, a problem-cause-solution pattern, a comparative advantage pattern, or Monroe's Motivated Sequence pattern.

Problem to Solution A problem to solution pattern divides information into two main sections. One section describes the extent of and harm created by a problem. The other section advocates a solution. The pattern is designed to compel the audience to make some kind of change in opinion or behavior by establishing that a problem exists, then providing a solution to the problem.

In his speech about the HPV vaccination, Stanley used the problem to solution organizational pattern. His speech was organized as follows:

Thesis: Parents should allow their children to be given the HPV vaccine.

I. Problem: Cervical cancer strikes about 12,000 U.S. women a year and kills around 4,000.
II. Solution: The American Academy of Pediatrics believes the cancer can be eradicated if girls in the United States are vaccinated between the ages of 11 and 12 years old.

Problem-Cause-Solution The problem-cause-solution pattern of organization can be useful when you are advocating a change by an institution or organization. The first main point presents the problem needing to be addressed, along with arguments about its significance. The second main point argues that the current policies are not effective in eliminating the cause of the problem. The third main point presents and advocates a solution to minimize the problem.

Monica, a student at the University of South Alabama, used a problem-cause-solution pattern to advocate a transit bus system on campus. Her speech was organized as follows:

Thesis: The University of South Alabama should implement a transit system to transport students to classes on campus.

I.   Problem: Parking on the main campus is congested near student parking lots and classroom buildings.

II. Cause: Many students who attend the University of South Alabama are commuter students, so many drive from building to building going to class.

III. Solution: Implementing a transit system would cut down on the need of commuters having to drive all over campus; which would, in turn, open up more parking spaces and alleviate traffic jams.

A comparative advantage approach is effective in a variety of settings.

Courtesy of Tom McCarthy/PhotoEdit.

191

Comparative Advantage Comparative advantage organization shows why the policy you are advocating is more beneficial than existing policies. Jeanette used the comparative advantage pattern to advocate the use of nuclear power. Her speech was organized as follows:

Thesis: Nuclear power is the best answer to our energy crisis.

I. Nuclear power is better than solar power because it is more reliable.
II. Nuclear power is better than solar power because it produces more energy for less cost.
III. Nuclear power is better than solar power because it can more easily be transferred to a centralized grid system, which already provides much of our electricity.

Monroe's Motivated Sequence Alan Monroe (1935) developed the motivated sequence pattern of persuasion over seventy years ago, and the persuasive strategy is still popular today. The sequence follows the stages of thinking people often go through while solving a problem or considering new ideas. The motivated sequence includes five main points: Attention, Need, Satisfaction, Visualization and Action.

Jasmine decided Monroe's Motivated Sequence pattern would be best used to persuade her audience to use social networking wisely. Here is how she applied the steps of Monroe's Motivated Sequence to make her case:

Thesis: Social networking sites are useful, but you must be mindful of how and when you use them.

Step 1: Attention [The attention step is focused on generating a willingness to listen to your message.]
    "By a show of hands, how many of you use a social networking site? How many of you log on to these sites at work? How many of you have ever, unintentionally, posted something someone else found offensive? According to a 2010 Proofpoint survey, 7 % of companies with over 1,000 employees terminated a worker due to a social media post. These numbers were up from 4% in 2008. In the same survey, 20 % of companies reported disciplining employees for violating social networking policies."

Step 2: Need [The need step is focused on identifying the relevance your topic has to your audience.]
    "Millions of people use social networking—including the majority of us in this class. Everyone who is a member of a social networking site is at risk of offending someone, or changing how others think about us, by what we post online. Social networking outlets can

be very useful. However, far too many people experience negative consequences as a result of using sites inappropriately."

Step 3: Satisfaction [The satisfaction step is focused on presenting how your ideas will fulfill the need you've identified.]
"Knowing how and when to use social networking can help you save your reputation and possibly your job."

Step 4: Visualization [The visualization step is focused on helping your listeners form a mental picture of the benefits of your persuasive message.]
"I will suggest strategies which will help you feel more comfortable with your social networking uses."

Step 5: Action [The action step is focused on you clarifying exactly what you want your listeners to do as a result of hearing your speech.]

"Here are some tips you should use when using social media:

1. Monitor your profile. Delete comments or photos posted by others you do not want to be seen by current or potential employers.
2. Set your privacy settings. Customize your privacy settings to limit who has access to your account.
3. If you work, know your employers social networking policy. Understand the position your company takes on social networking. Also remember, if you are using a company's technology to access social media accounts, it is likely your company has the right to monitor the activity used while using their property.

Using these tips will help improve your experiences with social networking."

Principle 6: Pitch to Your Audience's Emotions

You have a better chance of persuading your audience when you arouse their emotions.

We have all been moved by actions or words that generate anger, fear, surprise and joy. These experiences, while all subjective, are often accompanied by bodily arousal and sometimes, overt behavior. When developing your persuasive speech, you should look for opportunities to ethically arouse the emotions of your listeners.

It is likely that your best opportunities to use emotional appeal occur in the introduction and conclusion of your speech. Notice in the following example how emotional appeals are used in the introduction and conclusion of a speech urging listeners to boycott the circus:

Introduction:

Nine year old twins, Johniece and Johnny, saw a commercial advertising the circus, Ringling Bros., was coming to town. The twins became relentless in asking their parents to take them to the show. Their parents decided going to the circus would be a great family date-night, so they agreed to go. What these unsuspecting parents planning a family trip to the circus don't know about was the violent training sessions with ropes, bull hooks, and electric shock prods many animals endure to train for the circus.

After giving reasons for people to boycott the circus, the speech could be concluded by saying the following:

Conclusion:

As stated by the People for the Ethical Treatment of Animals (PETA) organization, elephants, tigers, and other animals do not voluntarily ride bicycles, stand on their heads, balance on balls, or jump through rings of fire. They don't perform these and other difficult tricks because they want to. They perform them because they're afraid of what will happen if they don't. For animals in circuses, there is no such thing as positive reinforcement—only varying degrees of punishment and deprivation.

Regardless of your affinity for pets, an audience would likely feel sadness after hearing how the animals are mistreated. We will have more to say about emotional appeals in Chapter 16.

Principle 7: Present Your Speech Well

You have a better chance of persuading your audience if you have an effective oral presentation style.

In Chapter 13 we discussed strategies for effective delivery. As you plan and begin to practice your persuasive speech, you should consider reviewing the chapter on delivery. Keep in mind, your delivery can make or break your speech.

SUMMARY

This chapter discussed persuasive speeches. Specifically, the chapter identified the seven principles related to effective speaking.

The first principle of persuasive speaking is the idea that you have a better chance of persuading your audience when they are convinced you believe in the goal of the speech and that your goal in is their best interest.

The second principle of persuasive speaking asserts that you will have a better chance of persuading your audience when your goal is aligned with their attitudes. Your audiences' attitudes will likely be in favor of your ideas, have no opinion about your ideas or will be opposed to your ideas. Your analysis of your audience members should give you a good indication of how your audience thinks about your topic.

The third principle stresses that your audience is more likely to be persuaded when your speech focuses on one specific claim. Your speech will either focus on a claim of fact, a claim of value, a claim of policy, or a claim of action.

The fourth principle emphasizes that your audience is more likely to be persuaded when you present good reasons and evidence to support your claims.

The fifth principle stressed you have a better chance of persuading your audience when your speech is organized in a way which is most persuasive to your audience. The most common organizational patterns for persuasive speeches are (1) problem to solution, (2) problem-cause-solution, (3) comparative advantage, (4) and Monroe's Motivated Sequence.

The sixth principle states you have a better chance of persuading your audience when you arouse their emotions. We have all experienced anger, fear, surprise and joy. These emotions, and other emotions like these, are amazingly effective in persuading listeners.

Finally, the seventh principle reminds you that you will have a better chance of persuading your audience if you have an effective oral presentation style.

REFERENCES

Beebe, S. A., & Beebe, S. J. (2006). *Public speaking: An audience-centered approach,* 6th ed. New York: Pearson.

Fraleigh, D. M., & Tuman, J. S. (2009). *Speak up! An illustrated guide to public speaking.* New York: Bedford/St. Martins.

McKerrow, R. E. (2007). *Principles and types of public speaking*, 16th ed. Boston: Person.

Monroe, A. H. (1938). *Principles and types of speech*, 1st ed. Glenview, IL: Scott Foresman.

PETA on circuses. (2012). Retrieved April 16, 2012, from http://www.peta.org/issues/animals-in-entertainment/circuses.aspx.

Rose, J. (2010). How to avoid getting fired due to social media. Retrieved on April 24, 2012, from http://www.flowtown.com/blog/how-to-avoid-getting-fired-due-to-social-media.

Chapter 16
Persuasive Strategies

Courtesy of Win McNamee/Getty Images.

WHY ARE PERSUASION STRATEGIES IMPORTANT TO YOU?

Persuasion pervades every aspect of your life. Advertisers make appeals to you to buy their product. Politicians seek to entice you to vote for them. Teachers try to persuade you to follow the syllabus, read the assignments and come to class prepared. The U.S. government attempts to convince you to be honest when filling out your tax return. Somebody close to you, who cares about you, tries to persuade you to take your pursuit of graduation seriously. Environmental groups try persuading you to protect the environment and also to conserve energy. The list of persuasive attempts in your life goes on and on. Of course, you must be able to carefully evaluate these attempts in order to make the right choices for yourself. This evaluation, however, requires understanding and skill in persuasion if you are to successfully navigate through it.

You will also make arguments on your behalf in numerous situations. You will have to persuade an employer to hire you over all the other candidates for a position. You may need to persuade the boss to buy you a new computer. You may seek to persuade a friend to vote for the candidate of your choice. You may need to persuade an instructor to reconsider a grade on your examination. You may persuade a classmate to help you on a project. And finally, if you choose to marry, you will persuade the person to marry you. Again, we could go on and on with situations in which successful persuasion is very important. Here is one final reason to understand how to be persuasive. You will want to achieve success and the grade you would like on your persuasive speaking assignments in this class.

Here is our plan to help you learn the many aspects of persuasion so these goals can be achieved. We will present a number of strategies that, if followed, should lead to success. We will begin with the issue of credibility and how to present yourself to achieve it. The credible speaker will be more successful than the speaker whose credibility is in doubt. Next, we will move to strategies for using evidence successfully. Third, we will present strategies and standards to follow for sound reasoning. This will include a discussion of various kinds of reasoning, as well as fallacies—logically unsound reasoning. Finally, we will present strategies that use emotions and needs to persuade. Now, let us turn to credibility.

BUILDING CREDIBILITY

Credibility has been a long-time concern of those who teach people how to be effective persuaders. This concern can be traced back to the Greek philosopher Aristotle, who wrote about it over 2,000 years ago. His term for credibility is *ethos*, the speaker's believability that is based largely on his or her reputation. Thus, **credibility** is the degree to which a receiver finds a speaker to be believable. This believability is based on the speaker's perceived competence and character (O'Keefe, 2002).

Competence in persuasive speaking is related to three factors—expertise, knowledge of the subject and intelligence. **Expertise** is the significant skill or knowledge resulting in his or her extensive study, observation of the topic and credentials. The speaker is experienced with the subject or proficient in the skills suggested by the topic. Knowledge of the subject is a separate category because a speaker can obtain this without direct experience with the topic. A speaker who has done the requisite research on a topic can claim to be knowledgeable. **Knowledgeable** means the person has significant understanding of the topic or issue because of his or her research and, possibly, direct experience with these. You as a speaker always have access to this source of credibility. **Intelligence** with regard to persuasive speaking is not an IQ factor. It is the understanding of how to craft an excellent argument. Of course, you will have this source of credibility when you effectively apply the strategies of persuasion and other topics we present here.

Character in persuasive speaking is seen as the speaker's sincerity, trustworthiness, and concern for the well-being of the audience. **Sincere** means to us that the speaker is being genuine, earnest and free from falseness (truth-telling). So, how does a speaker seem sincere to his or her audience? We believe sincerity comes, in part, from how you present your message. For example, if you deliver a persuasive speech with relatively constant eye contact on your notes, instead of on the audience, it is hard to believe you are sincere. We think the audience expects more. They are likely to expect that, if you are sincere, you have taken the time to have whatever you want to say firmly in your memory. There is no urgency to your message when you are not able to present it in a compelling way. **Character** also means that you are telling the truth. This factor is easily enhanced by having done your research and providing excellent support from reliable sources. **Concern for the well-being of your audience** suggests to us showing empathy for their experience by using it appropriately to illustrate and bolster your points.

Enhancing Credibility

Your credibility is based on the factors that define it. In other words, your credibility is based on your perceived competence and character. Here is some practical advice on enhancing your credibility.

Explain Your Competence   This is a task you will want to take care of in your introductory comments. Perhaps you are an expert on the topic. If so, say so. Realistically, most of us are not experts on the topics we will present. But, you may have special expertise? You might say, "I have personally experienced the effects of a learning disability since my brother has difficulty learning. I will bring some of my experiences into my speech to help you understand the seriousness of the problem." Perhaps you have done careful research on the topic. Describe this research without boasting. You can show that you have selected competent sources by presenting their credentials regarding the point you are supporting. Finally, describe your experience with the topic if it is significant.

Establish Common Ground   **Common ground** is established when you identify with your audience by showing that you share experiences, beliefs and/or values that are similar to theirs. Generally, you would want to establish common ground at the beginning of your speech.

Perceived similarity between people is a powerful source of trust and respect. In an interpersonal relationship it is well-known that perceived similarities are a significant source of attraction (Wilson, 2012). Sharing common grounds with your audience gives you the opportunity to affirm their view (in regard to some aspect of this topic) and show respect for their idea. Even if some of your audience members are opposed to your position, you can begin to build credibility if you can find common grounds and work from there. For example, if you are speaking about gun control and some of your audience members are against it, you may build common ground by reference to their concern about the rising crime rate. Of course, establishing common ground does not mean that you compromise your beliefs, but, instead, you are calling attention to beliefs you share with them.

Show Open-Mindedness   We know from research on persuasion that a well-educated audience will know that there are likely to be two sides to any issue. What this means is that you need to acknowledge the opposing side or the audience may think you are hiding something. Generally you would present the other side and show how that is not as effective as what you are proposing. You are showing you have been open to other views, studied them, and have determined that your position is better.

Deliver Your Speech Well   We suppose that you would find no difficulty believing that a well-delivered speech is more persuasive than one that is not. You would be right. There is a great deal of research that supports this (Perloff, 1993). Your audience will expect you to deliver your speech fluently and expressively. They will also expect significant eye contact.

Establishing common ground helps ensure that you persuade your audience.

Research has found that fluent, moderately fast vocal delivery, spoken with conviction, suggests intelligence and confidence. In contrast, a speaking style that includes vocalized pauses, "ums" and "uhs," with a slow speaking rate and monotonous tone produces the opposite effect (Perloff, 1993).

Your nonverbal body language is also something that can have a significant impact on your credibility. Research points out the power of eye contact for example. Direct eye contact has been found to create an impression of self-confidence and interest in the listener. (Hall, 1959; Kelly, 1972; Beebe, 1974) Also, confidently walking up to the podium and establishing brief eye contact with the audience before you begin your speech conveys self-confidence. You will also have impact on your credibility if you use the same routine when you finish your speech.

Appearance is the last physical issue. You can enhance your credibility when you wear certain clothing. Seriously; this is not a joke. Let us explain.

In the U.S. culture, attractive people are seen as more competent, well organized, and confident. Of course, we cannot do anything about some aspects of our appearance. We can be well-groomed and well-dressed however. Larson (2012) notes that speakers who are dressed more or less formally versus very casually or sloppily are seen as more credible.

Use Strong Evidence Charles U. Larson (2012) reminds persuaders that use of evidence from highly credible sources will increase the persuader's credibility. It turns out that strong evidence is crucial in a persuasive speech. The stronger the evidence is; the stronger your credibility will be. Strong evidence suggests to your audience that you have researched well, so in a sense you get a boost in your own credibility.

Use of Evidence

We addressed the topic of kinds of evidence in Chapter 6, Gathering Materials. Here we will talk specifically about the options you have as you provide evidence. Think of this as going one step farther to focus specifically on persuasion.

Be Specific   We know that stating your evidence specifically rather than generally will pack more persuasive punch (Reinard, 1988). For example, you could say, "Many people over 20 years old carry too much weight." Or you could say, "The National Institute of Diabetes and Digestive and Kidney Disease reported in a 2007–8 survey that 68% of the people in the United States are considered over weight. That leaves only 32% who are considered to be at a healthy weight." We believe that you see a difference here and that the second statement is much more powerful than the first because it is specific.

Use Credible Sources   Be sure you do not present evidence form a biased source. A **biased source** is the kind that has reason to present data in a way to promote their cause or put their organization in a favorable light. We say they have a self-interest in making their particular statement or releasing their data. If you use this kind of information it will be suspect unless it is backed up with data from other reliable sources. Trust us; use of reliable sources is very important. There is a great deal of evidence showing that audiences find evidence from competent, credible sources more persuasive than evidence from less qualified sources (Reynolds & Reynolds, 2002).

Be Sure the Evidence Relates to the Point You Are Making   This is one problem that speakers who have not had a lot of experience in constructing persuasive speeches find themselves having. There may be a connection, but it is not clear to the audience. You see a connection between the point you are making and the evidence, but they do not. As a speaker, you cannot count on your audience to draw the same connection you have made or, perhaps, any conclusion at all. This fact has been demonstrated in several studies (O'Keefe, 1999). You should be sure to be clear on the connection between the point you are making and your evidence.

EFFECTIVE REASONING

Reasoning is the process of drawing conclusions based on evidence. Reasoning is important to you because you will present conclusions to your audience at various points in your speech. These are a result of putting evidence and ideas together that lead to a conclusion *that you hope your audience will accept*. Do you suppose that your audience will take the things you say and come up with the same conclusion? They might. And, they might not. What do you suppose will make the difference between accepting and not accepting your conclusion? We can answer that question for you. The deciding factor will be the quality of your thought, the quality of your reasoning. Let's look at the major types of reasoning and thought to understand the factors you must consider.

Reasoning Based on Specific Instances

Reasoning using specific instances progresses from a number of particular facts, specific instances, to a general conclusion. A **specific instance** is a brief example of something. You need to have several specific instances that illustrate your point. Generally, this type of reasoning will not stand alone as proof. Obviously, there may be instances that exist that are the exception to the specific instances you cite. Specific instances point to a trend, a likelihood, so they are very useful to your persuasive effort. But, no matter how many specific instances you cite, and in a speech you will only have time for several, there may be exceptions.

Here is a brief argument that shows this kind of reasoning. Suppose that you are interested in the U.S. Space Exploration Program. One of the things that you have discovered in your research is that it has produced over 30,000 "spin-off" products since its inception in 1958; many of these are significant. This is a point you wish to support by arguing from examples. Here are the specific instances you select to use to make your point.

> The U.S. Space Program has produced over 30,000 "spin-off" products since its inception in 1958, many of them significant. Here are some inventions NASA sees as important to society's practical needs: new fire-fighting suits with better breathing systems; a device that can warn of pending heart attacks; digital imaging that enables a more accurate medical diagnosis; a longer-lasting running shoe; and scratch resistant contact lenses.

Here is another example of reasoning by specific instances. A district attorney may argue that Maude killed her husband, Hector.

> Maude killed her husband, Hector. We believe this is true because:
>   Maude had an insurance motive.
>   Maude told her friend, Alice, she intended to kill Hector.
>   Maude's fingerprints are on the knife used to kill Hector.
>   Ada Jeffers says she saw Maude do it.

Any one or two of these taken alone would not necessarily be sufficient to make this case. The case is more solid with all four of these specific pieces of evidence (instances).

Considerations in the Use of Specific Examples to Draw Conclusions

1. We said that specific instances often cannot stand alone.

Bolster your argument with other types of proof, such as statistics and testimony.

2. Do not make sweeping conclusions when your evidence does not support this.

An unqualified statement might be strong, but you should qualify it if necessary so not to overstep the bounds of your evidence.

3. One reasoning error is called hasty generalization.

A **hasty generalization** is one that reaches a conclusion when there is insufficient evidence to allow for the statement. When using specific instances you should not be reasoning from two or three instances. Although there is no specific rule as to how many instances you need, we think at least four or five are needed.

Reasoning Based on a Principle

Stephen E. Lucas (2010) has labeled deductive reasoning, in the form of a syllogism, reasoning from principle. **Reasoning from principle** is an argument that begins with an idea that is believed to be affirmed by audience members (an idea about how something—the principle—is), and then moves to a presumed specific incident of that principle, with a conclusion that follows these two elements. This is an excellent way to think about deductive reasoning because it is easy to understand. It follows this form: a general principle, a specific instance that represents the principle, and a conclusion. Here is an example of this reasoning that follows this form:

Suppose you decide to give a speech about Susan B. Anthony, one of the major forces in securing voting rights for women. You see, the right for women to vote in the U.S. was not fully secured until 1920. This right is now guaranteed through the Nineteenth Amendment to the U.S. Constitution. Susan B. Anthony traveled from state to state in 1872 and 1873 making her arguments based on reasoning from principle. Understanding that this was the basic structure of her arguments is helpful in understanding her effort in this area. Her reasoning from principle looks like this:

Principle: The Constitution of the United States gave all citizens the right to vote.

Specific Instance: Women are United States citizens.

Conclusion: Therefore, the Constitution guarantees women the right to vote.

Reasoning from principle is a very powerful strategy because if the principle is something your audience accepts, it will be very difficult to argue against the specific instance and conclusion you will make. The logic here is compelling.

Considerations in the Use of Arguments from Principle to Draw Conclusions

We said this type of reasoning is based on the assumption that your audience accepts the general principle. You may know they accept your general principle if your audience analysis has been thorough or you know your audience well. If you do not know that they agree completely with the principle, it would be a good idea to bolster it with additional evidence before you move to the specific instance you hope to be accepted. If you are still in doubt, you may also want to provide support for your specific instance as falling within the principle.

Reasoning Based on Causes

Causal reasoning attempts to establish a relationship between causes (the impetus for something) and its effects. In everyday life, we will find ourselves using this reasoning often, sometimes reversing the order here—effect to cause. You may think of something that is happening in our world, say our favorite football team's latest defeat, and then ask yourself what may have caused this divergence from their normally great playing. As we said, causal reasoning can be used in the cause-to-effect format or the effect to the cause format.

Here is another example. You might center an argument on the lateness of students for class based on how campus transportation runs. On an average, it runs five minutes late. Therefore, this could explain the fact that one-third of students show up for class late.

Here is an example of reasoning from cause. The topic of this speech was the drug methamphetamine, often called "meth." The speaker was attempting to persuade her audience that methamphetamine causes drug problems that are even more serious than those associated with the use of crack. The speaker said,

> There are four factors that make the use of methamphetamine cause more serious problems that those associated with the use of crack.
>
> 1. Smoking meth is easier than smoking crack because it does not need to be converted to a base form like crack.
> 2. Smoking meth packs a bigger, faster wallop than smoking crack because of its extreme volatility.
> 3. Smoking meth hooks the user faster than smoking crack because of the drug's rapid tolerance by the body.
> 4. Smoking meth is more likely to harm or even kill the user than smoking crack because of its long duration of action in the body.
>
> Taken together these factors allow us to conclude the use of methamphetamine causes more serious problems than those associated with the use of crack.

Considerations in the Use of Causal Reasoning to Draw Conclusions

In order to be a cause, one factor must be linked and follow the other. We would expect to see the same cause to follow the same results over a number of cases. For example, we believe heavy cigarette smoking is a significant causal factor of lung cancer. This is a pretty safe argument because many cases of these two have been linked numerous times in research so much so that we can claim a causal relationship. What you cannot do, however, is to argue from too few cases. Although there is no specific rule, you would want to see the cause of the cause-effect relationship you are arguing as a cause in a significant number of cases.

Another consideration is prompted by the question, "Are there other things that may have been causing this problem?" Just because one event occurs in close proximity to the other does not mean that one has caused the other, even if they seem related. There is a common saying that crossing the path of a black cat causes bad luck. One of your authors knows a police officer who would stop his patrol car and take another direction if he saw a black cat cross the road. Suppose you crossed the path of a black cat on the way to school to take an exam and did poorly on the exam. This police officer, if this were to happen to him, would claim this poor performance was a result of crossing the path of this poor, black cat. Would you? This is obviously a case of false causality. This is clearly a reasoning problem, but not all are this clear. Always ask if other things could have caused the effect.

A final consideration is to assess whether the effect may have multiple causes. In general, most complex problems have multiple causes. Understanding and discovering the multiple causes is something you will certainly want to do before you deliver your speech. The problem comes not from the multiple causes, but only if you do not recognize them. Suppose you decide to craft a persuasive speech on the causes of the current economic down-turn. This is obviously a complex problem. You would want to consider the multiple potential causes in your speech. These might include things such as interest rates, housing sales, gas prices, consumer confidence and the like. Complex problems have multiple causes. That is just the way it is.

Reasoning from Analogy

Reasoning from analogy is argument that compares two similar cases of something, perhaps a parking problem on your campus with one on a near-by campus, and infers that what is true of one is true of the other. This kind of analogy is called a **literal analogy.** So, you might reason that the near-by university solved their problem in this way and so we can solve our problem by following their lead. A politician might argue, and one has recently, that families have to keep their spending in line with their income, so the government can live within its resources also. Both of these examples may violate important considerations regarding use of analogies to persuade. The importance is that the situations actually must be similar.

Another use of analogy is to not for comparison, but to help the audience understand an essential aspect of a problem by comparing it to similar situations. This is called a **figurative analogy**. Senator Edward Kennedy has been known for years for his efforts to support gun control. Here is an analogy he used in one of his early speeches on the topic (U.S. News and World Report, 1972, p. 69)

> Opponents of firearms laws insist that gun licenses and record-keeping requirements are burdensome and inconvenient. Yet, they don't object to licensing automobile drivers, hunters, or those who enjoy fishing. If the only price of gun licensing is record-keeping requirements, an inconvenience to gun users, then the public will have received a special bargain. Certainly, sportsmen will gladly tolerate minor inconvenience in order to protect the lives of their families, friends, and neighbors.

Senator Kennedy asserts that gun licensing is like automobile, hunting, and fishing licensing in the essential characteristic of inconvenience.

A Consideration in the Use of Analogy to Draw Conclusions

The main consideration in using analogies is the similarity of the cases you are using. Your reasoning does not hold if they are not *very closely* similar. In the school parking analogy, we would need to know more to assess the validity of the conclusion. Presumably the audience members should be familiar with both schools so they could assess whether they are similar in the important aspects. If they are, the analogy is valid. In the second example, the reasoning is very questionable. It seems obvious that family finances and state or federal government finances are very different. For example, families do not have to pay for national defense, they do not have to pay for most of the roads they drive on, and they cannot create money like the government can. We would have to classify this second analogy as a "false" analogy.

We are certainly not saying that analogies are a means of support to be avoided. Analogies are very powerful tools when use appropriately. Use an analogy if the essential elements of the situations are similar.

FALLACIES

A **fallacy** is a misleading or unsound argument. These are arguments to be avoided as you will see. We will address seven of these.

Ad Hominem

Ad Hominem is a Latin word that is translated as "against the man." This would mean an attack against the person, instead of attaching the other's argument. The speaker who falls into this fallacy, whether he or she intends this or not, leads the audience to focus on certain actions negatively because of an alleged character quirk or flaw in the person. You might hear something like this in a speech on protecting American businesses from environmental regulation. "You know, these regulations were created by the nature freaks and governmental bureaucrats who care more about saving a tree than allowing business to make a decent profit." Notice that there is no evidence presented in this statement. Instead, it is an attempt to discredit by name-calling. Obviously, there is no logical connection here. Perhaps another example will help clarify this type of reasoning. A persuader says, "Obviously you cannot trust anything the Senator says about this bill to alleviate poverty in the inner cities of our state. Remember that he comes from a wealthy family who has not experienced a day of being poor." This effort to transfer the focus of the issue to the "messenger" is dishonest and unethical and may be easily recognized by an audience member who is listening and evaluating carefully.

Red Herring

A red herring is a fish with a strong scent. The word comes from a practice many years ago when red herring was used to distract and divert dogs from the trail of game so that poachers could claim the prize for themselves. The poachers would drag the herring across the trail of the game so the dogs would encounter and follow it instead of the game. In public speaking, the **red herring** is an irrelevant issue that the speaker brings up to divert the audience's attention from the real issue. A speaker might say, "Why should we be devoting so much time and energy to the issue of endangered species of animals when we could use our energy, and ought to do so, to finding ways to reduce the killing of thousands of people in automobile accidents each year?"

Perhaps you can imagine a lawyer from a tobacco company presenting this argument. "I cannot understand why the government spends so much time and energy suing tobacco companies, claiming that tobacco is poisonous. It is clear that drunk driving is far more dangerous. Drunk drivers kill about 20,000 people each year and we do not see the government suing whisky makers." Clearly, this is another case in which the arguer is trying to divert the attention of the listeners to an irrelevant issue.

Either-Or

The **either-or fallacy** is one in which the speaker presents an issue as if there are only two options when, in truth, there are many more. In the 1960s a group arguing a civil rights issue claimed, "You are either for us or you are against us." Of course, they were trying to encourage those who were certainly not against them to join them in the cause or be "branded" as insensitive, uncaring about this important issue, and against them. Obviously there is a great deal of middle ground between these two positions. Most issues and problems are, in fact, complex— not a choice between this or that. We also heard recently, "We must raise taxes or cut services." Of course, this is over simplifying another issue. Perhaps cost saving plans can be put in place that do not require cutting services.

Bandwagon

An advertiser may point out that twice as many consumers use their product than the second most popular product. The underlying message is this: "Since twice as many consumers use our product it must be the better product. So, use our product." The **bandwagon fallacy** asks people to assume that since something is popular it is good, correct, or desirable and join in it. Popular following or opinion cannot be taken as proof. At one point in our history, it was a popular belief among a segment of the U.S. population that women should not attend college with men. As a result there were several colleges that only admitted women. Today, we doubt that you would want to jump on that bandwagon.

Slippery Slope

The slippery slope fallacy gets its name from the image of taking a step off level ground down a steep hill. Once the first step is taken, the person is committed and will have to take a second, third, and so forth, until reaching the bottom. Of course, the assumption is that when committed a person must continue or risk falling.

In persuasive speaking, the **slippery slope** refers to taking the first step with an issue and, because of taking that step, becoming committed to taking more and more steps. Those who oppose gun control have often argued, "Once you ban one type of gun, it is easier to go on and ban another. We must not take that first step because it can easily lead to violating our constitutional right to bear arms." Of course, it would seem that there is no evidence to support this assertion. If there is, the speaker needs to present it if his or her audience is to believe his or her reasoning.

Hasty Generalization

To **generalize** means to infer a principle or trend from facts, statistics, or the like. A **hasty generalization** is a conclusion that is reached based on insufficient evidence.

A speaker who was opposed to home schooling said, "Home schooling doesn't work. I know a child who is being home schooled and can't read or write at her grade level." Obviously, one case is not enough to make a valid argument about home schooling. The audience would have no reason to believe this is a typical case. This speaker would have to offer evidence that shows a considerable number of cases to support this assertion.

False Analogy

A **false analogy** is a claim that two situations are similar, based on minor similarities between two cases, when there are major differences that are being ignored.

One student presented an argument about dealing with crimes committed on cruise ships. He argued the U.S. victim's rights programs should be implemented on cruise ships because there are U.S. citizens aboard that need to be protected. He argued further that U.S. laws have been proven effective in the U.S and these should be implemented to protect them on these cruise ships.

What this student failed to understand is that these situations are not similar because cruise ships sail on international waters and many are registered in other countries. So, even if these programs have been effective in the U.S., it is unlikely that they could be implemented on cruise ships.

Now that you have a firm understanding of reasoning, we turn to our fourth strategy—emotions.

APPEALS TO EMOTIONS

Your audience may be convinced you have a point, that is they believe your arguments, but may not be moved to action. Why? Logic alone rarely moves an audience to action. Logic and emotion used together create a more powerful speech than logic alone. Rhetoricians have recognized this relationship for a very long time. George Campbell, an early, well-known rhetorician wrote, "When persuasion is the end, passion [emotion] also must be engaged" (Campbell, 1988). What does this tell you? You will make your persuasive speech more powerful and more successful if you figure out how to touch your audience's emotions.

Using Emotions to Persuade

What is an emotional appeal? In today's terminology an **emotional appeal** would be described as a psychological appeal. The speaker attempts to assess the audience's emotional state in relation to the topic and crafts an emotional appeal that targets those states.

Charles U. Larson (2012) believes that our emotional states are directly related to our values. He suggests we use the virtues cited by Aristotle to identify appropriate appeals to emotions. Here is Larson's analysis with each value identified by italic font:

1. *Justice* involves respect for laws, people's right to have what belongs to them, tolerance, and related attributes.
2. *Prudence* relates to how one gives advice or demonstrates good judgment. For example, former NBA star Dennis Rodman seemed to lack prudence, or good judgment, whereas, a seemingly humble star such as Michael Jordan is thought to have good judgment—as being prudent.
3. *Generosity* involves having an unselfish attitude at home, at work, in one's community, in government, or in international relations. This virtue lies behind the ongoing debate about the U.S. roles in the world's defense and environment. Are we to be the world's police force? How much leadership can we give to save the world's environment?

4. **Courage** means doing what you think is right, even under pressure—not backing away from unpopular issues or positions when we believe they are right. An example would be a President's veto of a popular bill because it violates some principle of fairness or wisdom.

5. **Temperance** includes self-restraint and moderation in areas of human conduct. The temperate person is in control of his or her emotions and desires. Such people are open-minded and willing to consider all sides of a situation and try to be empathic with the other person's point of view.

6. **Magnanimity** is the willingness to forgive and forget, the desire to seek ways to better the world, and the ability to rise above pettiness. The ability to be as gracious in losing as in winning is a sign of magnanimity. Politicians, athletes, and others must appear magnanimous—when they win, they complement their opponents, and when they lose, they must congratulate and vow to support the winner.

7. **Magnificence** is the ability to recognize and be committed to the better qualities in human beings and to encourage them. History abounds with examples of magnificent persuaders—Washington, Lincoln, Roosevelt, Crazy Horse, Martin Luther King, Jr., and others. Their magnificence came from their ability to encourage the best in themselves and others.

8. **Wisdom** is more than just knowledge or intelligence; it is associated with good judgment, character, and experience.

Logic and emotion used together create a more powerful speech than logic alone.

Here is an example from a speech by a student who closed her speech of disabled persons and how they are victimized with a powerful emotional appeal. See if you can identify which of these values were used in this appeal.

Linda Wilson, a woman who lives in Mobile, Alabama, has a partially paralyzed left leg. She is in a good deal of pain which she tries to beat back with medications. These medications only partly work so she is constantly in some pain. She has had hip surgery that is helping some with the pain, but needs a knee replacement. Walking is often very difficult for her and so she was able to secure a scooter to assist her and a lift for the back of her car to carry it. This is her only means to walk distances. If Linda did not have this scooter, she would not be able to visit stores and purchase the things she needs. This is because her long-distant walking ability is so difficult that she could not do it without her scooter. (We are so fortunate and do not always recognize this because we can easily secure from the various stores the necessities of daily life because we walk normally without any pain.)

Not long ago a lady crashed into the back of Linda's car, seriously damaging her lift and scooter. Linda got out of her car and walked as fast as she could toward the lady standing in the road. This lady, who crashed into the lift and scooter, jumped into her car, backed up and sped around Linda and her car, leaving the accident scene. The lady actually got away with this horrible deed.

Linda, who suffered the loss of her scooter's transportation, found that her insurance company would fix the lift and scooter, but it would cost her a $500 deductible—money that she really didn't have. What kind of human being would stoop this low and treat a disabled person this way?

This real-life story may seem to not be typical, but remember we have not heard the whole speech. The speaker made a case earlier about the number of disabled people in the U.S and how they were treated by those who were not disabled. Although we would like not to think about it, you or somebody you love could be the disabled person and a person victimized by uncaring people in our society. This story was a powerful emotional appeal to close this speech.

We think this real-life story appeals to four of values and emotions we spoke about, above. We see it as appealing to justice—respect for people; generosity—an unselfish attitude; courage—doing what is right; and magnificence—commitment to the better qualities of human beings. This is why this was a very powerful conclusion to the speech.

Ethics of Using Emotions to Persuade

Some people in our culture have suggested that emotional appeals are too powerful a weapon and should be avoided when a speaker is advocating his or her position. They suggest a speaker should stick to the facts and logical arguments. They point to people like Adolf Hitler and the forces of Nazism and the hatred he stirred with emotional appeals in Germany. Yes, it is impossible to deny the damage caused by Hilter's emotional appeals—these are powerful tools for persuasion. The problem here is not the emotional appeals, but the ethics of the speaker who is using them.

We believe when you make your case you should be operating on the basis of *magnificence*. In other words, we assume that you are committed to the better qualities in human beings and to encourage them. This would mean to us that your motives are for the good of your fellow human beings. Since this is the case, the answer of the question regarding use of emotional appeals rests on the type of persuasive speech you will deliver. We believe you should steer clear of emotional appeals it you are making a speech on a question of fact. These appeals are not necessary and only muddle the question of fact. Stick to the evidence in this type of speech. Emotional appeals are necessary when persuading on questions of policy. Emotional appeals are also necessary if you want your audience members to do something as a result of your persuasion. This means that they are almost always appropriate to a problem-solution speech when you want your audience to be involved in your solution.

Keep in mind that you always have the obligation to build a case for your appeal. This means you will also craft a speech that is grounded in facts and logic. Why is this so important? The reason is a very simple one, but important. You need to reach your audience on the logical *and* emotional level if you are to achieve the success you desire. Careful and thoughtful listeners will not appreciate your attempt to stir their emotions if you have not built a reasonable case for your proposition. Please remember you need to be ethical in your appeals so that you meet the standards we laid out for you in Chapter 2. Now, we move to the topic of needs—our final persuasive strategy.

APPEALS TO NEEDS

Your audience members will have some underlying motivations to buy into or not buy into your persuasive appeal. **Motivations** are the desires, drives or needs that move a person toward a goal or, perhaps, away from some negative outcome. You can build a stronger persuasive appeal and achieve the success you desire if you make use of the motivations that move them toward your persuasive appeal. Of course, the first step in achieving this aim is to understand what some of the common motivations or needs your audience may have.

Common Needs that Motivate People

Here are eight of the common needs that motivate people. Of course, there are more.

1. *Love and esteem are two of the most basic needs we experience.*

All of us want to love and be loved, to have good friends, and to be esteemed at work and in our social connections.

2. *Our health is of great concern to us.*

We all want to be reasonably free from sickness, to maintain our fitness and health, and to live a long time.

3. *Our safety is vital to our well-being.*

We want to be protected from violence and crime, and to be assured that products we use will not injure or kill us.

4. *We want to be successful.*

Success is one of the top aims of this book—to help you be successful in the public speeches you deliver. Of course, success may mean different things to different people. Yet, we can count on most people wanting to achieve the best possible outcome for themselves and ones they love.

5. *Self-improvement is important to us because we all want to be the best we can be.*

We are speaking of all areas of our life—learning a new skill, learning ways to cope with problems we are experiencing, achieving fulfillment in any area of our life.

6. *Financial security is something we all desire.*

This is one of the things that motivate us to seek a college degree. Financial security also allows us to secure things that can help us meet needs in several of these other areas.

7. *We need recreational pleasure and relaxation to balance our lives.*

You can easily see how this relates to other areas we have mentioned—health is one of these. We need to get away from the stress and our occupation with work and relax. Taking vacations, going to movies, eating out, and so forth, are all ways we achieve these needs.

8. *We all have a need to be altruistic—that is, to engage in unselfish concern for or devotion to the welfare of others.*

There are many circumstances that encourage us to be altruistic. This is what motivates you to send money or food to the victims of a hurricane or tornado or give blood or anything else you do for the welfare of others.

Using Needs to Persuade

There are two considerations that will help you achieve success in your effort to use needs to persuade. *First, appealing to multiple needs will help you motivate more listeners.* Audience members who are not reached by one motive may very well respond to another. It is just that simple. You increase your chance to persuade your audience.

Second, it should be clear to you that there are degrees of strengths among motivational appeals. You should attempt to identify not only the needs you can appeal to, but also the strength of those needs. Of course, be sure to appeal to the strongest motivations possible.

Ethics of Using Needs to Persuade

Being ethical in persuading is a big deal. Not being ethical can really sabotage your success. We pointed out the ethical considerations, above, when we discussed the ethics of appealing to emotions. What we said there applies here also. Thus, we conclude our discussion of persuasive strategies.

COUNTER PERSUASION

What would be your best tactic to arm your audience against those who seek to challenge an argument you make? Suppose you made a speech where the argument was against raising fees at your university. You would be wise to use the counter persuasion technique to help your audience hold fast to your position. **Counter persuasion**, also called **inoculating**, is a technique in which the speaker presents a message to his or her audience that is meant to forewarn them about attempts to refute the argument.

There are several strategies that you will find useful to accomplish counter persuasion aim. First, a straight-forward warning helps audience members resist. A direct warning might be, "My opponent will attack me and my argument." Another direct warning might be, "My opponent will tell you that I am being unrealistic about arguing to hold our fees where they currently are." This forewarning is equally effective whether the counter persuasion is imminent or will come later.

The other strategy you might employ is to arm your audience with arguments and knowledge that they can bring to the situation of counter persuasion. You could say, "My opponent is likely to argue that a fee increase is absolutely necessary. Here is the information that shows this is not true." [Present the information.] Benoit (1994) points to research conducted by Hirt and Sherman that found individuals who have greater knowledge are more resistant to refutational arguments. Thus, if you wish to increase the potential resistance to counter arguments, arm your audience with information about the issues.

SUMMARY

This chapter focused on helping you understand the many aspects of creating successful persuasive strategies. We began with the issue of building credibility. High credibility will lead you to a more persuasive argument. Credibility is based on expertise, knowledge, and intelligence with respect to your topic. Character is, perhaps, the most difficult of these to understand. It requires sincerity, delivering your speech well, truth-telling, and showing concern for the well-being of your audience. Beyond these we provided advice on ways to enhance your credibility. These include; explaining your competence, establishing common ground, showing open-mindedness, delivering your speech well, and use of strong evidence. You can strengthen your evidence by being specific, using credible sources, and being sure your evidences relates to the point you're making.

Next, we addressed strategies for creating effective reasoning. Reasoning is the process of drawing conclusions based on evidence. The specific kinds of reasoning are: reasoning from specific instances, reasoning from principle, reasoning from cause, and reasoning from analogy. Here are specific considerations we offered to allow you to use each kind of reasoning effectively.

Considerations for use of Specific Examples:

- Specific instances generally cannot stand alone.
- Do not make sweeping conclusions when your evidence does not support this.
- Avoid making hasty generalizations.

Considerations for use of Arguments from Principle:

- Discover what principles your audience may accept.
- Bolster the principle with additional evidence if you are concerned about their agreement.

Considerations for use of Causal Reasoning:

- There must be a number of cases where the cause and effect are closely linked.
- Ask if there are other things that might be causing the problem.
- Assess whether the effect may have multiple causes.

Considerations for use of Reasoning from Analogy:

- The two cases you are using for this kind of reasoning must be similar.
- A figurative analogy must be linked in a way that it creates understanding of one situation by referring to the other.

We next addressed fallacies. These are errors in the reasoning process. *Ad hominem* is an attack against the person, instead of attacking the other's argument. A *red herring* is an irrelevant issue the speaker brings up to divert the audience's attention from the real issue. An *either-or fallacy* is one in which the speaker presents an issue as if there are only two options when, in truth, there are many more. A *bandwagon fallacy* asks the audience to assume something popular is good, correct, or desirable and to join in it. A *slippery slope fallacy* refers to taking a first step in an issue and finding it difficult not to take more steps. A *false analogy* is a claim that two situations are similar, based on minor similarities between the two cases, when there are actually major differences being ignored.

A third strategy we addressed is the use of emotional appeals to persuade. Some central emotions that may be used are justice, prudence, generosity, courage, temperance, magnanimity, magnificence, and wisdom. We also identified needs that you can use to motivate your audience.

These include love and esteem, health, safety, success, self-improvement, financial security, pleasure and relaxation, and to be altruistic.

We advised you to avoid using emotional and need appeals when arguing a question of fact. We advised you to use these appeals in speeches advocating policies and attempting to move your audience to action.

REFERENCES

Beebe, S. A. (1974). Eye contact: A nonverbal determinant of speaker credibility. *Speech Teacher*, 23, 21–25.

Benoit, W. L. (1994). "Forewarning and Persuasion." In Alan. M. and Preiss, R. W. (eds.) *Forewarning and persuasion: Advances through meta-analysis.* Dubuque, IA: Brown and Benchmark, pp. 159-184.

Campbell, G. (1988). *The philosophy of rhetoric.* Bitzer, L. F. (ed.). Carbondale, IL: Southern Illinois University Press, p. 77.

Hall, E. (1959). *The silent language.* Garden City, NY: Doubleday.

Larson, C. U. (2012). *Persuasion: Reception and responsibility,* 13th ed. Belmont, CA: Wadsworth.

Kelly, F. D. (1972). Communication significance of therapist proxemic cues. *Journal of Counseling and Clinical Psychology*, 39, 345.

Meyers, P., & Nix, S. (2011). *As we speak: How to make your point and have it stick.* New York: Atria Books, p. 113.

O'Keefe, D. J. (2002). *Persuasion: Theory and research,* 2nd ed. Thousand Oaks, CA: Sage, (pp. 182–184).

Perloff, R. M. (1993). *Dynamics of persuasion.* Hillsdale, NJ: Lawrence Erlbaum, 145–149.

Reinard, J. C. (1988). The Empirical study of the persuasive effects of evidence: The status after fifty years of research. *Human Communication Research*, 15, 37–38.

Reynolds, R. A. & Reynolds, J. L. (2002). Evidence. In Dillard, J. P. and Pfau, M. (eds.), *The persuasion handbook: Developments in theory and practice.* Thousand Oaks, CA: Sage, pp. 429–430.

Wilson, G. L. (2011). *Let's talk it over: Communication in interpersonal relationships,* 7th ed. Boston: Pearson.

Chapter 17
Speaking on Special Occasions

Courtesy of Stock Foundry/Alamy.

A special occasion speech turns out to be an important assignment. This is your opportunity to shine since this is often an honor to be selected for this type of speech. There are a variety of speeches in this category—all of which are designed for a different purpose from informative to persuasive speeches. These speeches often serve the general purpose of celebration. Graduations, award ceremonies, weddings, christenings, inaugurals, retirement dinners, and funerals are occasions of this type. Funerals may not seem to you to be a time of celebration, but they are often seen as a time to celebrate the person's life.

A graduation address is given to inspire graduates to achieve their best as they reach out to future goals. An employee is honored for his or her achievements as employee of the year. A family member gives a toast to the bride and groom. A family celebrates the sacrament of infant baptism. A president delivers an inaugural address to share his or her vision for the next four years. An endeared employee retires and is honored for years of devoted service. A eulogy is given to honor the life of a deceased loved one. There are many occasions for this type of speech, so we hope you can see the likelihood is high for you to have the opportunity to give one. You will want to be successful on these important occasions.

This chapter addresses the speech of introduction, the speech of presentation, the speech of acceptance, the speech of commemoration, the speech of eulogy, the speech of inspiration, and the after-dinner speech.

THE SPEECH OF INTRODUCTION

You are making a **speech of introduction** when you present a speaker to an audience. This may be a very simple introduction like, "Ladies and Gentlemen, the President of the United States." It is obvious that the President is well-known and so does not need more of an introduction. A longer introduction under these circumstances would be ill-advised.

Most other situations will call for more than brevity. Long-winded introductions, however, are not in order. Your job is to set the stage for the speaker, so no more than two or three minutes is enough. This speech may be shorter if the speaker is well-known.

Your main tasks are to gain the attention of the audience and arouse interest in the speaker and his or her topic. Here is an elaboration on what this means.

Research the Background of the Speaker

You will want to do research into the background of the speaker so that you can draw attention to some of his or her accomplishments. Of course, this research may not be necessary if you already know the speaker well. In this case, you may want to ask the speaker if there are special accomplishments he or she wishes to be cited. You might also ask if a résumé is available. A final source of information is to ask the event organizer what about the speaker should be cited. Of course, be sure to get the information correctly so you will not embarrass yourself or the speaker.

Adapt Your Presentation to the Audience

Ask yourself what connection the speaker has with the audience. Put yourself in the place of an audience member. What would you want to hear about the speaker? What makes this speaker particularly interesting or special to the audience?

Adapt Your Presentation to the Speaker

Generally, it is a great idea to check with the speaker to ensure what you are going to say fulfills his or her expectation. Perhaps something could be added to emphasize what will be presented in the speech. Perhaps you have exaggerated his or her accomplishments. This could very well embarrass the speaker. Perhaps you are going to include some personal information about the speaker. The speaker may see your remarks in poor taste if they are too personal. If what you have said distresses the speaker, there may be a few awkward moments as the speech begins.

Create a Sense of Anticipation

If the speaker is not well-known to your audience, just some significant information about the person's credentials as related to the topic will suffice. On the other hand, if the speaker is well-known to the audience, you may have to dig a bit deeper for something that will create a sense of anticipation. You might talk to the speaker beforehand to discover some interesting, but not generally known facts that connect the speaker and his or her topic.

Do not start out your speech by naming the speaker. Save this for the last lines of your introduction, unless there is some reason to do otherwise. Your last words should be to welcome the speaker and include his or her name. Say, something like, "Please join me in welcoming the well-known author of the Harry Potter series, J. K. Rowling."

Speeches of introduction are not usually elaborate since the expectation is that they will be brief. Here is an example of a typical speech of introduction.

> Our speaker tonight is best known for being the state's foremost expert on criminal liability. In addition to being an attorney, she is also the mother of two children, so she shares our deep concern for the rights of children. Her grandfather lived in Loxley, and she tells me she still remembers the delicious Loxley strawberries that she enjoyed as a child. Let's welcome Judge Donna DeOliveria whose heritage is linked to our community. She will speak on the topic, "Law and Disorder."

SPEECHES OF PRESENTATION

The **speech of presentation** is given to acknowledge some achievement. The introduction to various Academy Award Oscar winners is a well-known presentation of this type. Here are some considerations you will want to address when you give this speech.

Explain the Significance of the Award

There are several ways you might accomplish this. You might, for example, name some of the well-known recipients of the award. You might emphasize prestige surrounding the award.

Tell Why the Person or Group is Receiving the Award

Here you might speak of or announce the other nominees for the award if that is appropriate. You might also briefly review the criteria for giving the award and tell how the awardee fulfills these standards of excellence.

Here is a speech of presentation that was delivered by President Bill Clinton when he presented the Congressional Gold Medal to South African President Nelson Mandela at a ceremony in the Rotunda of the United States Capitol in Washington, D.C.

> To my friend, President Mandela, Americans as one today, across all the lines that divide us, pay tribute to your struggle, to your achievement, and to the inspiration you have given us to do better. Today we offer a man who has received the Nobel Prize, the highest honor within the gift of this country. . . .
>
> Those of us who share his vision and lift him up in honor today owe it to him to build a permanent partnership between Americans and Africans—for the education of our children, for the solution of our problems, for the resolution of our differences, for the elevation of what is best about us all. . . .

In forgiving those who imprisoned him, he reminded us of the most fundamental lesson of all—that in the end apartheid was a defeat of the heart, the mind, the spirit. It was not just a structure outside and jail houses within which people were kept; it was a division of the mind and soul against itself. We owe it to Nelson Mandela not simply to give him this award. But to live by the lesson he taught us and to tear down every last vestige of apartheid in our own hearts—everything that divides us, one from another. For those of us who have been privileged to know this remarkable man, no medal, no award, no fortune, nothing we could give him could possibly compare to the gift he has given to us and to the world. The only gift that is true recompense is to continue his mission and to live by the power of this profound and wonderful example.

Now, as prescribed by the law, it is my privilege to present the Congressional Gold Medal to President Nelson Mandela.

THE SPEECH OF ACCEPTANCE
The purpose of a **speech of acceptance** is to give thanks for an award. Sometimes you will be receiving a prize or gift. Here are some things you will want to accomplish in this speech.

Thank Those Who Have a Part in Bestowing the Award
There are two groups of people you would generally recognize—those who have selected you for the award and those who have helped you achieve the award. Beyond this you should plan to say what achieving the award means to you from a personal perspective, both now and into the future.

The Difficulty with this Speech
This speech can be difficult because you want to express your gratitude without sounding as if you are egotistical. Don't exaggerate your appreciation. Doing this often sounds insincere and so will detract from the honor. Also, be brief. Most audiences will have the expectation to hear a few sincere remarks.

Here is the acceptance speech delivered by Nelson Mandela upon receiving the Congressional Gold Medal Award. This acceptance speech is a bit lengthy, but the occasion would seem to warrant this kind of response.

Thank you, President Clinton, Mr. Speaker, distinguished members of the Senate and the House, ladies and gentlemen . . .

It has been my great privilege to serve the people whose bondage to an inhumane system evoked the solidarity of all those who love freedom and justice, a people whose triumph over the divisions of racist doctrine has given new life to humanity's hope for a world without hatred and discrimination. I am conscious that in bestowing the Congressional Gold Medal upon me you are evoking these bonds between our nations and paying tribute to the whole South African nation for its achievements in realizing our shared ideals.

It is in that spirit that I humbly accept the award, aware at the same time of the great honor you do me by using me as the vehicle of a unique distinction conferred by this hallowed institution of American democracy. As one who has dedicated his life to the pursuit of unity, I am moved by the consensus in your nation's regard for the achievements of my people. And I feel a great pride in the fact that with a few citizens of other countries who have received this high honor, the name of an African is now added.

President Mandela is known for both strength and humility.

The award with which you honor me today is an expression of the common humanity that binds us, one person to another, nation to nation, and people of the north to people of the south. I receive it with pride as a symbol of partnership for peace, prosperity, and equity as we enter the new millennium. I thank you.

THE COMMEMORATIVE SPEECH

A **commemorative speech** is sometimes called a speech of tribute. These are speeches of praise or celebration that honor a person, group of people, or an idea. Examples of these would be a Memorial Day address, Fourth of July speeches, testimonial addresses, a tribute to a person retiring, or a eulogy. Here are some basics for you to consider in constructing these speeches.

Stir Sentiments and Feelings

This is a speech of celebration, so you will want to convey joy and hope. This is why the speaker at a memorial service will approach his or her remarks as a celebration of the person's life. Your purpose is to inspire the attendees to sense the goodness of the person and his or her achievements.

Likewise, you would express your good wishes and the anticipation of a bright future if you were delivering a commencement address. It is a celebration of the years of hard work and the excitement the future will bring.

Do Research to Secure Supporting Materials

It is the supporting material that makes this kind of speech excellent—like every great informative speech. It is the details of a person's accomplishments, the way the person lived his or her life, that makes a great speech of tribute. You will want to include some memorable quotations from people who are close to the person being honored. These are the kind of things that reveal the essence of the person. This advice also holds true for a speech you would craft to honor the fiftieth year of your school or university.

One of the great speakers of our time was President Ronald Reagan. During his term of office, the United States experienced the tragedy of the space shuttle *Challenger* exploding when it lifted off. The whole thing was witnessed by many Americans who were watching the liftoff on national television.

Notice that he called these astronauts by name. Notice also that he calls them heroes and brave and dedicated pioneers.

He tells the families who lost loved ones that we feel their loss, even if we cannot bear it as they do. He also attempts to help the school children of the country understand the tragedy as painful, but that painful things happen. He declares that tragedies like these are part of the process of exploration and discovery.

His closing is especially powerful. Reagan provides an excellent comparison. Notice, especially, his eloquent, moving, and poetic wording in the final sentence of this speech.

Here is a transcript of President Reagan's speech commemoration from the video, Great Speeches, Volume V.

> Ladies and gentlemen, I'd planned to speak to you tonight to report on the State of the Union but the events of earlier today have led me to change those plans. Today is a day for mourning and remembering. Nancy and I are pained to the core by the tragedy of the shuttle *Challenger*. We know we share this pain with all the people of our country. This is truly a national loss.
>
> Nineteen years ago, almost to the day, we lost three astronauts in a terrible accident on the ground. But we've never lost an astronaut in flight; we've never had a tragedy like this. And perhaps we've forgotten the courage it took for the crew of the shuttle; but they, the *Challenger* seven, were aware of the dangers, but overcame them and did their jobs brilliantly. We mourn seven heroes: Michael Smith, Dick Scobee, Judith Resnik, Ronald McNair, Ellison Onizuka, Gregory Jarvis, and Christa McAuliffe. We mourn their loss as a nation together.
>
> [For] the families of the seven, we cannot bear, as you do, the full impact of this tragedy, but we feel the loss, and we're thinking about you so very much. Your loved ones were daring and brave, and they had that special grace, that special spirit that says, "Give me a challenge and I'll meet it with joy." They had a hunger to explore the universe and discover its truths. They wished to serve, and they did. They served all of us.

We've grown used to wonders in this century. It's hard to dazzle us, but for twenty-five years the United States space program has been doing just that. We've grown used to the idea of space, and perhaps we forget that we've only just begun. We're still pioneers. They, the members of the *Challenger* crew, were pioneers.

And I want to say something to the school children of America who were watching the live coverage of the shuttle's takeoff. I know it is hard to understand, but sometimes painful things like this happen. It's all part of the process of exploration and discovery. It's all part of taking a chance and expanding man's horizons. The future doesn't belong to the fainthearted; it belongs to the brave. The *Challenger* crew was pulling us into the future, and we'll continue to follow them.

President Reagan was well-known for his excellent speeches.

I've always had great faith in and respect for our space program, and what happened today does nothing to diminish it. We don't hide our space program. We don't keep secrets and cover things up. We do it all up front and in public. That's the way freedom is, and we wouldn't change it for a minute.

We'll continue our quest in space. There will be more shuttle flights and more shuttle crews and, yes, more volunteers, more civilians, more teachers in space. Nothing ends here; our hopes and our journeys continue.

I wish to add that I wish I could talk to every man and woman who works for NASA or who worked on this mission and tell them: "Your dedication and professionalism have moved and impressed us for decades. And we know your anguish. We share it."

There's a coincidence today. On this day 390 years ago, the great explorer Francis Drake died aboard ship off the coast of Panama. In his lifetime the great frontiers were the oceans, and an historian later said, "He lived by the sea, died on it, was buried in it." Well, today we can say of the *Challenger* crew: Their dedication was, like Drake's—complete.

The crew of the space shuttle *Challenger* honored us by the manner in which they lived their lives. We will never forget them, nor the last time we saw them, this morning, as they prepared for their journey and waved goodbye and "slipped the surly bonds of earth" to "touch the face of God."

You may listen to the entire speech at www.historyplace.com/speeches/reagan-challenger.htm.

Lest you think that crafting a speech such as this is beyond you, consider this first-hand experience and a tribute, presented by a student, telling how family can be experienced in the face of a devastating natural disaster—Hurricane Katrina.

Here's to You Kat

[Introduction] "I seldom end up where I wanted to go, but almost always end up where I needed to be." This is a quote from Douglas Adams, a well-known British author, accessed from thinkexist.com. The concept of fate, destiny, or whatever you prefer to call it, exudes in daily life in blessings, miracles, celebrations, grievances and distress.

For me, it took moving to a new part of the country. Within two months my life was changed forever by only four feet of water and hurricane-force winds. I remember the day vividly—August 29, 2005—a day most everyone can recall, a day that the entire gulf coast underwent a natural disaster. I remember vividly the distress I felt, for other families whose losses exceeded my own, and for my own family and our new home that succumbed to Katrina.

I remember the damage vividly. But the most powerful memory I have is watching the pile of our debris stack on the side of the road of the saturated dry wall and insulation and how hollow I felt. I also remember vividly the process of rebuilding not only our home but our life. Although Hurricane Katrina wreaked havoc, the experience changed my life and the way I looked at life. The event influenced my perspective. It revealed the true meaning of family and it encouraged me to be a "survivor."

[Transition] The most profound effect Hurricane Katrina had upon me was my perspective.

[Body; Main Point 1] Katrina made me experience for the first time loss. She influenced my perspective in a positive manner, enlightening me. She changed the way I approached devastation. I had never experienced natural disaster. I had to choose to wallow in pain, or be buoyant and give my all to improve the situation for my family and me. I had to physically and emotionally rebuild my life. She changed the way I perceived my destiny. Things happen for a reason. Search for it, learn from it and embrace it. Everyone experiences both good and bad. Destiny is unknown for an individual, but is right in the end.

She changed my demeanor. I focused more on my attitude towards things and had to transition from negative to positive. Things aren't always as they appear. I needed to stop being so detached from life and dig deeper for meaning and purpose. It instilled in me a key value of performance at home, in my academics and in relationships.

[Transition] Also key in perspective is appreciation.

[Main Point 2] Hurricane Katrina further stressed the value and role of family in my life. It is a common saying that you can choose your friends, but not your family. My mother quoted this to me since I was 22 months, when my first brother was born. My family will always be involved in my life, so I need to show them more gratitude. Friends can be close, but the bond and love within a family is the greatest of all. While I had always adored my family, I never realized how much they contributed to my character. They keep me buoyant. They support me in all my endeavors. They keep me busy and give me feedback. There are eight of us. I am the oldest of six. Being the oldest, I have to set an example. I have to take the initiative to help get things done. Even though there are so many of us, Katrina made me realize the company my family gave me and how lonely I would be without them. We are a quilt. We need all the pieces to function as a network warm with love.

[Transition] Katrina emphasized my family in my life, as well as acceptance and rising to the occasion.

[Main Point 3] Hurricane Katrina encouraged me to accept that sometimes lousy things happen and that I am a survivor. Situations in your life can't define who you are as a person, but rather your reaction and attitude towards it. Yes, our home was damaged, but I didn't let her become an excuse to perform less in other aspects of my life. One must think rationally and act thoughtfully. More often than not, how someone receives and responds to destined events is most defining to their character and determining fate, rather than what that destiny is. You can achieve anything or make anything of yourself. You can rise above your situation and improve it the best you can. Take responsibility. You control your actions; you are the final motivator. Take the initiative. The sooner you get up and are optimistic, the sooner laughter and joy will flow back into your life. Healing is a timely process. It's okay to cry. Just do your best to compose yourself. Practice gratitude in all aspects of life.

[Conclusion] All in all, Hurricane Katrina was a devastating event that stripped me of everything allowing me to evaluate myself and discover the true values in life.

Hurricane Katrina was a natural disaster that shook the entire gulf coast. My welcome wagon, her winds and waves damaged our new home. But in cleaning the debris, I came to new insight, new appreciation for my family and a proactive approach to coping with devastation.

So, here's to you Kat. You destroyed my life. You made moving to a new part of the country even more overwhelming. You took my comfort from me-- a nice home, a comfortable bed and roomy kitchen. I loathe you for the damage you caused in so many lives. I resent you for the pain you put me through.

But, here's to you Kat. To you I raise my gratitude. You were in my destiny, to my dismay, but I didn't let you control my fate. But I was meant to be here and you delivered the message I didn't know I needed to hear. So, for you Kat, here is my final statement, one that is inspired by you: Yes, good can sprout from bad. The manure of life can be rank, but from it, too, a rose can grow. The thorns are a memory of pain passed. The bloom is vibrant and sweet smelling, a new and beautiful life!

THE SPEECH OF EULOGY

A special type of the speech to commemorate is the eulogy. The **eulogy** is a tribute in which you seek to praise someone who died. This is a celebration of the person's life in which you draw attention to how this person was special to you and others he or she knew. You might deliver this speech at the person's funeral service or on an anniversary of the person's birth or death. This speaking opportunity is a time for praise. In fact, the word, eulogy, comes from the Greek word that means "to praise." You will find this to be a challenging speech when you have the opportunity to give it because the person was likely to be a close friend and your job will be to console close family and friends while commemorating and celebrating the person's life.

There are two points to keep in mind as you construct this speech.

Give Specific Examples of the Person's Life

You will want to point out the accomplishments of this person and put them in a positive light. Keep in mind that this is not a biography of the person's life. Focus on the significant aspects of the person's life. Frequently asked questions that point you in the right direction are, "How did the person enrich our lives? What inspiration or lessons can we draw from the person's life?"

Balance Effective Delivery and Your Emotional State

There can be a tendency if the person was close you to become overly emotional. Your assignment is to help the audience members be inspired by the person's life and closure, not being drug down by the loss. Do your best to stay in control.

Here is a eulogy written by Megan Sparks to honor her Aunt Florence.

Aunt Florence

Before preparing this brief speech I asked myself, "How will Aunt Florence be remembered?" A few qualities immediately came to my mind.

Aunt Florence was dedicated.

She was welcoming and caring.

She was smart and determined.

The last quality is the love she shared with her husband of seventy years, John.

Dedicated Aunt

Aunt Florence's house was the central hub. The entire extended family would gather at her house. We would eat, play cards and visit each other. Many happy memories were made on Erskine Boulevard.

We always had slumber parties as kids at Aunt Florence and Uncle John's home. We loved going to her house because we could drink as much soda pop and eat as much junk food as we pleased. In addition, we could stay up as late as we wanted. And then when we finally did get up in the morning, there was a breakfast feast waiting for us.

As the nieces and nephews grew older, we didn't play cards quite as much. But she still was feeding us and telling us stories about our grandparents and the good ole days. We'd stay up to all hours looking at old photographs and just talking. Those are the memories we will keep safe. To say she was good to her nieces and nephews is an understatement. She brought the family together and opened her home to us all.

Caring

Aunt Florence had a very rare talent. She cared for the sick in a compassionate manner. Her mother lived with her for the last several years of her life. She took care of other family members in their time of need. She cared for her sister, Dorothy, when she was battling cancer. She cared for her sister-in-law, Thelma, when she was sick as well. Her brother, Ed, lived with her in his last years as well. I always admired how there was never a hesitation. If a family member needed help, she was there willing to serve and never complained. She had a selfless attitude as the caretaker of the family.

Smart and Determined

Not only was Aunt Florence welcoming and caring but she was also very smart and determined. She was the valedictorian of her high-school class. She was extremely sharp and no one could take advantage of her. She was independent. She worked as a book keeper for a plumbing company. I am sure every penny was accounted for. She was meticulous and took pride in every aspect of her life.

The Love of Her Life

Aunt Florence and Uncle John had a deep love for each other. It's hard to remember one without the other. They were an amazing couple. They complemented each other so well. Aunt Florence was more outspoken and direct; Uncle John was calm, gentle, and easy going. Both had such wonderful spirits.

[End with a poem...]

In those quiet moments in the still of the night
Remember to rejoice and celebrate life
Do not think of me gone and weep
I am not there, I do not sleep
I am a thousand winds that blow

I am the diamond glints on snow
I am the sunlight on the grain
I am the gentle autumn's rain
When you awaken in the morning hush
I am the swift uplifting rush
of quiet birds in flight
I am the soft stars that shine
You will hear my gentle voice
and remember to rejoice
Never give up your fight
and remember always
to Celebrate Life.

-- Author Unknown

THE SPEECH OF INSPIRATION

You will find the speech of inspiration is one of the more common special occasion presentations. The **speech of inspiration** has as its aim to inspire and raise the spirits of an audience. A most familiar setting for this type of speech is in religious venues.

A sales manager might use an inspirational speech to introduce a new product to the marketing department, highlighting its competitive advantages and potential because of its "cutting edge" features. The aim is to inspire them, and thus encourage them to help the product reach its full potential. The goal, of course, is to raise their enthusiasm high and cause them to work with "great zeal" to identify potential customers.

This kind of speech might be delivered in times of adversity to challenge the audience to be strong. One such speech was delivered on April 17, 2007, by Nikki Giovanni, Virginia Tech faculty member and poet. Her purpose was to encourage the university community to be strong in the wake of 32 students and faculty being killed at the college.

This kind of speech might also be delivered at a political convention to praise the party and inspire the candidates and delegates to strive to put out their best effort to win the election. Major addresses at conferences often fall into this category too. One such address was presented by Hillary Rodham Clinton to the United Nations Fourth World Conference on Women at Beijing, China.

Here are several goals you will want to keep in mind when you are called upon to deliver a speech of inspiration.

Touch the Deep Feelings of Your Audience

The speech of inspiration relies heavily on pathos. Notice that Chapter 16, Persuasive Strategies, addressed the power of an emotional appeal. Inspiring your audience has more to do with the emotions than it has to do with logic.

Some common emotional appeals are these. Appeal to:

- Justice
- Prudence
- Generosity
- Courage
- Temperance
- Magnanimity
- Magnificence
- Wisdom

You might choose to review these emotional states addressed in Chapter 16.

Your Credibility is a Key

Often these speeches urge purer motives and harder effort and remind us of the common good. To arouse such feelings the audience members often have to identify with the speaker. Credibility is an issue because of this. Your audience must respect you if they are to be positively disposed to follow your urgings. For help on this topic, refer to Chapter 16 where we discussed ways to build your credibility.

Use Language that Appeals to Emotional States

Emotional states are aroused by vivid illustration, stories and artful use of repetition, alliteration, metaphor and parallelism in your language. Real-life stories are especially powerful appeals to emotional states. We are moved by examples of ordinary people who strive to succeed, whether that be overcoming adversity or achieving their dreams. An excellent example of this is our President introducing ordinary people who have achieved great things as illustrations when delivering the State of the Union address.

Use a Vigorous Delivery Style

A speech that lacks energy will lose its potential persuasive punch. You will have to be enthused if your audience is to be enthused. This is an essential characteristic of an inspirational speech.

Close with Inspiring Ending

Ask your audience to rise to the challenge. Ask them to achieve excellence. Quote something or somebody's inspiring words. For example, the late Martin Luther King, Jr. ended his "I Have a Dream" speech by quoting an old Negro spiritual, "Free at last! Free at last! Thank God almighty, we are free at last!"

We urge you to make use of this information when creating a speech of inspiration. We will leave this topic by providing two examples of excellent speeches of this kind. The first is by Nikki Giovanni and the second is by Hillary Rodham Clinton.

We are Virginia Tech

Nikkki Giovanni, April 17, 2007

We are Virginia Tech.

We are sad today, and we will be sad for quite a while. We are not moving on, we are embracing our mourning.

We are Virginia Tech.

We are strong enough to stand tall tearlessly, we are brave enough to bend to cry, and we are sad enough to know that we must laugh again.

We are Virginia Tech.

We do understand this tragedy. We know we did nothing to deserve it, but neither does a child in Africa dying of AIDS. Neither do the invisible children walking the night away to avoid being captured by the rogue army, neither does the baby elephant watching his community being devastated for ivory, neither does the Mexican child looking for fresh water, neither does the Appalachian infant killed in the middle of the night in his crib in the home his father built with his own hands being run over by a boulder because the land was destabilized. No one deserves a tragedy.

We are Virginia Tech.

The Hokie Nation embraces our own and reaches out with open hearts and hands to those who offer their hearts and minds. We are strong, and brave, and innocent, and unafraid. We are better than we think and not quite what we want to be. We are alive to the imaginations and the possibilities. We will continue to invent the future through our blood and tears and through all our sadness.

We are the Hokies.

We will prevail.

We will prevail.

We will prevail.

We are Virginia Tech.

Hillary Clinton is known to be a strong advocate for women and children

Address to the United Nations Fourth
World Conference on Women

Hillary Rodham Clinton

An excerpt. . .

As an American, I want to speak up for women in my own country—women who are raising children of the minimum wage, women who can't afford health care or child care, women whose lives are threatened by violence, including violence in their own homes.

I want to speak up for mothers who are fighting for good schools, safe neighborhoods, clean air and clean airwaves; for older women, some of them widows, who have raised their families and now find that their skills and life experiences are not valued in the workplace; for women who are working all night as nurses, hotel clerks, and fast food cooks so that they can be at home during the day with their kids; and for women everywhere who simply don't have time to do everything they are called upon to do each day.

It is also a coming together, much the way women come together every day in every country.

Whether it is while playing with our children in the park, or washing clothes in a river, or taking a break at the office water cooler, we come together and talk about our aspirations and concerns. And time and again, our talk turns to our children and our families. However different we may be, there is far more that unites us than divides us. We share a common future. And we are here to find common ground so that we may help bring new dignity and respect to women and girls all over the world—and in so doing, bring new strength and stability to families as well.

By gathering in Beijing, we are focusing world attention on issues that matter most in the lives of women and their families: access to education, health care, jobs and credit, the chance to enjoy basic legal and human rights and participate fully in the political life of their countries.

There are some who question the reason for this conference.

Let them listen to the voices of women in their homes, neighborhoods, and workplaces.

There are some who wonder whether the lives of women and girls matter to economic and political progress around the globe.

Let them look at the women gathered here and at Huairou—the homemaker, nurses, teachers, lawyers, policymakers, and women who run their own businesses.

It is conferences like this that compel governments and people everywhere to listen, look and face the world's most pressing problems.

Wasn't it after the women's conference in Nairobi ten years ago that the world focused for the first time on the crisis of domestic violence?

Earlier today, I participated in a World Health Organization forum, where government officials, NGOs, and individual citizens are working on ways to address the health problems of women and girls.

Tomorrow, I will attend a gathering of the United Nations Development Fund for Women. There, the discussion will focus on local—and highly successful—programs that give hard-working women access to credit so they can improve their own lives and the lives of their families.

What we are learning around the world is that if women are healthy and educated, their families will flourish. If women are free from violence, their families will flourish. If women have a chance to work and earn as full and equal partners in society, their families will flourish. And when families flourish, communities and nations will flourish.

That is why every woman, every man, every child, every family, and every nation on our planet has a stake in the discussion that takes place here.

AFTER-DINNER SPEECHES

After dinner speeches are also referred to as speeches to entertain. The **after-dinner speech** strives to make a serious point even though they have the purpose of entertaining. This suggests that they are not rambling or frivolous, even though the treatment of the topic is light.

The name, "after dinner," comes from the early tradition in England, during the early 1800s, where the speeches were delivered after dinner. The tradition has changed so you are likely to find this kind of speech delivered after any meal.

The audience's expectation is that they will not hear a presentation about weighty issues, but a light speech that includes humor. However, any topic that is suitable for an informative or persuasive speech is suitable for an after dinner speech as long as you treat it in a lighthearted manner. A major difference between this kind of speaking and other kinds of speaking is that the supporting material is chosen primarily for its entertainment value. Although your treatment of the topic will often be described as light and whimsical, the organization of it should not be rambling. This speech requires careful preparation and organization.

Make a Serious Point

All speeches are delivered to make a point. The after-dinner speech is not an exception to this rule. Consider what your thesis statement will be. You probably will not explicitly state this as you would in other speeches, but by the end of your speech the point should be clear. You should strive in your speech to make a thoughtful point.

Using Humor

Your speech is not to be a stand-up comedy routine. Rather it should include humor that will cause smiles and chuckles with occasional laughter. Some of us find it difficult to create a speech that will evoke laughter. That is okay. Laughter is not essential in this type of speech. You will do just fine if you create an interesting speech with vivid and colorful details and clever phrasing.

Recognize the Occasion

An after-dinner speech is often centered on some occasion. Your audience is gathering for an event. Recognize the event and be sure to make mention of it in your speech.

Here is an excellent example of an after dinner speech.

Assumptions
A National Championship Speech, 1987

Kim Roe

When I was about this tall, no, that was last year. [Laughter] When I was about this tall, my mom used to buy me story-records-with-bing-turn-the-page-go-along books. You know them, you loved them, you had them. Allow me to share with all of you one of my favorite books, Goldilocks and the Three

Bears. The three bears and a blond bimbo meet in a bedroom. [Laugher] And Goldilocks, trembling with anticipation ran into her mother's arms and said, "Bing turn the page." [Laughter]

Naturally, I assumed that this was the ending, the climax, Goldilocks catharsis. And even when I played it backwards it said: Mersh dea shea ner Goldilocks is Satin. [Laughter and applause.] Which wasn't as important to what I had done. I had assumed.

And I am assuming that you're all assuming that my speech is on assuming. Can I make that assumption? I assume so. When an assumption is made it lays the foundation for disappointment. And I'm sure we've all heard that when we assume we make an ass out of you and me—and well that's pretty much about it. [Laughter]

To better understand assumptions let's first take a look at, well, why we make asses out of ourselves, how it affects you, and ways to stop. Written, directed, and delivered by me. [Laughter]

Now I have to believe that each and every one of you here today already knows what an assumption is. And, if you don't, at least you have a good example of one. [Laugher] Some would go as far as to say, "What Assumptions! Phaat." And if you're one of those you just might want to get that checked out. [Laugher] Or, check out this true historical example. President Franklin Delano Roosevelt left a stack of papers on his desk with the top page saying, "Watch the borders." A presidential advisor, upon seeing this, quickly sent troops to secure the Mexican border. And, that wouldn't have been such a bad idea except that "Watch the borders" had been left for FDR's typist. And as my mother would've said, "Damn it to hell, somebody's going to get an ass-chewing." [Laughter]

One assumption. A potential disaster. One big question, why? Why do we make asses out of ourselves? Well, one reason is that we, for the most part being normal human beings, like very little surprise in our lives. [Not] knowing what is out there, or what's in store for the future, or what really goes into a hot dog, is frightening. We feel the need to fill the gaps in our lives with our assumptions.

Another reason why we assume is that there has been a lack of communication and understanding. Now, a prime example of this can be seen through the story of the Trojan Horse.

"Yo, fellow Trojans. A gift has been bestowed—A gift—We just got a present."

"Read the card, read the card!"

"Who's it from, who's it from?" [Laughter]

And as we all know that was one trick pony. [Laughter]

And finally, we assume because we rely on past experience and knowledge. And it's fair to say whenever Geraldo Rivera bursts on the screen to unveil another fast-breaking news story, the networks assume the ratings will go sky-high. So, I too, like millions, tuned in to watch his riveting on-the-spot coverage of the uncovering of Al Capone's vault. Which turned out to be as entertaining as paste. [Laughter] As did Geraldo's underwear when he opened that empty vault. [Laughter] [Nothing there.]

As children we are taught that monkeys live on bananas alone. But movies such as Planet of the Apes contradict this assumption.

"Cornelius, [Laughter] would you like a Chicken McNugget? [Laughter] So right away we assume and fill in the gaps and probably don't know all the facts, and, hell, I like Roddy McDowell. [Laughter]

Now that we know why we assume, let's see how it affects you, oh, what the heck, me too. Usually, negative.

Assumptions can hurt us interpersonally, inside, right here where it counts, because we read into something, because deep down we want it to turn out our way. And when that doesn't happen we feel hurt and disappointed. And believe me, I know, because I have always thought that I could sing, so naturally I assumed that I was going to get a part in my ninth grade variety show, especially singing this beautiful love ballad. [Laughter]

I'd like to dedicate this to my boyfriend, Chuck. [Laughter] "Some say love, [Laughter] it is a river that drowns a tender reed. [Laughter] But with the sun's love, in the spring it becomes a rose." [Applause] I ushered, rather than sing. [Laughter]

Now, assumptions can not only affect ourselves but others as well through stereotyping. There is this guy in my high school—some called him Pete. He was the president of the chess club, math club, Eagle Scout Troop 411, and the head hall monitor. I don't think you understand; you see Pete monitored everyone in the hall. [Laughter]

What do you assume? (A) Pete's athletic, and beside his chess knowledge, he's one lady-killer. (B) Well, Pete's a partier, and after a rough day in the hall, hey, it's Miller time. (C) Ha. Ha. Ha. Pete's hung like a horse. [Laughter]

Now, although stereotyping can be harmful, or gosh, pretty darn entertaining as well, misunderstood conclusions can lead to disaster. To illustrate, let's look at a page in history. [Laughter] You might want to stand up in the back. Okay, let's talk about it. Well, it's an average size piece of paper and it's got some bold letters on it and a lot of words on it. The year, 1948. The event, the presidential election.

The assumer was the Chicago Tribune. Now this newspaper released over one hundred thousand copies each with the headline, "DEWEY DEFEATS TRUMAN." Dewey lost the election. I'm sorry. I don't care how charismatic he was, who would ever vote for Donald Duck's nephew? I mean Huey and Louie, maybe Dewey? He was like Pete. He was a dork of a duck. He is a dork of a duck.

And from this example we can see that assuming can lead to big problems. And because I said it was a problem, you probably think there's going to be a solution. Well look, I don't want you to leave empty-handed so let me give you some simple solutions, and I'm not talking saline. [Laughter] Well, I guess that one just leads itself to it. [Laughter] Oh, they were written by me.

First of all, our assumptions come from an alternate source, and it's important for us to evaluate and validate our sources. For example, my Aunt Beulah told me that professional wrestling is real. Now, do I consider my aunt, who is also an ex-roller derby queen to be a reliable source? Well, yeh. She's toothless, but she's family. [Laughter] And besides, to see Aunt Beulah fly across the room and complete that flying-scissor-hook-combination-body-slam makes you want to believe.

So after you have considered the source, get accurate information. Because acting upon an assumption can lead to real disaster. I didn't want to be in that show anyway!!! [Laughter] If they could see me now. [Laughter]

So what's the point? An assumption in itself is harmless. It's harmful when acted upon. Quite simply, don't act upon assumptions. Consider the source, find out the information, get the facts, and act upon well-thought-out, educated information. And, hopefully, with this information we can turn our misplaced assumptions into directed conclusions. So that we no longer have to hear that when we assume we make an ass out of you and, oh all right, me too. But only once.

Well, my Kimberly. You certainly have filled us in on assumptions. And all in less than ten minutes. Simply amazing.

Don't put me on the spot silly-artificial-story-telling voice; just turn the page. Bing. Kim's speech is over. [Applause]

SUMMARY

The special occasion speech turns out to be an important assignment. This is an opportunity to shine since it is often an honor to be selected for this type of assignment. These speeches so often serve the general purpose of celebration. This chapter addressed the speech of introduction, the speech of presentation, the speech of acceptance, the speech of commemoration, the speech of eulogy, the speech or inspiration, and the after-dinner speech.

A speech of introduction presents a speaker to an audience. The main tasks are to gain the attention of the audience and arouse interest in the speaker and his or her topic. This requires research into the background of the speaker, adapting the presentation to the audience, and creation of a sense of anticipation.

A speech of presentation is given to acknowledge some person's achievement. The introduction to various Academy Award Oscar winners is a well-known presentation of this type. The speaker should explain the significance of the award and tell why the person (or group) is receiving it.

The acceptance speech gives thanks for an award. Sometimes it will be thanks for a prize or gift. The speaker will want to thank those who have had a part in bestowing the award. Recognize that this speech can be difficult because the speaker wants to express gratitude without sounding egotistical.

A commemorative speech is sometimes called a speech of tribute. These are speeches of praise or celebration that honor a person, group of people, or an idea. The two basic considerations in constructing these speeches are the need to stir sentiments and feelings and collecting information to adequately present the person's accomplishments.

A special type of commemorative speech is the eulogy. The eulogy is a tribute in which the speaker seeks to praise someone who died. This is a celebration of the person's life in which the speaker draws attention to how this person was special. This speech might be delivered at the person's funeral service or on an anniversary of the person's birth or death. This speaking opportunity is a time for praise. Two points to remember are to give specific examples of the person's life and to seek balance between effective delivery and the speaker's emotional state.

The speech of inspiration is one of the more common special occasion presentations. This speech has as its aim to inspire and raise the spirits of the audience. Several goals the speaker should keep in mind are to touch the deep feelings of the audience, establish credibility, use language that appeals to emotional states, use a vigorous delivery style, and close with an inspiring ending.

Finally, we addressed after-dinner speeches. These speeches are also referred to as speeches to entertain. They strive to make a serious point even though they have the purpose of entertaining. This suggests that they are not rambling or frivolous, even though the treatment of the topic is light. A major difference between this kind of speaking and other kinds is that the supporting material is chosen primarily for its entertainment value. Although the treatment of the topic can be described as light and whimsical, the organization should not be rambling.

GLOSSARY

abstract   type of summary of the content of the article that may be written by someone other than the author.

active listening   a listening technique that requires you to "will yourself" to pay attention. This means to pull your mind to what the speaker is saying and force yourself to keep it there. One way to do this is to review in your mind what the speaker has been saying.

ad hominem   a Latin word that is translated as "against the man." This would mean an attack against the person, instead of attacking the other's argument.

after-dinner speech   a speech that strives to make a serious point even though it has the purpose of entertaining.

application speech   a type of speech that is part of a class of demonstration speeches.

appreciative listening   listening we do for enjoyment or pleasure.

articulation   the degree to which we pronounce letters in words correctly and clearly.

atlas   a book that provides maps of the world.

attending   the selective act of focusing on stimuli.

attention getter   the opening of a speech; its goal is to increase the audience's interest level and encourage them to listen to the rest of the speech.

attitude   where your audience stands on a continuum from in favor to opposed to your topic and ideas.

attitude modification   accomplished by allowing you to complete several lessons on how to develop a speech, and then allowing you to complete drill and practice sessions until you are comfortable with the speech.

audience-centeredness   planning a speech so that it relates to the audience's experience. In other words, what you say connects with the experience of the members of your audience.

bandwagon   a fallacy. Asking people to assume that since something is popular it is good, correct, or desirable and join in it.

bar graph   consists of horizontal or vertical bars that contrast two or more variables.

brainstorming   a timed procedure for generating a large number of ideas quickly. It's important to remember that the goal of brainstorming is quantity, not quality.

brief example   a short, specific instance.

captive audience   a situation where the people are required to attend a speech. Your classmates compose a captive audience, as do your colleagues if your boss requires them to attend a presentation.

card catalog   a system of indexing collections of books by devoting a single card to each holding, such as books in a collection. Libraries housed these in cabinets with numerous drawers filled with alphabetized cards

causal pattern   shows the cause and effect of a situation or phenomena. In short, it looks at why something happens and the impact of it.

causal reasoning   attempts to establish a relationship between causes (the impetus for something) and its effects.

channels   the mediums through which the messages are sent and they can be verbal (a radio program) or nonverbal (a newspaper).

character   in persuasive speaking this is seen as the speaker's sincerity, trustworthiness, and concern for the well-being of the audience.

chronological pattern   organizes main points based on time, sequence or steps.

cliché   an expression whose effectiveness has been lost due to overuse.

clearinghouse question   asks the interviewee to talk about something you failed to ask.

cognitive restructuring   a strategy that helps you replace irrational thoughts with rational ones. For example, you can accomplish this by identifying negative self-statements and replacing them with positive statements.

colloquialism   an expression that is appropriate to everyday speech, but not to formal speaking or writing.

community   a group of people with a common background or with a shared interest.

comparative advantage   a consideration of two or more alternatives to demonstrate that the argument being advocated is better than the others.

comparison   a process of examining two items by pointing out their similarities. The speaker uses a familiar object, person, place or concept to help the audience understand an unknown object, person, place or concept.

competence   in persuasive speaking this factor is related to three things—expertise, knowledge of the subject and intelligence.

comprehensive listening   involves listening for understanding of the message.

conclusion   statements at the end of a speech that are used to summarize the points made during the speech. It often has a concluding statement that ties the speech together.

connotation   the emotional overtones that an individual associates with the word.

context   where communication takes place.

contrast   a process of showing the difference between two or more things, ideas, factors, or issues.

counter persuasion   (often called inoculating) a technique in which the speaker presents a message to his or her audience that is meant to forewarn them about attempts to refute his or her argument.

credibility   the degree to which a receiver finds a speaker to be believable. This believability is based on the speaker's perceived competence and character.

credibility statement   an explanation as to why the speaker is qualified in regard to the topic.

critical listening   sometimes called discriminative listening. What we engage in when evaluating a message for the purpose of accepting or rejecting it.

decoding   the listeners interpreting the verbal and nonverbal content of a message to give it meaning.

definition   explains the essential qualities of a word or terminology. It often determines the boundaries of the term—what is in and what is out. In other words, it tells what the term means and what it does not.

delivery   the vehicle speakers use to transmit ideas to listeners and it is both verbal and nonverbal.

delivery outline   a more condensed version of the formal outline using short words and phrases to guide the speaker during his or her presentation.

demographic analysis   a technique used to draw inferences about your audience based on categories of information you have available. This analysis allows you to make decisions about various aspects of your speech as related to your audience.

demonstrate   to show how something is done, how something works or how something is made. The goal of a demonstration speech is to teach the audience how something works or how to do something—to create understanding or provide application.

denotation   the literal meaning or dictionary meaning of a word.

description speech   an informative speech designed to provide a clear picture of a person, place or event.

dictionary definitions   a formal and concise statement of the meaning of a word.

either-or fallacy   a statement in which the speaker presents an issue as if there are only two options when, in truth, there are many more.

emotional appeal   a psychological appeal.

empathic listening   hearing and understanding a person, thereby providing emotional support for the speaker. When a friend comes to you to talk about a problem he or she is experiencing, empathic listening is in order.

encoding   putting ideas or information into specific language the sender selects to convey his or her ideas.

enunciation refers to how we articulate and pronounce words.

ethical communication is that which fosters "truthfulness, fairness, responsibility, personal integrity, and respect for self and others"

ethical listening   behaving responsibly when receiving and processing what the speaker is saying.

ethos   the character of the speaker.

etymology   defining a word by telling the history of the word.

example   a specific case used to represent or illustrate an idea, condition, experience or a group of people.

exercise anorexia   a medical condition brought on by taking exercise to the extreme so that it becomes dangerous to the person's health.

expert testimony   a quotation or paraphrase of a statement by an acknowledged authority in his or her field.

expertise   the significant skill or knowledge gained from a person's extensive study, observation of the topic and credentials. The speaker is experienced with the subject or proficient in the skills suggested by the topic.

explanation   an elaboration on an idea with the purpose of making it understandable and clear.

extemporaneous delivery   speaking with carefully planning and practice, using brief notes to deliver a speech.

extended example   a narrative or story developed at some length with more detail than a brief example. Telling a story is an excellent use of this technique.

eye contact   direct, visual contact with another's eyes.

fallacy a misleading or unsound argument.

false analogy a claim that two situations are similar, based on minor similarities between two cases, when major differences are being ignored.

feedback the information the receiver sends back to the sender to let the speaker know how well the message is being understood. Feedback can be verbal (an answer "yes" to a question) or nonverbal (a smile).

figurative analogy claims two things are similar, but only in certain essential aspects.

focus group a gathering of selected individual participants who are encouraged to talk in an unstructured way about questions posed by a facilitator.

follow-up secondary questions asked in an interview to expand on a primary question.

formal outline a formatted full-sentence, content plan of your speech ideas.

frame of reference our personal set of interlocking facts, ideas, beliefs, values, and attitudes that we use to filter what we hear and then make sense of it if we allow it to register in our brain.

functional one of the best ways to define a word is to use the word in context.

gazetteer a geographical dictionary.

general encyclopedias a book that provides general information about what is known, arranged alphabetically by topic.

hasty generalization a conclusion that is reached based on insufficient evidence.

hypothetical example an imaginary example that is based on fact and, therefore, plausible.

impromptu speaking speaking "off the cuff;" a casual speech delivered with little or no time for preparation.

indirect methods observations made by asking people other than the targeted group to provide information or reviewing written documents to gather information

informative speech a presentation intended to help an audience gain understanding.

inoculating a technique in which the speaker presents a message to his or her audience that is meant to forewarn them about attempts to refute his or her argument.

intelligence in persuasive speaking it is the understanding of how to craft an excellent argument.

internal summary a transitional device that gives a thorough recap of the main point before moving on to another idea.

jargon technical language of a group of people.

knowledgeable   a person has significant understanding of the topic or issue because of his or her research and, possibly, direct experience with it.

line graph   uses a horizontal and a vertical scale to show trends and the relationship between two variables.

listening   an active process of receiving verbal and nonverbal messages. It has five components: sensing, attending, understanding, remembering and responding, each of which is essential to effective listening.

literal analogy   comparison in which identical items are asserted to be alike and therefore useful for basing a conclusion.

main points   major ideas that flow from the thesis statement. They elaborate on or develop the statement. Main points express the key ideas of the speech and directly support the thesis statement.

manuscript speaking   a presentation by reading a text which has been prepared in advance.

memorable ending   a final statement that emphasizes the overall purpose of the speech.

memorized speaking   a presentation from memory using a prepared written text that is repeated from memory.

message   the information the sender and receiver send to each other. These messages can be verbal (talking) and/or nonverbal (a head nod).

Monroe's Motivated Sequence   Alan Monroe (1935) developed the motivated sequence pattern of persuasio. The sequence follows the stages of thinking people often go through while advocating a position.

motivations   desires, drives or needs that move a person toward a goal or, perhaps, away from some negative outcome.

name-calling   the use of abusive words to demean or defame another person.

negation   definition by negation clarifies a meaning of a word by telling what something is not.

noise   any interference that distorts the message exchange. It can be physiological or psychological. Noise can be internal (thought processes) or external (the hum of an air conditioner).

pandering   merely telling an audience what you think they want to hear or indicating agreement with the audience on all issues when you really don't.

paraphrasing   restatement, rewording or a summary in your own words of what somebody said or something printed in a text.

passivity syndrome   condition where the listener believes that the speaker is entirely responsible for the meaning and does not participate actively because of this belief.

pauses   the silence between words which are important for effective speech delivery.

peer testimony   support of a fact or statement that is given by ordinary people like us. Of course, we may have credentials in some area to warrant expert status.

persuasive speech   a presentation designed to influence an audiences' beliefs, attitudes or actions.

physical noise   distractions from such things aches, pains, or other discomforts like a room that is so hot that people are feeling uncomfortable and sleepy.

pie chart   a circle representing 100 percent and divided into segments of various sizes.

piecing together   selecting material from several sources, taking them word for word and joining them together in a way that makes sense. It is often referred to as "cut and paste."

pitch   described as the highness or lowness of the tone of our voices.

plagiarism   the act of using another's ideas or language as if it is your own.

posture   the position or bearing of your body. There are two extremes with posture—rigidity and sloppiness.

preparation outline   consists of short sentences and phrases to help guide you in developing a formal outline. A preparation outline is much like a rough draft.

preview statement   a sentence or sentences that alerts the audience to the main points of the speech. The preview statement prepares the audience for what they will hear and also gives them a structure of the speech.

primary question   the initial question used in an interview for an area of your topic.

problem to solution   a pattern used in constructing a speech that divides information into two main sections. One section describes the extent of and harm created by a problem. The other section advocates a solution.

problem-cause-solution   a pattern used in constructing a speech where the speaker is advocating a change by an institution or organization. The first main point presents the problem needing to be addressed, along with arguments about its

problem-solution pattern   a speech construction that establishes a problem or dilemma and then offers an answer or fix to the problem or issue.

projector   a device that uses lenses and light to project an enlarged image on to a screen.

pronunciation   a contrast to articulation, refers to how the letters of a word sound and where the stress falls when the word is spoken.

psychological noise   distractions that come from worry or concern. These concerns occupy some of the psychological space that would normally be devoted to listening to the speaker.

public speaking   the process of speaking to a group of people in a structured, deliberate manner that is intended to inform, persuade, or entertain listeners.

quoting   the use of another's exact words or a text.

reasoning from analogy   argument that compares two similar cases of something.

reasoning from principle   an argument that begins with an idea that is believed to be affirmed by audience members (an idea about how something is—the principle), and then moves to a presumed specific incident of that principle, with a conclusion that

reasoning   the process of drawing conclusions based on evidence.

receiver   the person who listens to the message (the decoder).

red herring   an irrelevant issue that the speaker brings up to divert the audience's attention from the real issue.

relaxation techniques   help you reduce your apprehension by helping you associate relaxed feelings, instead of anxious feelings, with public speaking.

remembering   the process of recalling by an effort of memory.

repetition   articulating words, phrases or sentences the exact same way in different instances to make impact and enhance communication.

responding   giving observable feedback to a speaker.

restatement   reinforcement of an idea using different words that communicate a similar message.

rhetorical question   an inquiry that does not seek a response. Its purpose is for the audience to reflect about the subject material before the speaker discusses it.

search engine   an Internet device that uses a key work or words based on what you type in the search box to retrieve information. One commonly used search engine is Google.

selective attention   suggests that we focus on something to the exclusion of other things.

sender   the person who talks or sends the message (the encoder).

sensing   receiving information through the five senses.

shared meaning   both the sender and receiver have a similar understanding of the messages delivered in the communication.

sincere   a state in which the speaker is being genuine, earnest and free from falseness (truth-telling).

slippery slope   refers to taking the first step with an issue and, because of taking that step, becoming committed to taking more and more steps.

spatial patterns   information is arranged based on physical space, direction or location. For example, you could arrange your main points based on physical space such as West to East, inside out or top to bottom.

specialized encyclopedias   books that provide in-depth coverage of a particular field of study.

specific instance   a brief example of something.

speech of acceptance   a speech given to give thanks for an award, prize, or gift.

speech of commeration   a speech of tribute, praise, or celebration that honors a person, group of people, or an idea.

speeches of definition   a presentation used when the speaker's aim is to clarify the meaning of a word, phrase or idiom. A definition-type informative speech usually focuses on an object, an event, or an idea.

speeches of eulogy   A tribute in which the speaker praises and honors someone who died.

speeches of inspiration   a speech that has the purpose of inspiriing and raising the spirits of an audience.

speeches of introduction   a speech where you present a speaker to an audience.

speeches of presentation   a speech given to acknowledge some person's achievement.

statistics   numerical ways of summarizing information or facts.

stimulus   something that incites your senses to their functional activity. We think primarily of audio and visual stimuli, but of course there are others.

sub points   ideas that provide proof or evidence to bolster your main points.

supporting material   information that expands on the main and sub points. It is meant to explain the point, provide an illustration or example of the point, and/or provide evidence as proof of an argument made by the point.

template   a list of all the components of the speech from the introduction to the conclusion used by a speaker to plan his or her presentation.

testimony   the statement or declaration of a witness, often used in support of a fact or statement. Testimonies can come from peers or experts.

thesis statement   an idea presented in a single sentence that reveals the core idea of a speech.

topical pattern   planning a presentation by dividing the thesis statement into subtopics or categories.

transactional   a back and forth "negotiation" of meaning. The speaker and listener are responding to each other as they seek to create a common understanding.

transitions   words, phrases or sentences that connect one idea to the other.

understanding   the interpretation and evaluation of what you choose to attend to.

visual aid   any physical item that reinforces the speaker's ideas visually.

visualization   a technique used to help reduce communication apprehension by helping you create, or recreate, sensations associated with your speaking experience.

volume   the loudness or softness of your speaking voice.

yearbooks   annual publications that report information from the previous year.

Index

Speaker's Name: _____

Was the thesis/central idea clear?
☐ Yes   ☐ Improve   ☐ No
Was there a clear pattern of organization?
☐ Yes   ☐ Improve   ☐ No
Was there support for the information?
☐ Yes   ☐ Improve   ☐ No
Was the overall delivery strong?
☐ Yes   ☐ Improve   ☐ No
Were the transitions clear?
☐ Yes   ☐ Improve   ☐ No
Did the conclusion reiterate the theme of the speech?
☐ Yes   ☐ Improve   ☐ No
Did the speaker make eye contact with the audience?
☐ Yes   ☐ Improve   ☐ No

Name two (or more) things the speaker did exceptionally well.

Name two (or more) things the speaker needs to work on for next time.

Speaker's Name: _____

Was the thesis/central idea clearly stated?
☐ Yes   ☐ Improve   ☐ No
Was there a clear pattern of organization?
☐ Yes   ☐ Improve   ☐ No
Was there support for the information?
☐ Yes   ☐ Improve   ☐ No
Was the overall delivery strong?
☐ Yes   ☐ Improve   ☐ No
Were the transitions clear?
☐ Yes   ☐ Improve   ☐ No
Did the conclusion reiterate the theme of the speech?
☐ Yes   ☐ Improve   ☐ No
Did the speaker make eye contact with the audience?
☐ Yes   ☐ Improve   ☐ No

Name two (or more) things the speaker did exceptionally well.

Name two (or more) things the speaker needs to work on for next time.

Speaker's Name: _____

Was the thesis/central idea clear?
☐ Yes   ☐ Improve   ☐ No
Was there a clear pattern of organization?
☐ Yes   ☐ Improve   ☐ No
Was there support for the information?
☐ Yes   ☐ Improve   ☐ No
Was the overall delivery strong?
☐ Yes   ☐ Improve   ☐ No
Were the transitions clear?
☐ Yes   ☐ Improve   ☐ No
Did the conclusion reiterate the theme of the speech?
☐ Yes   ☐ Improve   ☐ No
Did the speaker make eye contact with the audience?
☐ Yes   ☐ Improve   ☐ No
Name two (or more) things the speaker did exceptionally well.

Name two (or more) things the speaker needs to work on for next time.

Speaker's Name: _____

Was the thesis/central idea clear?
☐ Yes   ☐ Improve   ☐ No
Was there a clear pattern of organization?
☐ Yes   ☐ Improve   ☐ No
Was there support for the information?
☐ Yes   ☐ Improve   ☐ No
Was the overall delivery strong?
☐ Yes   ☐ Improve   ☐ No
Were the transitions clear?
☐ Yes   ☐ Improve   ☐ No
Did the conclusion reiterate the theme of the speech?
☐ Yes   ☐ Improve   ☐ No
Did the speaker make eye contact with the audience?
☐ Yes   ☐ Improve   ☐ No
Name two (or more) things the speakers did exceptionally well.

Name two (or more) things the speaker needs to work on for next time.

Speaker's Name: _____

Was the thesis/central idea clear?
☐ Yes   ☐ Improve   ☐ No
Was there a clear pattern of organization?
☐ Yes   ☐ Improve   ☐ No
Was there support for the information?
☐ Yes   ☐ Improve   ☐ No
Was the overall delivery strong?
☐ Yes   ☐ Improve   ☐ No
Were the transitions clear?
☐ Yes   ☐ Improve   ☐ No
Did the conclusion reiterate the theme of the speech?
☐ Yes   ☐ Improve   ☐ No
Did the speaker make eye contact with the audience?
☐ Yes   ☐ Improve   ☐ No

Name two (or more) things the speaker did exceptionally well.

Name two (or more) things the speaker needs to work on for next time.

Speaker's Name: _____

Was the thesis/central idea clearly stated?
☐ Yes   ☐ Improve   ☐ No
Was there a clear pattern of organization?
☐ Yes   ☐ Improve   ☐ No
Was there support for the information?
☐ Yes   ☐ Improve   ☐ No
Was the overall delivery strong?
☐ Yes   ☐ Improve   ☐ No
Were the transitions clear?
☐ Yes   ☐ Improve   ☐ No
Did the conclusion reiterate the theme of the speech?
☐ Yes   ☐ Improve   ☐ No
Did the speaker make eye contact with the audience?
☐ Yes   ☐ Improve   ☐ No

Name two (or more) things the speaker did exceptionally well.

Name two (or more) things the speaker needs to work on for next time.

Speaker's Name: _____

Was the thesis/central idea clear?
☐ Yes   ☐ Improve   ☐ No
Was there a clear pattern of organization?
☐ Yes   ☐ Improve   ☐ No
Was there support for the information?
☐ Yes   ☐ Improve   ☐ No
Was the overall delivery strong?
☐ Yes   ☐ Improve   ☐ No
Were the transitions clear?
☐ Yes   ☐ Improve   ☐ No
Did the conclusion reiterate the theme of the speech?
☐ Yes   ☐ Improve   ☐ No
Did the speaker make eye contact with the audience?
☐ Yes   ☐ Improve   ☐ No
Name two (or more) things the speaker did exceptionally well.

Name two (or more) things the speaker needs to work on for next time.

Speaker's Name: _____

Was the thesis/central idea clear?
☐ Yes   ☐ Improve   ☐ No
Was there a clear pattern of organization?
☐ Yes   ☐ Improve   ☐ No
Was there support for the information?
☐ Yes   ☐ Improve   ☐ No
Was the overall delivery strong?
☐ Yes   ☐ Improve   ☐ No
Were the transitions clear?
☐ Yes   ☐ Improve   ☐ No
Did the conclusion reiterate the theme of the speech?
☐ Yes   ☐ Improve   ☐ No
Did the speaker make eye contact with the audience?
☐ Yes   ☐ Improve   ☐ No
Name two (or more) things the speakers did exceptionally well.

Name two (or more) things the speaker needs to work on for next time.

Speaker's Name: _____

Was the thesis/central idea clear?
☐ Yes　　　☐ Improve　　　☐ No
Was there a clear pattern of organization?
☐ Yes　　　☐ Improve　　　☐ No
Was there support for the information?
☐ Yes　　　☐ Improve　　　☐ No
Was the overall delivery strong?
☐ Yes　　　☐ Improve　　　☐ No
Were the transitions clear?
☐ Yes　　　☐ Improve　　　☐ No
Did the conclusion reiterate the theme of the speech?
☐ Yes　　　☐ Improve　　　☐ No
Did the speaker make eye contact with the audience?
☐ Yes　　　☐ Improve　　　☐ No

Name two (or more) things the speaker did exceptionally well.

Name two (or more) things the speaker needs to work on for next time.

Speaker's Name: _____

Was the thesis/central idea clearly stated?
☐ Yes　　　☐ Improve　　　☐ No
Was there a clear pattern of organization?
☐ Yes　　　☐ Improve　　　☐ No
Was there support for the information?
☐ Yes　　　☐ Improve　　　☐ No
Was the overall delivery strong?
☐ Yes　　　☐ Improve　　　☐ No
Were the transitions clear?
☐ Yes　　　☐ Improve　　　☐ No
Did the conclusion reiterate the theme of the speech?
☐ Yes　　　☐ Improve　　　☐ No
Did the speaker make eye contact with the audience?
☐ Yes　　　☐ Improve　　　☐ No

Name two (or more) things the speaker did exceptionally well.

Name two (or more) things the speaker needs to work on for next time.

Speaker's Name: _____

Was the thesis/central idea clear?
☐ Yes　　　☐ Improve　　　☐ No
Was there a clear pattern of organization?
☐ Yes　　　☐ Improve　　　☐ No
Was there support for the information?
☐ Yes　　　☐ Improve　　　☐ No
Was the overall delivery strong?
☐ Yes　　　☐ Improve　　　☐ No
Were the transitions clear?
☐ Yes　　　☐ Improve　　　☐ No
Did the conclusion reiterate the theme of the speech?
☐ Yes　　　☐ Improve　　　☐ No
Did the speaker make eye contact with the audience?
☐ Yes　　　☐ Improve　　　☐ No
Name two (or more) things the speaker did exceptionally well.

Name two (or more) things the speaker needs to work on for next time.

Speaker's Name: _____

Was the thesis/central idea clear?
☐ Yes　　　☐ Improve　　　☐ No
Was there a clear pattern of organization?
☐ Yes　　　☐ Improve　　　☐ No
Was there support for the information?
☐ Yes　　　☐ Improve　　　☐ No
Was the overall delivery strong?
☐ Yes　　　☐ Improve　　　☐ No
Were the transitions clear?
☐ Yes　　　☐ Improve　　　☐ No
Did the conclusion reiterate the theme of the speech?
☐ Yes　　　☐ Improve　　　☐ No
Did the speaker make eye contact with the audience?
☐ Yes　　　☐ Improve　　　☐ No
Name two (or more) things the speakers did exceptionally well.

Name two (or more) things the speaker needs to work on for next time.

Speaker's Name: _____

Was the thesis/central idea clear?
☐ Yes　　☐ Improve　　☐ No
Was there a clear pattern of organization?
☐ Yes　　☐ Improve　　☐ No
Was there support for the information?
☐ Yes　　☐ Improve　　☐ No
Was the overall delivery strong?
☐ Yes　　☐ Improve　　☐ No
Were the transitions clear?
☐ Yes　　☐ Improve　　☐ No
Did the conclusion reiterate the theme of the speech?
☐ Yes　　☐ Improve　　☐ No
Did the speaker make eye contact with the audience?
☐ Yes　　☐ Improve　　☐ No

Name two (or more) things the speaker did exceptionally well.

Name two (or more) things the speaker needs to work on for next time.

Speaker's Name: _____

Was the thesis/central idea clearly stated?
☐ Yes　　☐ Improve　　☐ No
Was there a clear pattern of organization?
☐ Yes　　☐ Improve　　☐ No
Was there support for the information?
☐ Yes　　☐ Improve　　☐ No
Was the overall delivery strong?
☐ Yes　　☐ Improve　　☐ No
Were the transitions clear?
☐ Yes　　☐ Improve　　☐ No
Did the conclusion reiterate the theme of the speech?
☐ Yes　　☐ Improve　　☐ No
Did the speaker make eye contact with the audience?
☐ Yes　　☐ Improve　　☐ No

Name two (or more) things the speaker did exceptionally well.

Name two (or more) things the speaker needs to work on for next time.

Speaker's Name: _____

Was the thesis/central idea clear?
☐ Yes　　☐ Improve　　☐ No
Was there a clear pattern of organization?
☐ Yes　　☐ Improve　　☐ No
Was there support for the information?
☐ Yes　　☐ Improve　　☐ No
Was the overall delivery strong?
☐ Yes　　☐ Improve　　☐ No
Were the transitions clear?
☐ Yes　　☐ Improve　　☐ No
Did the conclusion reiterate the theme of the speech?
☐ Yes　　☐ Improve　　☐ No
Did the speaker make eye contact with the audience?
☐ Yes　　☐ Improve　　☐ No
Name two (or more) things the speaker did exceptionally well.

Name two (or more) things the speaker needs to work on for next time.

Speaker's Name: _____

Was the thesis/central idea clear?
☐ Yes　　☐ Improve　　☐ No
Was there a clear pattern of organization?
☐ Yes　　☐ Improve　　☐ No
Was there support for the information?
☐ Yes　　☐ Improve　　☐ No
Was the overall delivery strong?
☐ Yes　　☐ Improve　　☐ No
Were the transitions clear?
☐ Yes　　☐ Improve　　☐ No
Did the conclusion reiterate the theme of the speech?
☐ Yes　　☐ Improve　　☐ No
Did the speaker make eye contact with the audience?
☐ Yes　　☐ Improve　　☐ No
Name two (or more) things the speakers did exceptionally well.

Name two (or more) things the speaker needs to work on for next time.

Speaker's Name: _____

Was the thesis/central idea clear?
☐ Yes   ☐ Improve   ☐ No

Was there a clear pattern of organization?
☐ Yes   ☐ Improve   ☐ No

Was there support for the information?
☐ Yes   ☐ Improve   ☐ No

Was the overall delivery strong?
☐ Yes   ☐ Improve   ☐ No

Were the transitions clear?
☐ Yes   ☐ Improve   ☐ No

Did the conclusion reiterate the theme of the speech?
☐ Yes   ☐ Improve   ☐ No

Did the speaker make eye contact with the audience?
☐ Yes   ☐ Improve   ☐ No

Name two (or more) things the speaker did exceptionally well.

Name two (or more) things the speaker needs to work on for next time.

Speaker's Name: _____

Was the thesis/central idea clearly stated?
☐ Yes   ☐ Improve   ☐ No

Was there a clear pattern of organization?
☐ Yes   ☐ Improve   ☐ No

Was there support for the information?
☐ Yes   ☐ Improve   ☐ No

Was the overall delivery strong?
☐ Yes   ☐ Improve   ☐ No

Were the transitions clear?
☐ Yes   ☐ Improve   ☐ No

Did the conclusion reiterate the theme of the speech?
☐ Yes   ☐ Improve   ☐ No

Did the speaker make eye contact with the audience?
☐ Yes   ☐ Improve   ☐ No

Name two (or more) things the speaker did exceptionally well.

Name two (or more) things the speaker needs to work on for next time.

Speaker's Name: _____

Was the thesis/central idea clear?
☐ Yes   ☐ Improve   ☐ No

Was there a clear pattern of organization?
☐ Yes   ☐ Improve   ☐ No

Was there support for the information?
☐ Yes   ☐ Improve   ☐ No

Was the overall delivery strong?
☐ Yes   ☐ Improve   ☐ No

Were the transitions clear?
☐ Yes   ☐ Improve   ☐ No

Did the conclusion reiterate the theme of the speech?
☐ Yes   ☐ Improve   ☐ No

Did the speaker make eye contact with the audience?
☐ Yes   ☐ Improve   ☐ No

Name two (or more) things the speaker did exceptionally well.

Name two (or more) things the speaker needs to work on for next time.

Speaker's Name: _____

Was the thesis/central idea clear?
☐ Yes   ☐ Improve   ☐ No

Was there a clear pattern of organization?
☐ Yes   ☐ Improve   ☐ No

Was there support for the information?
☐ Yes   ☐ Improve   ☐ No

Was the overall delivery strong?
☐ Yes   ☐ Improve   ☐ No

Were the transitions clear?
☐ Yes   ☐ Improve   ☐ No

Did the conclusion reiterate the theme of the speech?
☐ Yes   ☐ Improve   ☐ No

Did the speaker make eye contact with the audience?
☐ Yes   ☐ Improve   ☐ No

Name two (or more) things the speakers did exceptionally well.

Name two (or more) things the speaker needs to work on for next time.

Speaker's Name: _____

Was the thesis/central idea clear?
☐ Yes ☐ Improve ☐ No
Was there a clear pattern of organization?
☐ Yes ☐ Improve ☐ No
Was there support for the information?
☐ Yes ☐ Improve ☐ No
Was the overall delivery strong?
☐ Yes ☐ Improve ☐ No
Were the transitions clear?
☐ Yes ☐ Improve ☐ No
Did the conclusion reiterate the theme of the speech?
☐ Yes ☐ Improve ☐ No
Did the speaker make eye contact with the audience?
☐ Yes ☐ Improve ☐ No

Name two (or more) things the speaker did exceptionally well.

Name two (or more) things the speaker needs to work on for next time.

Speaker's Name: _____

Was the thesis/central idea clearly stated?
☐ Yes ☐ Improve ☐ No
Was there a clear pattern of organization?
☐ Yes ☐ Improve ☐ No
Was there support for the information?
☐ Yes ☐ Improve ☐ No
Was the overall delivery strong?
☐ Yes ☐ Improve ☐ No
Were the transitions clear?
☐ Yes ☐ Improve ☐ No
Did the conclusion reiterate the theme of the speech?
☐ Yes ☐ Improve ☐ No
Did the speaker make eye contact with the audience?
☐ Yes ☐ Improve ☐ No

Name two (or more) things the speaker did exceptionally well.

Name two (or more) things the speaker needs to work on for next time.

Speaker's Name: _____

Was the thesis/central idea clear?
☐ Yes ☐ Improve ☐ No
Was there a clear pattern of organization?
☐ Yes ☐ Improve ☐ No
Was there support for the information?
☐ Yes ☐ Improve ☐ No
Was the overall delivery strong?
☐ Yes ☐ Improve ☐ No
Were the transitions clear?
☐ Yes ☐ Improve ☐ No
Did the conclusion reiterate the theme of the speech?
☐ Yes ☐ Improve ☐ No
Did the speaker make eye contact with the audience?
☐ Yes ☐ Improve ☐ No
Name two (or more) things the speaker did exceptionally well.

Name two (or more) things the speaker needs to work on for next time.

Speaker's Name: _____

Was the thesis/central idea clear?
☐ Yes ☐ Improve ☐ No
Was there a clear pattern of organization?
☐ Yes ☐ Improve ☐ No
Was there support for the information?
☐ Yes ☐ Improve ☐ No
Was the overall delivery strong?
☐ Yes ☐ Improve ☐ No
Were the transitions clear?
☐ Yes ☐ Improve ☐ No
Did the conclusion reiterate the theme of the speech?
☐ Yes ☐ Improve ☐ No
Did the speaker make eye contact with the audience?
☐ Yes ☐ Improve ☐ No
Name two (or more) things the speakers did exceptionally well.

Name two (or more) things the speaker needs to work on for next time.